The Serendipity *of* Hope

The Serendipity *of* Hope

Edited by
Simon Lee
and Ian S. Markham

PICKWICK *Publications* · Eugene, Oregon

Pickwick Publications
An Imprint of Wipf and Stock Publishers
199 W. 8th Ave., Suite 3
Eugene, OR 97401

www.wipfandstock.com

PAPERBACK ISBN: 978-1-6667-3706-6
HARDCOVER ISBN: 978-1-6667-9614-8
EBOOK ISBN: 978-1-6667-9615-5

Cataloguing-in-Publication data:

Names: Lee, Simon [editor]. | Markham, Ian S. [editor].

Title: The serendipity of hope / edited by Simon Lee and Ian S. Markham.

Description: Eugene, OR: Pickwick Publications, 2023 | Includes bibliographical references.

Identifiers: ISBN 978-1-6667-3706-6 (paperback) | ISBN 978-1-6667-9614-8 (hardcover) | ISBN 978-1-6667-9615-5 (ebook)

Subjects: LCSH: Christian universities and colleges | Christian education | Christian universities and colleges—United Kingdom | Christian education—United Kingdom

Classification: LC427 L44 2023 (print) | LC427 (ebook)

JULY 3, 2023 11:18 PM

"Go and open the door," by Miroslav Holub, *Poems Before & After: Collected English Translations*, trans. Ian & Jarmila Milner et al., is reproduced with permission of Bloodaxe Books.

This book is dedicated to the memory of founders of S. Katharine's and Notre Dame—pioneering women in the nineteenth century.

Contents

PARITY OF ESTEEM
Inclusivity and Change

PIONEERING LEARNING AT A DISTANCE AND IN PARTNERSHIPS

SERVING ALONGSIDE THE MARGINALIZED
Walking On, with Hope in Our Hearts

Acknowledgements

THE EDITORS ARE GRATEFUL to the many people who made this project possible. For the graciousness of Professor Gerald Pillay (vice-chancellor of Liverpool Hope University), who attended the consultation. For the many participants who came together to engage in an exercise of serious reflection on the impact of an institution in their lives.

The initial conference was a three-hour Zoom event. The subsequent book was much improved by our research assistant the Rev. Lauren Banks, who edited each chapter and much improved each chapter and took charge of handling all the logistics.

We are grateful to Pickwick Publications and our commissioning editor, Robin Parry, who saw potential in this project.

In addition, the editors are grateful for the following permissions.

For Miroslav Holub: Poems Before & After: Collected English Translations, Trans. Ian & Jarmila Milner et. al. Reproduced with permission of Bloodaxe Books. www.bloodaxebooks.com @bloodaxebooks (twitter/facebook) #bloodaxebooks.

For Charles Causley, 'Ten Kinds of Hospital Visitors' from Collected Poems 1951–2000 by Charles Causley (Macmillan), reproduced by permission of David Higham Associates.

We are both grateful to our respective institutions; for Professor Lee, the Open University, and for Dr. Markham, Virginia Theological Seminary. In both cases, these institutions supported this project that was, appropriately enough, celebrating the value of institutions.

Finally, any institution in the present owes a debt to the past. Liverpool Hope was a result of courage and vision. The women who founded the original colleges that became Hope were in a very real sense pioneers of Hope, who deserve our gratitude.

Simon Lee and Ian S. Markham

Introduction

INSTITUTIONS ARE FRAGILE, YET so important. They are fragile because stability and strength are dependent on many factors that are often beyond the control of any leadership team. They are important because they are vehicles. Without the House of Commons and its practices, there would not be a vehicle for government accountability. Without the Marylebone Cricket Club (and we ask our American readers to tolerate the abundance of British illustrations), the game of cricket might not have survived and remained as strong as it is in the United Kingdom. Without parishes where people gather, Christianity might have gone the way of ancient Greek religions and disappeared. And without universities, there would not be a vehicle for learning and formation that leads to individual growth and a civic sensibility.

This collection of essays explores the impact of one such institution – a relatively small university in the north of England. It explores through a set of 'experiences' the impact of a university that was seeking to survive and thrive at the turn of the century from 1995 to 2003.

The title essay, which follows this introduction, sets out Simon Lee's reflections on both serendipity and the idea of a university. As the head of the institution from 1995 to 2003, and as the person who proposed the name Hope, he sets the scene for the rest of this book, but the essay can also stand in its own right.

This is true of all the other contributions also. Essays can be read on their own or the book can be read in a number of ways, chapter by chapter, section by section, all in one go or a few pages at a time. In this introduction, we explain the remaining sections, with a sentence or two about each chapter, but our primary purpose is to spell out the ways in which we believe the book can have a significance for different readers in different ways, in addition to the most obvious group, those who have a connection to Hope themselves. On the one hand, they will know the characters and have a direct interest. On the other, they do not need to learn these stories as they will have their own. This book, however, is intended to appeal to diverse readers.

Our primary readership is anyone who is studying or working in any university. It does not have to be Hope in particular, or even another church college. Those in secular universities will also recognise issues of mission, of student-centred staff, of the need for and challenges of change. As we rightly widen participation in universities, it is necessary to widen and deepen the appreciation of the true value of higher education. Otherwise, those with the least family background in university life might miss out on some of the most enduring lessons of a university experience.

A second group of readers is those whose days of studying at university are over. There is still time to retrieve from memories aspects of the experience that have affected alumni, decades after they happened. We would like to see a change in the current mis-match at many reunions, where institutions look for donations but alumni look for meaning. If the institutions would embrace the wider stories, the donations might even follow. Our reunion, twenty-five years after the name change of Hope, was not about raising funds. It has led to this collaboration and enriched each of us in diverse ways.

Given that Hope was founded by the churches, a third readership is all those involved in faith communities. Often pioneers of, for instance, education and medical care, many religious communities have generously handed over their institutions to the state or to independent trustees, but it is worth recalling the origins of religious involvement in the development of the whole person, in mind, body, and spirit, and it is worth reflecting on what the faith communities can learn in return.

A fourth group is those who are not in higher education or in the churches but who are open to the lessons here for their institutions and communities. Schools are an obvious example, but there are many charities and other organisations that face similar issues and create similar opportunities. Some of these, such as the National Trust, have seemed to be caught between those who wish them to lead social change and those who wish them to resist it.

There are two subgroups of these four categories for whom the timing of this book might have a special relevance. So the fifth group is all those who are reflecting on how the experiences of the pandemic have given pause for thought.

The sixth, smallest, niche group is nonetheless a most powerful one. It is all those attending, or connecting with, the Lambeth Conference. This gathering of bishops in the worldwide Anglican communion takes place once a decade. The one scheduled for 2020 was postponed to the summer of 2022 because of the pandemic. It met in the wake also of #BlackLivesMatter. As editors of this volume, we each have a message in our essays for these church leaders, and for leaders of other denominations and faiths. Simon Lee points out that Hope and other church colleges were pioneers of inclusivity and diversity, for instance, through the prophetic conversation of Pro Torkington and Diana Neal, published in the year 2000, and in the Black Science Summer Schools. While the churches have much for which they need to repent, they should not be ashamed of pointing out also the pioneering work of their own universities, colleges and schools. Ian Markham, writing with his colleague Joe Thompson, explains how one Episcopal college, the Virginia Theological Seminary, has initiated a radical reparations process for the descendants of slaves who had been compelled to work on their campus.

In contrast, the seventh group we have in mind is the largest, namely those who are interested in, or affected by, the virtue of hope or, in its absence, by the challenges of despair, which could also be described as hopelessness. Simon Lee observes that what those who are socially excluded are ultimately excluded from is precisely a sense of hope. To understand this, it might help readers to see how those who studied and worked at Hope over two decades ago lived out the point made by the ecumenist, Cardinal Suenens, 'To hope is not to dream but to turns dreams into reality.'[1] For those who find that way of putting it is too theological, the political equivalent was well put by Robert F. Kennedy, attorney general of the USA, in a speech to South African university students in 1966: 'Each time you stand up for an ideal, or act to improve the lot of others, or strike out against injustice, you send forth a tiny ripple of hope and crossing each other from a million different centers of energy and daring, those ripples build a current that can sweep down the mightiest walls of oppression and resistance.'[2]

Turning to the remaining sections, the next one is by students of Hope. It has a short introduction from Suwani Gudawardena, who spent six years studying at undergraduate and postgraduate levels at Hope and

---

1. Suenens, *New Pentecost*, viii.
2. Kennedy, 'Day of Affirmation Address.'

is now a teacher and head of department in a London school. This seems an appropriate profession with which to begin, as the three founding colleges of Hope were each created as teacher training institutions, two for women in the mid-nineteenth century. The longer essays in this section begin with Debbie Woolfe's moving account of how she has battled through challenges before, during, and after her time studying at Hope. Debbie also became a teacher and has had a particular concern for those in care or otherwise disadvantaged. She has been pioneering in her responses, including introducing children to working with horses and now as a leader in the virtual school movement. Paola Barros and Lessandro Rodrigues came from Brazil to pursue a Masters in Contemporary Urban Renaissance. They have each returned to Brazil and have combined their work with their respective families, while also drawing on the charity Hope One World, now Global Hope, to make a difference in their communities. Michael Ford was an accomplished religious journalist and author when he decided to undertake doctoral research with the University of Liverpool's Philosophy Department and two of Hope's theologians, Ian Markham and David Torevell, as his supervisors. He had in his professional career interviewed Simon Lee, who took a particular interest in Michael's progress and referred to his research in the first graduation ceremony where students from Hope received doctorates alongside Michael. Rounding off this section, Sanjee Perera has both her undergraduate degree and her doctorate from her time at Hope, as well as having worked in a number of part-time jobs on the staff of Hope all through her studies, including teaching. Sanjee is now the archbishops' adviser on minority ethnic Anglican concerns. From Sri Lanka to Brazil, from a challenging school experience through to someone who had graduated from prestigious universities and was now, in mid-career, turning to a doctorate, our students offer diverse perspectives. Two of them featured in Simon Lee's essay on 'Impressions of Hope' for the 2003 book, edited by John Elford, *The Foundation of Hope*.

A bridge between these student experiences and the rest of the book, which draws on staff and partners, is Protasia Torkington's introduction to the next section, reflecting on the Black Science Summer School that she created and ran. Pro came to Liverpool from South Africa. Her work with Black teenagers changed Hope as well as changing their lives. The three longer essays in this section on parity of esteem, inclusivity, and change are by the head of Fine Art and Design, the director of Finance and Resources, and the pro-rector and provost of Hope at Everton. Alan

Whittaker writes about the significance of the creative and performing arts in Hope and in the city of Liverpool. Sean Gallagher, whose work is appreciated in so many of the other essays, does explain the value of professional support staff in a university but chooses to focus primarily on his experiences of walking pilgrimage routes. John Elford has written extensively about Hope in the book he edited in 2003 so is entitled to come at the topic from a different angle this time, exploring the elusive concept of collegiality.

The next section shows how the innovations of educational institutions during the pandemic were anticipated by Liverpool Hope twenty or more years ago. It begins with a short essay by Vicky Baker entitled 'Mothership', which says it all, both about how Hope pioneered learning through partnerships far away from its own campuses and about how homeschooling has been necessary during lockdown. Helen O'Sullivan's distinguished career in higher education has taught her the need to focus on our students' current needs and future prospects, rather than replicate the past. She is generous in recognising what she learned through the groundbreaking Network of Hope. Jan Jobling's timely essay explores pedagogy in the pandemic. John Crowley was the principal of St John Rigby Sixth Form College in Orrell, Wigan, who started the Network of Hope with Simon Lee. He discusses how Hope's dynamism helped its partner colleges develop their own self-confidence, as well as providing so many opportunities for study in Lancashire. Shannon Ledbetter completes the section by explaining her own journey from being 'alone and without hope' in Boston to researching for a doctorate and working at Liverpool Hope, leading some of our partnership-working in the community and creating charitable initiatives of her own.

In the final section of the book, we turn to some of the experiences of people who have left Hope and whose focus now is on the most marginalised of individuals and communities. The biblical comparisons, and especially the echoes of the company kept by Jesus, speak for themselves. Sr Maureen McKnight introduces the section by describing her visiting of prisoners. David Torevell analyses the respect shown in real life and in art to prostitutes; John Patterson is now the head of a radical school in Liverpool for those who are visually impaired. In America, Ian Markham and Joe Thompson describe their institution's pioneering approach to slavery reparations.

All these essays could have been in more than one section, which brings us back to the nature of Hope and the ambition of this volume. We are also very conscious of the fact that we restricted the symposium to twenty-five people, partly for the twenty-fifth anniversary, partly to fit on a Zoom gallery screen, and partly to give everyone five minutes to talk, and within that only some of the participants volunteered to write essays given other demands on everyone's time during the pandemic. So there are many others who could have enriched this collection, including tens of thousands of students. Nevertheless, these reflections of a cross section of a higher education community have some insights to offer readers which we trust will stimulate thinking about readers' own experiences. We conclude our introduction by highlighting just some of the lessons that have been brought home to us through our symposium and the process of contributors' five-minute talks becoming short or long essays.

An institution touches each person in different ways. For some, the place was formative in terms of education. The students grew as they studied at Hope. The education laid, as it should have done, a foundation for subsequent growth as a person and within a career. For others, the place is where their 'academic agenda' grows and develops. Drs Jobling and Torevell developed distinctive approaches to fundamentally important questions that have shaped their reputations in the academy. For a third group, there are the distinctive projects of this time – a network of hope, a community of hope, the Black Summer School, and the different pioneering approaches to education and learning. And finally, there is the moving biography of how a certain value of the institution became part of who they are – from Vicky Baker and motherhood to Sean Gallagher and a pilgrimage.

Institutions impact and reach out in countless different ways. One finishes this book in awe at the way in which a place can make such a difference. From scholarship of excellence to reparations to the individual life transformed, the ripples of Hope continue to be seen in Britain and across the world.

Bibliography

Kennedy, Robert F. 'Day of Affirmation Address, University of Capetown, Capetown, South Africa, June 6, 1966.' John F. Kennedy Presidential Library and Museum, 1966. https://www.jfklibrary.org/learn/about-jfk/the-kennedy-family/robert-f-kennedy/robert-f-kennedy-speeches/day-of-affirmation-address-university-of-capetown-capetown-south-africa-june-6-1966.

Suenens, Leo Joseph. *A New Pentecost?* Translated by Francis Martin. New York: Seabury, 1975.

1

The Serendipity of Hope in the Peripheral Vision of a University

Simon Lee

Serendipity and Hope

SERENDIPITY **CAME FIRST AND** *HOPE* came fifth in a survey of favourite words in the UK launched by Bob Geldof in the year 2000.[1] In an afterword to his book with Elinor Barber on *The Travels and Adventures of Serendipity*, Robert K. Merton, a leading American sociologist, observed that serendipity topping this poll was no mean feat, as '*Jesus* and *money* tied for tenth place.'[2]

The word *serendipity* had been coined by Horace Walpole in 1754 but had hardly been used by anyone else when Merton and Barber started writing their manuscript two hundred years later. Indeed, their exhaustive search failed to reveal any single use of it in writing for the first seventy-nine years after its creation by Walpole in a letter dated 28 January 1754. They completed their own text by 1958 but left it unpublished, although Merton referred to it and the authors were frequently asked when it would appear. It was first published in Italian in 2002; Merton then wrote an

---

1. This was part of a millennial fashion for polls or, depending on your point of view, a publicity stunt for the London Festival of Literature in partnership with the publishers, Bloomsbury, and the Globe Theatre.

2. Robert K. Merton, 'Afterword,' in Merton and Barber, *Travels and Adventures*.

afterword and died in 2003, before Barber saw it through to publication in English for the first time by Princeton University Press in 2004. This is intriguing. Questions abound. Why was their book not published in the 1950s? Why was it published in the early years of this millennium? Were its delay and its eventual publication serendipitous? What was happening in the second half of the twentieth century to explain the explosion in the use of *serendipity*?[3] Most importantly for the purposes of this essay, what is serendipity and how does it relate to hope? Less significantly, but more personally, what unpublished texts or insights from our own university experiences might be appropriately revealed now?

The fable of 'The Princes in the Serendips', which inspired Horace Walpole to invent the term *serendipity*, is a story of hope. Walpole seemed to think, and others have mostly followed his lead, that this is so widespread a tale that it has no particular author. Merton and Barber disagree. They identify the author in this version as Christoforo Armena in his *Peregrinaggio di tre giovani figlivoli del Re di Serendippo*, in 1557, based on the Hasht Bihisht work of Amir Khusrow, a Persian writer some 250 years earlier. They also disagree with Walpole's interpretation that it is a 'silly fable' in which the princes go out in search of a treasure or holy grail. It was not about a search for any material thing. It was more that, on their travels, to widen their appreciation of the diversity of human experience, they were observant and wise enough to make inferences based on what they saw:

> Their adventures resulted from the use they made, and that other people made, of their keen wits; and their 'discoveries', which were of the nature of Sherlock Holmesian insights rather than more conventional 'treasures', often proved valuable to those whom they encountered.

They inferred, for example, that a missing camel (a mule in Walpole's Westernised version of the tale and an elephant in Indian adaptations), which had strayed from its companions and which they had not seen, was blind in the right eye because the grass was chewed more on the left side of the path it had taken. The animal had various conditions that they identified in this manner. Anyone in education, not only in Liverpool

---

3. The answers are that they had other books and articles to write but got around to publishing this text only when Merton knew he did not have long to live. In between times, the major change was the exponential growth of scientific discoveries that were perceived to have had an element of serendipity.

Hope, who is committed to inclusivity will have honed such 'accidental sagacity' to discern when, where, and why students are lost or need to be brought back to their fellow students' pathway.

To hope, as Cardinal Suenens observed and I repeated incessantly at Liverpool Hope in my time there from 1995 to 2003, is not to dream but to turn dreams into reality. This means that hope looks towards a more just world and then inspires action to achieve that. On the grand scale, attributed to St Augustine, this can involve anger at injustice and the courage to create a fairer society. In everyday university life, however, it is often the tutor or administrator or chaplain or counsellor or coach who infers from some clue that a student might be dyslexic, or anorexic, or visually impaired, or distressed, or overburdened, or abused, or over-working, or undernourished, who can give that student and perhaps their whole family the hope of a more fulfilling life.

Serendipity is not about waiting for good luck, but rather, the original fable tells a story of using your wits, senses, spirit, and talents, your powers of observation, to spot clues and opportunities on your journey that others might miss but that might make a difference to someone else.

The Serendips is an ancient term for what was, in 1958 when Merton and Barber were writing, known as Ceylon and soon became Sri Lanka. The king who sent out the princes was doing so because he knew that they would develop as characters through the journey in meeting diverse people. To some extent, the princes make their own luck. Their father sets them in motion but does not determine their fate. He sends them out when they have shown sufficient wisdom and modesty to develop other virtues and to become well-rounded characters. They have to be open to learn from their experiences. In a way, a university sends out its graduates in that same spirit.

The Peripheral Vision of a University

The second part of this essay's title can be read in diverse ways. It is intended in part as a very faint echo of *The Idea of a University* by John Henry Newman, substituting *Peripheral Vision* for his *Idea*. In fact, Newman had two central ideas about universities – that theology was the queen of the sciences and that an 'university is an Alma Mater, knowing her children one by one, not a foundry, or a mint, or a treadmill.'[4] The

4. Newman, *Idea of a University*, 145.

former point is not accepted by many who pay lip service to Newman's idea, and the latter is sadly not always honoured in practice. *Mater* is understood as 'mother', but if *alma* is translated at all nowadays, it might be put as 'nourishing' or 'nurturing'. Its literal root meaning is breast-feeding, but an English expression that has come to mean the opposite of a good university education is 'spoon-feeding'. We do not want our universities to treat our students as babies. We do want our universities to inspire our students and staff, to care about them as a nurturing mother would, and to accept that they must leave the nest and follow their own path. Vicky Baker's essay title in this volume could be a modern transla-tion of alma mater: 'mothership'. Saint John Henry Newman was right on both his main points about universities and, incidentally, farsighted in being the first to use the phrase 'virtual Universities',[5] but a rounded understanding of universities also requires attention to peripheral vision.

A second significance is that, in 1995, Hope was on or beyond the periphery of university titles and hardly on the periphery of many people's consciousness, even in our home city of Liverpool. An exasper-ated young lecturer told me in one of many meetings in between my appointment and taking up the post that we were less famous than the nearest roundabout, the Fiveways. Most other universities were relatively unaware of us, or unconcerned with us, until we started to make ripples, if not waves. There was the name change, proposed on my first day, a Friday, 1 September, 1995, and agreed by the governing body at their first scheduled meeting of the academic year two months later, on 31 October 1995. Bishop David Sheppard kindly said in one of his memoirs, *Steps along Hope Street*, that I brought 'flair, imagination and a higher profile' to Hope. We were accorded parity of esteem by the city of Liverpool when given the Freedom of the City in 1996, alongside the University of Liver-pool and Liverpool John Moores University. In 1997, Hope was awarded one of the 1996 cycle of Queen's Anniversary Prizes for our students and staff volunteering through Hope One World each summer to teach Ti-betan refugee children in Ladakh, in northern India, in partnership with SOS Children's Villages. After those successes, one thing led to another and we became the first institution in the country, with Imperial second, to secure degree-awarding powers under the new, stringent process in-troduced by the Blair government, after it had taken office in 1997 and frozen the procedure in 1998.

5. 'We cannot then be without virtual Universities.' Newman, 'Prima Facie Idea.'

A third reading of this element of the title, however, is that Hope benefited from the peripheral vision of another university, Liverpool. Much of our recognition and progress was thanks to this other university, Liverpool, and in my time especially to the vice-chancellors, Professors Philip Love and Drummond Bone, and their representative on our governing body, Dr Jimmy Chubb. Just as their university had begun life as a university college, preparing students for examinations of the University of London, so they nurtured Hope and Chester to independent status as universities, awarding our students their degrees until the point where government policy forced Hope to acquire and use its own degree-awarding powers. For many years, the gold standard of a University of Liverpool degree meant that we could widen participation at entry level without being accused of weakening degree requirements. The University of Liverpool provided a benchmark of quality. Our students were dual citizens of Liverpool Hope University College and of the University of Liverpool. In due course, we were able to pass this spirit forward to our partnership with sixth form colleges in the Network of Hope, who were on the cusp, or the peripheries, of further and higher education.

A significant reason for this part of the essay title is that everyone who became aware of us would concede that we had a distinctive vision, but it could be dismissed as peripheral to the main thrust of most universities, whereas Newman's idea was celebrated as if it were *the* idea or ideal of a university. At one level, that was explicable because of Newman's own status as a scholar and a saint. At another level, however, it is curious that the pieties were observed by many others when quoting Newman, whose vision was assumed to be central, whereas Hope's was considered as peripheral. Incidentally, Liverpool Hope and the local MP (now Dame) Louise Ellman were included in the Window of the Hidden Saints by the parish of St Francis Xavier, Everton, their stained glass commemoration of their 150th anniversary, which was a generous act on the part of the parish. Like many who played a part in their history, even the poet Gerard Manley Hopkins who was briefly a curate there, perhaps the legacy of Hope will become known only decades later. Our vision and Newman's had two distinctive elements in common, neither of which was accepted by some of the noisiest of other vice-chancellors and universities. Theology was, according to Newman, the queen of the sciences. A university was not a research institute and was not an exam factory but knew its students one by one, cultivating their rounded development. Newman, creating a men-only small college in Dublin in the middle of the nineteenth century, put this as educating gentlemen. We described it as educating the whole person, in mind, body, and spirit, or 'education in the round'.

Another reading of this sense of peripheral vision, however, is that part of the vision of Hope in those days, part of the vision of this collection of essays, and a large part of my personal philosophy, is that pioneering, almost by definition, happens on the peripheries, the borders, the margins, the frontiers. This idea of peripheral vision, in other words, is not restricted to universities, or any other institutions, with Hope in their title. While in pursuit of vision, the lesson is to keep scanning the environment all around so as to identify and seize opportunities. This is what the princes did in the Serendips. This is what scientists do, in Merton and Barber's account of serendipity, when they discover something 'by accident'. This is what students, staff, and all involved in university life could do to take advantage of opportunities that could be described as examples of serendipity. This is also the stuff of hope, the stuff of life, an education in looking around. In all these senses, then, my claim is that the serendipity of hope can be seen to flourish in the peripheral vision of a university. Those on the peripheries have often been making points for decades before those in the centre are listening.[6] Peripheral vision, and thus serendipity, can be enhanced by coaching, as demonstrated by Dr Sherylle Calder at the highest level of rugby, time and again for different teams.[7] Similarly, I would argue, students, staff, and governors can improve their peripheral vision of a university.

First Impressions of Hope on Leaving in 2003

In my essay for *The Foundation of Hope* in 2003, I referred to two students without naming them as I did not want to embarrass them.[8] Some readers thought I was making them up, but they were real-life characters, and, decades later, I was delighted that they participated in our gathering via

6. Church leaders, for example, could have anticipated #BlackLivesMatter by listening in their own church colleges, twenty years before, to conversations such as this between Dr Protasia Torkington and Dr Diana Neal of Hope on 'The Black Woman in Church and Society.'

7. Kitson, 'Eyes Have It.'

8. I named two other students, Michael Ford and Suzanne Kelly, as I thought they could cope with being identified, as they were both, in different ways, in the media, as will become clear later in this essay and elsewhere in this book.

Zoom. It was only in that conversation, in 2020, that I realised neither of those students had read, or even had the slightest idea of what was in, my 2003 essay.

I framed that reflection, *Impressions of Hope*, from beginning to end, around a student who sent me a card thanking me for smiling and saying hello on campus and for her graduation in 2002, as she set off with First-Class Honours for her PGCE at Exeter. That student was Debbie Woolfe, who is now running pioneering virtual schools.

> This is just a little note to say thank you for my time at Hope. I got a D and an E for my A-levels and graduated with a First. I just wanted to let you know that I have thoroughly enjoyed my three years at Hope. I have made wonderful friends and have loved learning about new subjects. . . . Thank you for always smiling and saying hello when walking around campus. Finally, thank you for an amazing graduation. I think it was probably the most enjoyable day of my life. The best bit was leaving the Cathedral and being applauded by all the Hope staff. I felt so proud. Thank you.

The centerpiece of my essay was a student whose father, coming into our internet café in the Albert Dock in 1997, Hope on the Waterfront, for a coffee, was so impressed with Sean Gallagher, our director of finance and resources, volunteering to clean the tables and serve coffee on a weekend, that he sent her to study with us. He was visiting from Asia and had previously sent his daughter to another continent to study in Australia. That student was Sanjee Perera, who is now the archbishops' adviser on minority ethnic Anglican concerns.

These two stories are linked. As Professor Ian Vandewalle said of Hope on the Waterfront, in his generous citation for my honorary doctorate at Hope in 2016, it was 'probably the first internet café outside of London, in the Albert Dock . . . a learning laboratory, with touchscreen TVs to link to our academic programmes, a concept that was years ahead of its time.' But I would add that its beating heart, transmitting Hope, its soul, was Sean and colleagues, students and staff, smiling and saying hello.

It took me eighteen years to thank Debbie and even to find her. Her card has meant so much to me, but our interactions on the Pathway of Hope made a difference to each of us anyway, whether or not she knew of her impact on me, and everyone remembers their Hope graduation.

It has been easier to keep track of Sanjee as she is prominent on social media. We have worked together at the Open University and written a couple of blog posts for the William Temple Foundation together, prompted by #BlackLivesMatter, the toppling of monuments, and Sanjee's views on my 'privilege'.

Nobody can remove the memories I have of Sean as a guardian angel for Sanjee and for many other students and colleagues, just as Gillian Atkinson (now Dyche) and Sr Eileen Kelleher looked after, and were in turn inspired by, students from across the Irish Sea, and Professor Protasia Torkington is still in touch with students from our Black Science Summer Schools. Although I like the phrase 'guardian angel', another way of putting it is that these and other figures of Hope were 'an upholding presence.'

Sanjee's story led to this book's title of *The Serendipity of Hope*. Sanjee came to us from the Serendips, Sri Lanka. She came through the happenstance that Sean Gallagher was such an extraordinary director of finance and her father was such a judge of character and of where to have coffee that of all the gin joints/internet cafés in the world, he came into ours, Hope on the Waterfront, in 1997. That, in turn, could have happened only because we had taken a risk in casting our net out into the Albert Dock, doing it, if I may say so, with some style, reaching out to those who would otherwise never have heard of us or from us. Many students followed Sanjee from Sri Lanka and other continents, including Paula Barros and Lessandro Rodrigues from Brazil.[9] Paula and Lessandro have described in their essay for this volume how they came to Liverpool Hope. Neither from Sri Lanka nor Brazil did these students respond to a traditional recruitment process by a British university, sending out emissaries. We sent out ripples of Hope instead.

I concluded that 2003 essay with John Henry Newman's words, 'I do not ask to see / The distant scene; one step enough for me',[10] and then Debbie Woolfe's, 'This is just a little note to thank you for my time at Hope.'

---

9. For instance, Suwani Gunawardena, now head of Psychology and Sociology at Highams Park School in London, who is quoted in Sean Gallagher's essay in this book.

10. Newman, 'Lead, Kindly Light.'

Influences a Quarter of a Century after Starting at Hope

Every person leaving a university, as a student or member of staff, a governor or a partner, deserves the lasting legacy of being able to summon up memories that have some significance for them, in this case, as signs of Hope. Their top ten will change over time. Here are some of the memories I cherish, in just one (albeit very long) sentence each, avoiding stories revolving around fellow essayists or ones that are told by them elsewhere in this volume or ones that I have written about before.

1. Serendipity

When Bishop Michael Henshall, the bishop of Warrington, asked over dinner in the refectory the night before my interview why I had applied and I said that, given the ceasefire in Northern Ireland and with our children coming up to secondary school age, it was a good time to move on and then this ecumenical possibility arose so it seemed like fate, another governor, Pat Mullin, interrupted my answer in no uncertain terms, saying, 'It wasn't fate, it was the Holy Spirit.'

2. 'Can I just say?'[11]

A highlight of my first month was that when student freshers came into halls of residence on the weekend before their first lectures, they were met by our finance team led by Sean, Keith, Claudia, Anne, and Sue, alongside the deans of hall, resident tutors, chaplains, and the domestic services team led by Rita Lewis (and in later years joined by the communications and marketing team and almost all the support staff), giving up their family time, volunteering, helping the students and their families in all manner of ways, fetching and carrying, yielding up memories (and, in subsequent years, many photos recorded in Hope Direct and Hope Virtually Daily) of the sheer excitement when the first generation in a family goes to university (often with the rest of the family carrying their worldly goods), with families' thankfulness for this welcome being conveyed to me, after someone had pointed out that I was 'in charge', their invariable opening being, 'Can I just say your staff have been wonderful?'

---

11. In 1995, in my experience, 'Can I just say?' was always a lovely opening to a positive comment whereas somehow or other, a quarter of a century later, it is often an indignant interruption by somebody who is about to whinge about something and about the time it has taken for them to have their whinge heard.

3. An upholding presence

On the day we heard that Archbishop Derek Worlock had died, six months after I started, I suddenly felt the burden of responsibility for keeping Hope alive (as he was such a fearsome champion of our ecumenical witness that while he was alive we had seemed invulnerable) and two of our chaplains, Sr Phil and Fr Peter, understood that intuitively so just came to be with me in my office as an upholding presence,[12] which gave me a glimpse, beyond our daily morning prayer together, of how the chaplaincy team and wider student services would be astute to discern when students and colleague needed support.

4. Hope in the back pews

When Bishop John Packer succeeded Bishop Michael Henshall as Bishop of Warrington and as a governor, he supported our mission without any fuss by slipping into the back pews whenever he could to kneel in prayer, rather than officiating or sitting at the front, during our Foundation Hour (an opportunity to learn about certain mission-related activities) or other chapel services, a practice that reflected his humility but that also gave him perspectives from the peripheries, as he showed when asking acute questions in governing body meetings about the (un)fairness of policies that were widespread in higher education but that he thought disadvantaged the poorest students.

5. Graduated Hope

Prof. Philip Love had the biggest, loveliest, best sustained smile of any vice-chancellor at graduations, which is important for encouraging every single graduand to smile back (at the very moment when a photo, which will live with them forever, is taken over the vice-chancellor's shoulder), but his registrar wanted me to curtail the loud whistling, cheering, and stamping of feet by our graduands' families, which gave me the opportunity to suggest a change of venue, from the university's traditional setting of the Philharmonic Hall to the cathedrals, since those environments engendered a serenity but also, serendipitously, reinforced our distinctive mission.[13]

---

12. Causley's use of this phrase is quoted later in this essay, as is the fact that I learnt of it from Dr John Elford's book *The Pastoral Nature of Theology*, which has the subtitle of *An Upholding Presence*.

13. Previously, the registrar had wanted Hope students to have the same setting

6. Mature students' proud families

Speaking of proud families, Pat Mullin was also chair of governors at a primary school in inner-city Liverpool and took me to their breakfast club one Friday morning, where I sat next to a lively, challenging boy who told me (and it came tumbling out in this stream of consciousness) he was always in trouble but he wouldn't be because he had a secret that I would never guess but he would tell me, which was that his mum was a student at Hope and was going to be a teacher but, he explained to me, I wouldn't realise they were related because he and his mother had different surnames, something that clearly bothered him more than any thought that I might not know either surname.

7. Special kinds of Hope

It was humbling to visit a special school only a short distance from Hope that was under threat of closure, where they taught me three lessons: that the private sector Sainsbury's did more for their pupils than Hope or any-one else in the public sector offered, in work shadowing and experience, not just pushing trolleys but offering genuine, challenging opportunities; second, that the school gave back to the local community by striving to give people their first jobs, such as someone without a child in the school who was previously a stay-at-home mother, now recently divorced, who told me she was delighted to find work in their school office; and third, that they would prefer to work all year than to have holidays as their pupils regressed outside school terms.

8. Hope from Tibet to Oswestry

Hope One World, with support from Dr Susan O'Brien in stating their case, were recognised for their volunteering with Tibetan refugee children in Ladakh with a 1996 Queen's Anniversary Prize, which led to me sitting next to Michael Bichard, a permanent secretary in the civil service, at the awards dinner in 1997, which led him to suggest me for the new government's Standards Task Force on education, where I met a fellow member, Janet Warwick, headteacher in Oswestry, who made the point that while the government was promoting urban education action zones, it was her rural pupils who were more disadvantaged because they had

---

as all other Liverpool graduands, but this was tested to his limit when our widening participation families, often making their debuts at such events, responded as they might at a concert in the philharmonic or at a festival or a football match.

never seen a university, so I invited a group to come to Liverpool, where they saw the universities in the centre of town and spent the rest of their day in Hope, including a seminar with me on a case in the news, about whether to operate on Siamese or conjoined twins so that one might live and the other would die, or not to operate, which would mean they would both die, and when I asked these pupils how they would decide if they were judges in the Court of Appeal, their fifty-strong coachload argued well for the different outcomes and then voted twenty-five to twenty-five, inspiring me to write the book *Uneasy Ethics* but also to appreciate Janet's points that disadvantage is not restricted to the inner city and that the sight of a university can be transforming.

9. The art of Hope

After a visit by Bishop David and Grace Sheppard to their partner diocese of Akure, Grace and I were walking along the Pathway of Hope when she asked if we could help the women they had met in Nigeria who were taking art classes without sufficient supplies of paints, brushes, or canvasses, whereupon Peter Moore hove into view and offered to go there with colleagues and find suitable, natural, sustainable materials in the locality,[14] which they duly did, one of thousands of encounters on the pathway that could be described as fate or grace or a sign of hope or a miracle or serendipity or as Grace and Hope sending out tiny ripples of hope.

10. Honouring the dead

If Pope John Paul II's funeral had been at St Francis Xavier's in Everton, where we were creating our campus for the creative and performing arts, it would not have been the simple affair it was in St Peter's, Rome, as there would have been plumed black horses drawing the coffin on a carriage, with an elaborate floral tribute spelling POPE, so we knew Billy Thistlewood, who had been an altar server at SFX for eighty (yes, eighty) years and had been sceptical about our rescue of the church and development of a campus there, was not joking when he asked us to promise that his funeral would go ahead in the church should he die during our restoration works; thus reassured, he did indeed die only weeks later and we duly honoured his fervent wish, in a major operation suspending building and thereby challenging health and safety norms.

14. The traditional university or church approach to such a challenge might have been to organise a committee meeting to explore the costs of shipping conventional Western artists' materials.

Why are these memories illustrations of the serendipity of Hope and are there any common themes? They were moments of grace,[15] when a university experience brings you into contact with a wide range of people, often the families of students, and when either the nature of the foundation or of the people encountered or of the communal endeavour offers some glimpse of the divine, including the divine humour. It is easy to miss the clues, or to fail to draw the inferences, but one will benefit more from time at university, as a student or a member of staff, if one learns from the humanity of one's fellow travellers as well as about one's subjects of study. Indeed, it will not have escaped the notice of readers that these stories do not address the core of university degrees or research; they are examples of what I am calling the peripheral vision of university life. They taught me lessons. All of these ten examples are true and I record them now in case they help anyone else – but sceptics might prefer some verifiable and preferably tangible, visible or audible signs of Hope. I will, therefore, give five works of art, four books, three letters, two sounds of music, and one poem, which are among the legacies I value from Hope. Together with the ten memories, they amount to an illustrative twenty-five reminders of the influences on me over the twenty-five years since I first came to Hope.[16]

I have begun with these ten, however, as they show some ways in which Hope was distinctive and pioneering. For example, five of the ten involve governors, but it was only when I later encountered some poor governance by certain (but not all) 'business governors' who did not understand the 'business' of a university that I truly appreciated the support of Hope's governors who shared the institution's mission and values. I have not mentioned in these examples Sr Eileen Kelleher, Nigel Bromage, or John Kellaway, but they were outstanding governors who had all enjoyed successful careers (as a headteacher, in the Bank of England, and in Midland Bank, respectively), they came from different denominations (Catholic, Anglican, and Methodist, respectively), they had a vocation or calling now to help ecumenism and education behind the scenes, and they embraced radical change. Indeed, Sr Eileen embodied such change; she became the first woman to chair the governing body of Hope, which required a change in the constitution, under which the

---

15. They could also be described as grace notes in the sense used by Bernard Mac-Laverty in his 1997 novel *Grace Notes*, 'the notes between the notes'.

16. In keeping with my practice of, for instance, choosing sixty books to reread in the run-up to my sixtieth birthday.

position had rotated between bishops. To take one other dimension, five of these memories revolve around families or neighbouring or partner communities. If a university is really widening participation, perhaps by drawing in a mature student whose entire family has never known anyone at a university, or students from a school and town where they have never seen a university, it is making a difference to, and with, whole families and communities, and the little personal touches of dozens of staff will matter. Indeed, the staff themselves can have liberating opportunities through working for a university, not only those undertaking part-time postgraduate studies. When Hope was shortlisted for an equal opportunities award, for instance, some of the women in the catering team who represented us told me they had never been to London before that overnight stay. When my office team took on one of our wonderful modern apprentices, she had never been on a train.

Several of these encounters remind me of that poem quoted at the start of *The Pastoral Nature of Theology* by Dr John Elford, who was already a pro-rector when I joined Hope. John Elford and Charles Causley are both from Cornwall. John would not have written that book at that stage of his career without encouragement from a new colleague at Hope, now the co-editor of this volume, Professor Ian Markham, and myself. Causley describes ten kinds of hospital visitors, the first two of whom significantly are the enemies of hope, for

> The first enters wearing the neon armour
> Of virtue
> Ceaselessly firing all-purpose smiles
> At everyone present.
> She destroys hope
> In the breasts of the sick

while the second,

> in a melancholy splurge
> Of theological colours,
> Taps heavily about like a healthy vulture
> Disturbing deep-frozen hope'

and so on, with only one visitor, the sixth, understanding what is needed:

> The sixth visitor says little,
> Breathes reassurance,
> Smiles securely,
> Carries no black passport of grapes

And visa of chocolate, has a clutch
Of clean washing,
Unobtrusively stows it
In the locker, searches out more.
Talks quietly to the Sister
Out of sight, out of earshot, of the patient,
Arrives punctually as a tide,
Does not stay for the whole hour.
Even when she has gone
The patient seems to sense her there:
An upholding
Presence.[17]

The sixth hospital visitor is like all the people in my ten memories and like the three princes in the fable of the Serendips. My role at Hope was in part to create the conditions in which colleagues, governors, and partners could flourish through exercising their powers of observation to be an upholding presence for our students, for one another, and for the wider community.

The design of a campus does make a difference, for instance, ensuring that there will be encounters on a pathway, as do the structure of the day or week, the rhythm of the year, and the proper celebration of rites of passage, while the recruitment of diverse students, for instance, from across the Irish Sea, from Muslim communities across the Northwest, and from as many countries as possible, enrich the experience for all. Most of those encounters in any university experience remain invisible to those not immediately involved, unrecorded, perhaps even forgotten, but they will have made a difference, as this sample of ten has influenced me.

11–15. Art

One question that that 2003 essay has prompted is whether I have kept any other cards, letters, or memorabilia from my time at Hope, in addition to Debbie's card? Yes: for example, I am still buoyed up every day by five *visible* signs of the art of Hope dotted around our house: a study by Ghislaine Howard for her mural of the visitation, Ray Semple's sketch for the cross he created for the Anglican cathedral, a ceramic pot by Alan Whittaker, and portraits of me by Alastair Adams, commissioned by the governors and by a Hope student, Jenny Thewis (now Cussons), at the instigation of the fine art and design team.

17. Charles Causley, quoted in Elford, *Pastoral Nature of Theology*, "Introduction."

16–19. Books

There are also dozens of books that remind me of Hope but I will name only a sample quartet. I have a complete set of the works of Professor Kenneth Newport, for instance, and I especially value his book on the *The Branch Davidians of Waco*, partly for its generous preface but mostly because of the serendipity involved in a leading theologian visiting survivors in prison and engaging seriously with their interpretations of the book of Revelation. A second book on my shelves that always makes me smile is on *Coastal Dune Management*, edited by Sally Edmondson and Paul Rooney of Hope, together with J. A. Houston. Sally wrote, in my first month, the longest and most detailed letter telling me off that I have ever received, whingeing about the ecological vandalism,[18] as she and others saw it, of my proposal to make the walls level on the Anglican and Catholic sides of the campus, while Paul sent me the shortest letter of gratitude in my last month at Hope: 'thanks for the banter.' In between times, this book of theirs reminded me of the Sefton coast, which is where our children had many happy times with my parents-in-law, of the shifting sands of higher education, and especially of a case of plagiarism, where a student had 'borrowed' from a public library much of an old dissertation on these very dunes, not appreciating the fundamental points of not cheating and that the dunes change over the decades. A third book is Michael Ford's soulful biography of the fire service chaplain hero of 9/11, *Fr Mychal Judge: An Authentic American Hero*. Michael was encouraged to write this by one of Fr Mychal's friends who had found a copy of his biography of Henri Nouwen in the friar's room. If that is not serendipity, then what is? As Michael Ford relates, this was happening at the time of submitting his PhD thesis on Nouwen, who has also influenced me, and I continue to follow Michael's writing.

It is not only books written *by* colleagues that remind me of Hope, so my fourth example is that when I left Liverpool Hope in 2003, Dr Helen O'Sullivan was studying part-time for an MBA and kindly gave me, as a farewell gift, a book on *Metaphor and Organizations*, edited by David Grant and Cliff Oswick. Helen's inscription began, 'An exhaustive analysis of your management style reveals a love of metaphor to explain

18. In 2007, when I was vice-chancellor of Leeds Met, we won the inaugural People and Planet Award for the most environmentally friendly university in the UK, just saying. One of the neighbours who wrote to the local paper, protesting about the lowering of a wall at Hope, had decades earlier written to the same paper protesting about the wall being built.

your vision for the organization. I thought that you might therefore like an MBA-esque discussion of how metaphors are used in organizational science.' This insight was yet another indicator that Helen O'Sullivan would go far. During my time at Hope, Helen was a lecturer in biology who became our head of student services and deputy registrar, after helping the theology team through quality assurance. She is now deputy vice-chancellor and provost of the University of Chester, having served as pro-vice-chancellor at Keele and earlier as an associate pro-vice-chancellor at the University of Liverpool. The book itself did not complete my education in metaphors, although I did like its explanation that the concept of a metaphor is itself a metaphor and that the now widespread use of *literally* is in fact a metaphor. Not for the first time, I was reminded of that phrase by Leon Lipson that was cited by the Yale Law School professor Arthur Leff, 'Anything you can do, I can do meta.'[19] Indeed, I am tempted to quibble with the claim that metaphor was the essence of my approach. I would argue for the meta-metaphor claim that what I tried to do was to encourage the community to inhabit or live out parables. A parable, a story with a moral, is an extended metaphor.[20] Whether a fable, as in 'The Serendips', is the same as a parable, is itself a matter for debate. What I particularly enjoy is almost taking metaphors literally or, at least, pursuing the metaphor and preferably giving it visual expression and acting it out in real life, turning an idea into a story, which is compelling. Uniting a separated campus with the Pathway of Hope was both practical, making it safer to cross Taggart Avenue at one point with a pelican crossing, rather than the previous practice of hopping across at many places, and also aspirational, creating the conditions for encounters, with Debbie, Grace, Peter, and all-comers, so that serendipity could flourish.

20–22. Letters

Since I focused on students in that 2003 essay, I will turn to fellow members of staff this time, but with an eye also for those who might have seen themselves as on the peripheries. In using examples which are hitherto unknown to people other than the one who made contact and myself, I am grateful for their support and so take the liberty of putting into the public domain these illustrations of their generosity of spirit. I have kept many other letters in our garage and in my heart. When checking that the

19. Leff, 'Unspeakable Ethics, Unnatural Law', 1230n2.
20. Lee, 'Parables of University Life.'

letters say what I have taken from them, I have invariably found deeper wisdom and greater generosity and thankfulness alongside the phrase that I remembered.

A sister of Notre Dame wrote to me in my first month, telling me not to be disheartened by the whingeing that any new head of an institution will meet. Sr Kathleen Bishop described this practice as 'hector the rector'. That phrase did stick in my mind, but I am not sure that I decoded or grasped properly at the time her biblical reference: 1 Tim 4.12. In the Jerusalem Bible, the translation of which into English was overseen by Mgr Alexander Jones of what is now Liverpool Hope, this reads,

> Do not let people disregard you because you are young, but be
> an example to the believers in the way you speak and behave,
> and in your love, your faith and your purity.

Although I could now do with a biblical verse that begins 'Do not let people disregard you because you are old . . .', there is much still to ponder in Sr Kathleen's choice of text. As I had been appointed a professor at Queen's at thirty-one and head of Hope at thirty-eight, I was predisposed to give young colleagues opportunities, but I also chaired panels that appointed two registrars in succession who were each in their last few years before retirement.

Writing on 22 September 1995, three weeks after I started, our nursery manager Helen Rowlands picked out two points that she said were boosting morale in her beleaguered team:

> Firstly, that you have already made more changes in 20 days
> than we can remember over several years, and secondly that we
> (the nursery team) are involved in the whole process.

It was partly a matter of engaging all who wished to embrace change and partly conveying a sense of hope, purpose, determination, and enjoyment:

> Your enthusiasm for your work revived my own sense of pur-
> pose. It seems that my own restored spirit coupled with your
> regular correspondence to ALL colleagues has worked wonders.

I will spare you the many letters telling me off, but the phrase 're-stored spirit' captured the soul of Hope. We built a new nursery in partnership with Busy Bees, and any prior criticisms of the nursery team or their manager were seen to have been the fault of the unsatisfactory setting in which they had been operating. I appreciate that some will think I was a sucker for a letter from a team leader, but I prefer to think that we were evenhanded, whether teams were whingeing or welcoming change. If Helen was one of the most supportive managers, one of the most vociferously critical was Ray Semple of fine art and design, ably assisted by his deputy and eventual successor, Alan Whittaker, and their students whom they inveigled into a protest group for my first visit to their studios. My colleague Dr John Elford is a painter and an admirer of art and design, but when we walked round the studios together, John took a robust view of Ray's and Alan's demands for more space, suggesting that an alternative solution would be for the students to create smaller sculptures. I made a passing comment that Ray's prominently parked Porsche indicated that the artists were managing to survive despite protestations of underfunding. We supplied a £20-millon campus for the creative arts as soon as we could, by which time Alan Whittaker had succeeded Ray. When I left, Ray not only gave me a beautiful sketch of his processional cross but wrote in an accompanying note that he had sold one of the Porsche wheels to pay for the framing. Beneath the combative exteriors, Ray and Alan, and their colleagues, were full of humour, talent, hope, and goodwill. The nursery and fine art and design teams were across another road so they were on the periphery of the estate. The nursery moved on to the Pathway of Hope, and fine art and design moved into the Cornerstone of Hope at Everton, close to the centre of the city.

I knew that a full-page letter from Fr Kevin Kelly, written when I was leaving Hope eight years later, was full of thoughtful insights and generous praise, but I was pulled up sharp by one example of his humility and openness while checking my recollection of his profound last sentence: 'God's presence and grace is equally at home in a secular environment as in a church college.' Amen to that. I am involved in an initiative now that could well take that sentence as its leitmotif. Along the way, though, in writing about how grateful he was to come in to the campus after retirement and reflecting on watching the development of Hope, this brilliant theologian had the humility to say, 'I think I have learnt a lot from you.' While it is immodest of me to repeat Kevin's comment, my excuse is that it is salutary as I approach the age he then was to see how the foremost radical theologian of my own denomination in this country was still open to learning as he 'retired'. In this letter, he was referring to leadership within Hope, but Kevin Kelly was always lifting my spirits in my endeavours in the wider community in Liverpool, where he had decades of greater engagement. Within Hope, when I suggested naming the theologians' building after the former head of theology at Christ's

College, Mgr Alexander Jones, Kevin told me about Alexander Jones teaching him at seminary, while editing the translation of the Jerusalem Bible, and asking Kevin to read out draft passages in the school hall, ostensibly to hear whether the translation would work in liturgies but also to help Kevin overcome a stammer. Kevin also told me a reassuring story that, after all the checking in the world by a distinguished team, when Alexander Jones opened the first proof copy of the Jerusalem Bible in English, he found a typo in the first sentence.

23–24. *Songs of Hope*

Hope's music team, in particular, and the wider performing and creative arts, influenced me beyond measure by creating, without any help from me, an annual Cornerstone Festival at Everton, a concept that (together with the Network of Hope) inspired me to develop at Leeds Met a peripheral vision of a university of festivals and partnerships. Every university has a soundtrack. While often peripheral to the university authorities, music is often central to student life. The opening bars of two pieces of music immediately remind me of Hope, although neither is directly linked to the virtue of hope. More importantly, they remind me of two lessons: not to underestimate the aspirations of those who have not had the opportunity, for instance, to play a musical instrument; and to learn from students that some songs (and other phenomena) can best symbolise an experience for them even if you think there would be more relevant choices. The schoolchildren of Everton were given the option of any instrument to learn well enough to play in the opening of Hope at Everton. They could have chosen guitars or drums but opted for violins, which I found encouraging. Our head of music, Professor Stephen Pratt, arranged the opening of *Pavane* by Gabriel Fauré, the football theme tune of the year as the BBC's introduction to their coverage of the 1998 World Cup in France, and the pupils played in a mini-concert we relayed between Hope at Everton, Hope on the Waterfront, and Hope Park, again a prefiguring of many a lockdown concert. I trust that pupils and their families were inspired by this experience of the intensity and beauty of practising the violin and making music together. Our own students also had their own musical tastes. We tried to popularise a graduation song each year, to use on the website and at the celebrations. I am not referring here to the processional music, where Handel's 'La Réjouissance' from his *Music for the Royal Fireworks* is the classic, inspirational accompaniment, but at a more frivolous level, for instance, to play while students assembled for a team photo in the quadrangle and to be part of the soundtrack of the CDs of graduation days. While my favourites for this purpose each had an explicit message of Hope, *From a Distance* by Julie Gold and *Gimme Hope, Jo'Anna* by Eddy Grant, the students obstinately preferred *Daydream Believer* by the Monkees, which somehow, despite its odd story and lyrics, captured the joy of summer graduations and the spirit of Hope. On reflection, the words *dream* and *believer* were Hope-filled, and the more I think about university experiences, the more I empathise with the phrase 'oh, what can it mean . . . ?'

25. Poetry

This brings me to my twenty-fifth memory on the meaning of our shared time at Hope twenty-five years ago. A reunion can encourage people to revisit together their treasure trove of memories and see them in a new light, for instance, because the same incident is interpreted differently by various characters. What might have been peripheral twenty-five years ago becomes central now and vice versa. A fresh metaphor or parable to explain what I have in mind is that reflecting in this way on our experiences of university life is not just about sifting through old photos or prose but is more like returning to poetry. Having just read this passage from a foreword by that Cornish poet I quoted earlier, Charles Causley, I think his profound analysis holds true not only for poems but also for universities:

> A poem, by its nature, may hold certain qualities in reserve. It may not burn itself out, so to speak, in one brilliant flash of light. A poem is a living organism, capable of continuous development and the most subtle of changes. It may contain both a revelation and a mystery. We need to be aware not only of what is said, but also of what the poet has most carefully left unsaid.
>
> If we take poems to pieces and put them together again, unlike pieces of machinery they may give no reason why they 'work', nor are they obliged to do so. A poem has no single 'meaning'. This may differ with each reader, who interprets the piece in accordance with his or her own age, experience and sensibility. However many times we read a poem, no matter how seemingly familiar the text, it is perfectly capable of revealing some fresh quality, some resonance hitherto unnoticed in the course of a hundred earlier readings.[21]

21. Charles Causley, in Gibbs, *Macmillan Treasury of Poetry*, 15–16.

When we are the poet, or at least a co-poet, in having played a part in creating our own university experiences, and we are now rereading that poem in the company of other poets and critics, the metaphor may need adapting, but the spirit holds for this exercise. I appreciate that taking individual moments to pieces, or subjecting them to microanalysis, may similarly not explain how a university works.

There was serendipity involved in my coming across this passage and discerning a similarity between poems and universities. When I first read Causley's words, the connection occurred to me because I was in the middle of writing this essay. These observations by the poet Charles Causley come in his foreword to *The Macmillan Treasury of Poetry for Children*. Although this was published in 1997, I only spotted the book, with its bright and glossy but torn cover, at Farthingoe Tip (technically, a waste recycling centre) during lockdown in 2021. The serendipity in this chain of events is that Farthingoe was one of the few places we could visit on a weekend in lockdown, having brought goods to give away prior to our house move. I was drawn to the book by the name of the foreword writer. I knew who Charles Causley was because of those insightful words of his, quoted by John Elford, which I cited earlier. So I think it is timely to round off my twenty-five memories with a few lines of poetry. The poem that I have in mind is one chosen by Dr David Torevell in bidding me farewell in 2003, extracting from a longer work by Seamus Heaney:

> You were the one for skylights. I opposed
> . . .
> But when the slates came off, extravagant
> sky entered and held surprise wide open.
> For days I felt like an inhabitant
> of that house where the sick man of the palsy
> was lowered through the roof, had his sins forgiven,
> was healed, took up his bed and walked away.[22]

The Heaney household's disagreement on whether their roof should have skylights is part of the background to this, but the genius lies in linking it to the biblical story of the house that was so crowded that the sick man's friends could get him close to Jesus only by taking off the roof, and then there is Seamus Heaney's and David Torevell's shared humility in confessing their initial scepticism about change before graciously imagining the reactions of someone in that house when a miracle happened. Whatever the poet or the gift-giver meant, I have been sustained

22. Heaney, 'Skylight.'

by this over two decades as a parable of widening participation. Those of us engaged in taking the roof off higher education (or as it is sometimes put, smashing the glass ceiling, although in that metaphor the assumption is that the ceiling is broken from below), are not seeing ourselves as the messianic figure in the story but as one of the friends of the disadvantaged person on the periphery, who needs some help to get to the place where there is hope. The people already in the house might have initially wondered what on earth was happening when the roof opened up, but David's gift of this Heaney poem makes me think that those already in the house would have been energised by the faith of the one lowered into their midst and would have willingly drawn in others from the peripheries. Certainly, David himself is one of the inhabitants of the house of Hope who has always welcomed in people from the peripheries.

'We Are All Graduands'[23]

The underlying point I made one way or another at all graduations is that you leave a university not only with a certificate but with a cluster of experiences which will influence you over the long run. When I returned to a Hope graduation in 2016, this time as a grateful recipient of an honorary doctorate, I put it like this:[24]

> Twenty years from now, what will you recall from your time at Hope? Even when you receive your certificate, you will not know the full extent of your achievements, of what you take and what you have given. Indeed, the paradox is that the more profound an influence from university turns out to be in your later life, the less likely you are to have appreciated it at the time. Putting it more positively, there will be a slow release of hope buoying you up year after year, decade after decade.

23. A phrase I used persistently, despite imitations by repeat-attenders of Hope graduations in long-suffering staff, governors, and my family, of the way I said it and of my exegesis of the word, a graduand being someone who is in the process of transition from one stage of learning to another, my point being that while they were transformed from being a graduand to being a graduate by the ceremony, we all still continue to progress in our lifelong learning, as this book attests, for instance, by revisiting the poetry of our university experiences.

24. Metropolitan Cathedral of Christ the King, Liverpool, 26 January 2016, but similar passages are quoted in editions of the colourful photo-led magazine, *Hope Direct*, in 2001 and 2002, for example, where we reproduced aspects of graduation to appeal to students and their families in Clearing and then in our welcoming weeks.

This essay and this book test this hypothesis for staff as well as students. Despite the league table mentality and the educational establishment's obsession with first-destination statistics, it does not matter much where students go next after university, compared to the influence they have on society in the long run and indeed the long-run influences on them and on others of their education in the round. I do not even share the league table compilers' prejudice against those who do not complete a degree within three years, just as there is no reason to stigmatise those who do not complete a marathon within three hours. There have been some famous 'drop-outs' from university, including entrepreneurs lauded by governments, such as Bill Gates. On 11 July 2001, my graduation address was directed to our newly qualified teachers on the graduation day for our education deanery. I began with a homage to a 'drop-out', Saint Benedict:

> The Eleventh of July is the Feast Day of Saint Benedict. He was born in the fifth century. Exactly fifteen hundred years ago, at exactly the age of the majority of this week's graduands, he left the formal world of education, in his case in Rome, in his case because it appalled him. Unlike today's graduands, however, he decided to become a hermit and so he went to live in a cave.

> Just imagine if you were to choose that somewhat unorthodox lifestyle today. The Teacher Training Agency would regard you as 'wastage' and we would be in trouble with our first-destination employment statistics. Her Majesty's former Chief Inspector, Chris Woodhead, would blame liberal teacher training institutions for encouraging drop-outs . . .

> For someone who went to live in a cave fifteen centuries ago, St Benedict's influence has been enormous. He made a difference. He did so by daring to be different. St Benedict achieved this partly through his personal example and partly through his simple rule, or set of rules, of common sense about how to search for God and how to live in a community. The grace and insight to live harmoniously together can come from the space, the silence and the reflection of time spent alone. St Benedict was not a priest, he never left what we would now call Italy and the first two times he was called to lead a community, dissident forces in the staff room tried to poison him. Yet he overcame these little local difficulties and became patron saint of Europe.

> St Benedict's Rule has remained constant for fifteen hundred years, a remarkable statement to modern governments and

quangos who cannot seem to resist changing the rules every
few weeks.

The solitary elements of St Benedict's life serve as a reminder to students
that they do not always have to be in a big group partying to be extracting
value from student life, that there are times for reflection and retrench-
ment as well as for more public activity. The first word of his rule is 'Listen', which really means 'Observe' and is an instruction to be as alert as
were the three princes of the Serendips.

The next day, I based my address on another saint, a heroine who
did not herself benefit from university education, to make a point about
the inclusivity of Hope:

> On 12 July 1751, exactly 250 years ago this very day, Saint Julie
> Billiart was born. She is usually described as being of French
> peasant stock. She did not have the opportunity to study at
> university but worked as a farmhand in the fields, acquiring
> little money but a great love of sunflowers and fellow workers.
> She spent much of her adult life unable to walk and for some
> considerable time she was also unable to talk. Yet, in her fifties,
> she founded the Sisters of Notre Dame de Namur. Fifty years
> after that, the sisters came to Liverpool, to the other end of Hope
> Street, on the corner of Mount Pleasant, to establish a teacher
> training college. One hundred fifty years later, the college is one
> of three parts of Hope's foundation . . .
>
> St Julie lived through the French Revolution. Her disabilities
> were such that she is normally described as bed-ridden al-
> though this hardly does justice to someone who was carried
> from her bed and hidden under hay on a cart so that she could
> travel through riots. She founded her order in the year in which
> Napoleon was crowned emperor. Life in Belgium was fraught
> over the next couple of decades, especially after the Battle of
> Waterloo. All this puts in perspective the challenges graduands
> have overcome to achieve your degrees.
>
> Few people could have expected Julie to achieve very much.
> Some of those who did realise what she could do, by way of edu-
> cating young girls, tried to stop her. Those who tried to block
> her included powerful men in the church. The obstacles which
> face us may change in their precise form but the substance of
> them does not vary much through the centuries. Even today,
> there will be graduands in the cathedral who have succeeded

despite one or both of these two barriers to education, low expectations or high hurdles obstructing access.

Elsewhere in that address, and in other Hope graduations, I explained the philosophy of Hope in ways intended to be helpful to all graduands. Since we are all graduands, however, this essay concludes with how Hope led me along unexpected paths.[25]

Three Journeys of Serendipity

The three princes of the Serendips eventually come home. (Other metaphors are available to students who might prefer to see themselves as Homer's Odysseus or Tolkien's Bilbo Baggins in *The Hobbit*, who also come home after having learnt about themselves and others on their travels, or in real life, pilgrims on the Camino[26] or on their way to other holy places.) The journeys I have in mind take me back to Oxford, lead me to Cambridge, and take me back to Northern Ireland, in each case with a combination of serendipity and hope, with a sense that it is the peripheral vision of a university that matters. In each, there is more than one university involved. My account is intended to explain how I think I spotted and worked away at an idea or a connection, and then how one thing led to another. An idea from a widening participation class in Hope, or from the history of its founders, or from a tragic incident in modern times can lead to insights into the peripheral vision of Hope, of Oxbridge, or of other universities, helping to make sense of journeys of lifelong learning. Serendipity is what happens if we are truly, in the memorable taxonomy of the first chancellor of the Open University, 'open to people, places, methods and ideas.'[27]

25. I appreciate that there are more profound stories of serendipity in *research* at Hope, for instance as Kenneth Newport's work on *Apocalypse and Millennium* was followed by *The Branch Davidians of Waco*, but the premise of our reunion was to tell our own stories of what we took from Hope. I have told and do not repeat here my personal stories of influential people, places, and ideas from the peripheries of my own undergraduate days (including Cardinal Suenens on 'hope') in Elford, *Foundation of Hope*, and in my address in thanks for an honorary doctorate from Hope, cited in the preceding footnote.

26. As in Sean Gallagher's essay in this volume, 'Camino of Hope.'

27. Lee, 'Open and Shut Cases.'

My first sequence stems from my use of the metaphor or parable of lifelong learning being more of a marathon than a sprint in Hope graduations, welcomes, and open days:

> Whatever your start in life was like, education is a marathon, not a sprint, it is open to all, not an invitation only event. A commitment to both quality and equality, with world class scholars and lifelong learners reaching out to one another, creates an educational ethos similar to sport's London Marathon or Great North Run in which the world's elite athletes, on foot or in wheelchairs, participate in the same endeavor as those who are jogging for fun, for charity or to stretch themselves. It is simply not true, in education or distance running, that one group holds the other back. Instead, each enhances the occasion for the other and they do so by running at their own pace yet still making progress and enjoying the challenge together.

Although using sporting metaphors all my life,[28] this version evolved from one of our Hope students who was actually an Olympian sprinter over hurdles and eventually led me to half-marathons and, as a supporter of my wife and children, to marathons. The serendipity, or peripheral vision, or perhaps subversion, involved here was that I had been asked by Dr Pro Torkington to take a class with her Black Science Summer School pupils. She was trying to move away from the stereotypes of careers in sports, but I thought the power of the analogy was worth incurring the wrath of Pro when I saw that Diane Allahgreen was running against the Olympic gold medal-winning heptathlete Denise Lewis on the weekend before the summer school. So I recorded the race and showed it to the group. They were impressed that one of our students beat the Olympic champion, albeit in Diane's specialist event, and were delighted to meet Diane in person. Whereas I had thought that gliding over hurdles would work as a symbol for overcoming obstructions, the better analogy over time proved to be in distance running, perhaps because only accomplished athletes tend to hurdle, whereas many of us can become involved in charity runs.[29]

28. See, e.g., https://uptoyouskip.net/, a website chronicling my fiftieth season as a cricket captain, or my reference months *before* the 2003 Rugby World Cup Final to Jonny Wilkinson's exemplary commitment to practicing kicking, an acquired skill that enabled him to win that game in the last minute of extra time with a dropkick with his naturally weaker foot (in Elford, *Foundation of Hope*, 206).

29. Tracing this history is an atonement for any offence caused to sprinters and hurdlers by any inference they might have drawn from this metaphor praising distance

This story of lifelong learning as a marathon came to figure ever more prominently when I moved from Hope to Leeds Metropolitan University in 2003 and was asked by the then chair of governors, Nimble Thompson, to find a 'spike of excellence'. As one of the institutions merged into Leeds Met was the Carnegie physical education teacher training college, established in the 1930s, I set about developing sporting partnerships[30] and encouraging coaching. I suggested that the founder of the Great North Run, Brendan Foster, should be awarded an honorary doctorate by Leeds Met, as he had pursued his PGCE at Carnegie after his undergraduate degree at Sussex. This led to him becoming chancellor, in succession to Leslie Silver, an entrepreneur, philanthropist, and former chairman of Leeds United. We won various awards and were appointed as the national coaching centre of excellence, while I chaired Podium, the mechanism for encouraging all universities to become involved in the London 2012 Olympics. When we were the runners-up for the university of the year in the 2006 Times Higher Education Awards, Brendan Foster made the point as we left the awards evening that it is always good to come away from championships with a medal.[31] In seeing this recognition of our 'low-charging, high impact' policy as a silver medal, it lifted spirits as much as our gold medal in the same year for the outstanding contribution of a university to the community, for our partnership with Bradford City FC and their local Muslim community. By the time we had returned to Leeds from London, we had organised a gold-and-silver celebration.

---

running, that I was somehow suggesting their craft was easy. On the contrary, there is also much to learn from their commitment and the intensity of their events. Indeed, I learnt a lesson from Linford Christie, which might explain some of the rise of Hope and Leeds Met Carnegie and which might even explain why certain politicians seem to succeed, despite commentators thinking they should not. That is for another essay. The point here is that if the sixth-formers loved the athlete but could not relate to her event, look for a variation on the sporting metaphor that does appeal to them.

30. Wilson, 'From Ivory Tower.'

31. Brendan Foster had firsthand experience of this. Given our successes in athletics in this century, it may need pointing out that, at the Montreal 1976 Olympics, the men and women track and field athletes of Great Britain and Northern Ireland won only oe medal between them, which was Brendan's bronze in the 10,000 meters. Although he was gracious about Lasse Viren winning gold in the 10,000 and 5,000 meters, I could not help the less worthy thought that Nottingham winning 'university of the year' for cloning their main campus building in China was an oddly imperialist, and possibly Pyrrhic, victory.

A visitor to Carnegie from the Lawn Tennis Association, Andrew Thomas, was struck by this combination of excellence and inclusivity that the mass participation runs epitomise. When I left Leeds Met and started Level Partnerships with Dr Jill Adam, who had resigned as the Carnegie Dean of Education, we helped others create partnerships in this spirit, in Asia, Africa, and Europe. Through Brendan Foster, Jill and I had already met Haile Gebrselassie and I had conferred on him an honorary doctorate in the middle of the track during the African Athletics Championships. By now, Andrew Thomas had left the LTA to become the head of sports development at the University of Oxford, my alma mater. Sir Roger Bannister was the biggest draw for alumni and philanthropists there, but Andrew wanted to connect somehow this iconic figure to the more modest sporting memories of college life shared by alumni with limited sporting talents (such as myself) but perhaps with unlimited wealth to commit to philanthropy (unlike myself). He approached Level Partnerships, and I wrote *The Z to A of Oxford Sport*, which initially appeared as fortnightly essays on the Oxford Thinking website for the year running up to those Olympics and then became an audiobook. This process in turn led to Vincent's, the Oxford sporting club, asking me to write their history for their 150th anniversary. This was launched in 2014 by Sir Roger himself on the exact 60th anniversary of his historic sub-four-minute mile. He kindly wrote in the foreword:

> Having heard Simon Lee speak at an Oxford alumni weekend in 2011, I was pleased that Vincent's asked him to write a history of our Club. Lord Butler hosted a particularly friendly dinner in the House of Lords in 2012 when Simon Lee spoke specifically about Vincent's Olympians. Now, in 2014, we have this book by him which ranges more broadly and I commend it to members and to all who care about our sporting and educational institutions.[32]

In addition to the honour of meeting this great athlete, this was the point at which I realised how much I do indeed care about institutions, especially educational ones. It is the 'peripheral' activities of educational institutions, such as extracurricular sport or music-making or volunteering with Hope One World to help Tibetan refugees, that influence so many students for life. Sir Roger's words resonated with me partly

---

32. Roger Bannister, in Lee, *Vincent's 1863–2013*, foreword, page number unavailable.

because they echoed a phrase I associate with Ian Markham, who wrote about institutions mattering in *The Foundation of Hope* and who helped me at a difficult time in Leeds Met, when two of the London bombers of 7 July 2005 were identified as Leeds Met alumni, and when I left Leeds Met in 2009. In the former case, he flew across to address our staff development festival on Muslims and Islam. In the latter, he invited me to advise on his own institution, Virginia Theological Seminary, and then on their behalf to study other Episcopalian institutions in New York, Chicago, and Columbus, Ohio. This was a kindness to me more than a help to him, although my predilection for anniversaries did lead me to make one suggestion that he has taken on board spectacularly. He would be following this in the early 2020s anyway, of course, but back in 2009, it might have seemed peripheral that an institution founded in 1823 should develop a vision for its bicentenary in 2023. Ian, however, immediately created a pub on campus called the 1823 and has built up steadily, and more soberly, to 2023. I did not anticipate that Ian would still be in the same post by now or that he would be pioneering slavery reparations because of the nineteenth-century experience of slave labor on that campus. But I did know that institutions that care about revisiting and really understanding their history are all the more likely to flourish and to know when it is time for a radical change of direction.

Second, our record of widening participation at Hope and then at Leeds Met enabled me to speak at the University of Hiroshima in 2007 to an international audience of students with disabilities and of university staff committed to widening participation, which was when I retrieved my graduation address about St Julie. I visited the Peace Museum in Hiroshima, which had a profound effect on me.[33] In February 2014, my experience in the ecumenical setting of Hope was significant in my appointment as executive director of the Cambridge Theological Federation of nine colleges of diverse denominations, on the peripheries of two universities, Cambridge and Anglia Ruskin. Combined with my experiences of conflict in Northern Ireland, this led to me being invited to give the sermon in the university church of Great St Mary's in August 2014 as

33. Not only in the way intended. Its first exhibit is a huge photo of the atom bomb exploding. I came to this in the company of many Japanese schoolchildren. It seemed to me that while the devastating impact of the bomb was naturally the centerpiece, the relevant history might also have included explanations of Pearl Harbor and Japan's determination not to surrender until after the Hiroshima and Nagasaki bombs. Nonetheless, the museum traced the effects of the bomb over the ensuing decades in ways that moved me and have influenced a current project.

the university and city of Cambridge commemorated the centenary of the start of the First World War. I tried to interweave stories of the sacrifices and the signs of hope of both town and gown but also, inspired by Northern Ireland and by Hiroshima, referred to survivors, those working for peace and those showing grace to former enemies:

> The sermon here one hundred years ago, on the Sunday after the declaration of war, explained that, 'The noblest kind of courage is the courage that dares to be generous to a fallen foe. . . . It is an ancient and noble people that is arrayed against us—we think that it has been misled by false ideals. . . . We have offered our friendship these last few years; when these tragic events are past, over the graves of our dead we shall offer it again' . . .

> Eglantyne Jebb, of this city, with her sister Dorothy Buxton did something wondrous at the end of the Great War in creating the charity *Save the Children*, helped by writing to the pope, Benedict XV, and then travelling to Rome to meet him, holding an extensive conversation with him in French, an Anglican laywoman forging an ecumenical alliance with the pope. Benedict XV issued a call to be read out in every Catholic parish in the world to support this enlightened charity, including through a collection in every church. This was to support the children of the defeated Austro-Hungarian Empire, extending the hand of friendship to the children of our foes.

> Still lighting up the world decades after this war were those who survived with horrendous injuries. Disfigured, they became inspirational sources, transfiguring the lives of others. Here in this church, from 1957 to 1963, the organist was Douglas Fox, a Cambridge resident and Oxford organ scholar who had lost his right arm in the First World War. He had been taught by Charles Wood at the Royal College of Music. Another great musician, Charles Villiers Stanford, wrote to Douglas Fox's father, 'I am sure his art will come out somehow.' Douglas became director of music at Bradfield and then at Clifton College. He lived until 1978, more than sixty years without his right arm. Sir Thomas Armstrong's tribute was that 'Douglas stands, in a way, for the whole of that doomed generation, for all the men killed and maimed on . . . many fronts.' He observed of their courage that 'sometimes, it is a question of facing death, more often of facing life . . . '

When Douglas Fox returned from the war to Cambridge, thinking that his musical career was over, famous musicians Stanford and Hubert Parry asked another organ scholar to play with one arm strapped while they brought Douglas Fox into chapel to listen. Not being able to see the scholar in the organ loft, Douglas Fox appreciated the virtuosity, and when he saw that the playing had been without the use of one hand, he realised that music-making was still possible for him.

The first person to come up to me at the reception afterwards began with, 'Can I just say . . . ?', which could have had either a positive or a negative follow-up, and then said the ominous words, 'I knew Douglas Fox', which staggered me and made me fear that I had the wrong arm or the wrong person or the wrong details in some other way, but no, this retired theology don, Canon Brian Hebblethwaite, just wanted to say that he had been a boy at Clifton and that Douglas Fox was indeed an inspiration. I would never have met this distinguished theologian, a Gifford lecturer, who was taught by an inspirational musician maimed in the First World War, if I had not been blessed by my time at Hope.

Third, this is perhaps the tiniest of ripples in response to a tidal wave of injustices, but it is a memory I value because it illustrates how our journeys can come full circle and it revolves around the fragility of life and the significance (to me, at least) of 'peripheral' or 'marginal' conversations with students.[34] Almost all of the 180 law students in each year at Queen's

---

34. The last time a quango said anything interesting about university life was so long ago that it needs updating to include diverse students, not just young men in halls of residence, but mature women commuting to campus; it still bears retrieving from obscurity, however, because it has the right spirit about the soul of a university and its concept of citizenship: 'Notoriously the most subtle and potent educational influences in the older Universities of this country have been those which, being indirect, come not with observation, and originally were probably unforeseen and unintended. The excitement of being plunged into a new environment and a more spacious mode of life, with all its possibilities of congenial study and congenial companionship; the sense of privilege in being made heirs of a great tradition, citizens of no mean city, with the freedom of "its streets where the great men go"; above all, the informal discussions of a few friends about all things in heaven and earth up to all hours of the night or morning, where the argument is followed whithersoever it leads; the clash of mind between the youthful historian, medical student, chemist, theologian, and engineer, members often of different social classes and bringing into the pool different experiences and different prejudices, with the resulting recognition of the existence of different points of view and of the need of taking account of them; and in all this the exhilarating sense of intellectual daring and adventure: these are the influences which stimulate thought and enlarge its boundaries, develop the faculty of judgment and arouse in students that energy of the soul which Aristotle found the essence of true well-being. To evoke

University Belfast matriculated as eighteen-year-olds with three A grades at A-level. Some are now leading figures in the practice of law, in politics, and in universities. Much the same applied to the students I had taught at King's College London and in Oxford. At Queen's, there were only a few mature students,[35] but their stories of determination inspired me to move into the universities that were opening up higher education to those on the peripheries. I had taught one of those mature students at Queen's, Sheena Campbell, in a small tutorial group in her first year, discussing the issues of the time, including the broadcasting restrictions on Sinn Fein. Before coming to university, Sheena had stood for Sinn Fein in the Upper Bann by-election when David Trimble, then on the staff of the law school at Queen's, had been elected as the MP. Sheena Campbell was murdered by a loyalist terrorist who followed her out of the law library one Friday evening. She was twenty-nine, with a son at primary school. As dean, I went to the hospital that night and then, this being Northern Ireland where funerals happen swiftly, to her funeral on the Sunday.

The oldest law student at Queen's in my time was a remarkably accomplished woman, Bernadette Grant,[36] who was more than twice Sheena's age, indeed twice my own age at the time, more my own age now. She was inspirationally returning to study to qualify as a solicitor, having earlier trained to be a teacher. Bernadette had retired as both a teacher and as a SDLP councillor in Omagh. We often talked about the Troubles and prospects of a ceasefire as we walked around the campus. She encouraged me to carry on with my observations in the media and my involvement in grassroots community movements for peace and justice. Bernadette kindly gave me a shield of the coat of arms of Omagh when I left Queen's in 1995. In starting Hope across the Irish Sea, with Paul Rafferty, Gillian Atkinson (now Dyche), Sean Gallagher, and Sr Eileen Kelleher, assisted by Eddie and Chris Ferguson based in Northern Ireland, it was natural that we drew students first from Omagh, Derry, Belfast, and other communities around Northern Ireland where we had links, before Sr Eileen soon took Hope into communities in the counties on the other side of the border.[37]

---

in its students such an energy of the soul in pursuit of excellence must be a principal aim of any University' (Millet, review of *English Universities*).

35. In UK higher education, 'mature' students are those who start at age twenty-five or over.

36. D'Arcy, 'Lives Remembered.'

37. This was, in itself, a homecoming for part of Hope's foundation. In the same

Three years later, one of those Hope students, Suzanne Kelly, was seriously injured in the Omagh bomb. At the end of her first year with us, in her summer vacation after the 1998 Good Friday Agreement had seemingly marked the ending of the Troubles, she was out shopping with her mother in her hometown. I was on our family holiday in Italy when I heard the news that both Suzanne and her mother had been caught up in the blast. Hope ensured that Suzanne's tutor, Tim Griffiths, was able to fly out to visit her in hospital, and he continued to support her magnificently. We did not want to overwhelm Suzanne or her family with visitors but liaised through Tim. Hope provided Suzanne with a laptop computer, and she worked from hospital and home for six months, more than twenty years before universities adapted to lockdown for all students. Suzanne was studying for the four-year bachelor of education degree and graduated on time, three years later, having lived in one of the rooms at Everton designed for disabled access. Sean Gallagher and the Hope across the Irish Sea team made sure discreetly that if we could help in any other way, we did. We respected Suzanne's wish that she did not want publicity and did not want to be defined by the bomb. She did, however, choose herself to give one interview just before graduation, to *The Irish Times*. When she walked across the stage, most of the families in the cathedral would not have known the challenges that she had overcome.

When the news of the bomb had broken back in the summer of 1998, in life before the widespread use of email,[38] I sent a postcard from Italy addressed simply to 'Mrs Bernadette Grant, Omagh', confident she was so well known that it would reach her, which it did, and my office also made contact. I asked Bernadette if she would pop into the hospital on my behalf to let Suzanne know that she was in our thoughts and prayers. Even though Suzanne had many visitors, including Bill Clinton, she told me on her graduation day that she really appreciated Bernadette Grant's

---

decade as Newman's famous lectures, now known as *The Idea of a University*, and his attempts to create a Catholic university in Dublin for gentlemen, young Irish women who had fled the famine to Liverpool were given educational opportunities by the Sisters of Notre Dame who came from the Continent to establish a teacher training college opposite the poorhouse, at the intersection of Mount Pleasant and Hope Street. One of Her Majesty's Inspectors concluded in 1896 that 'for teaching, it stands first in England. . . . I had long had an ideal of teaching and failed to find it until I came here this year and gave the "excellent" mark in nearly every case.'

38. In the last century, I had argued unsuccessfully for giving every student a laptop and a Hope email address; this was opposed by those who thought students should be free to use any pseudonym and not compelled to adapt to modern technology

kindness. Bernadette Grant was the model 'sixth visitor' of Causley's poem, an upholding presence. At times like that, there is not much that the head of an institution can do, but asking a former student to help was a little gesture of solidarity. It was serendipitous that I knew such a responsible and generous former student in Omagh.

I cannot explain why bad things such as the Omagh bomb happen, but wherever there is trauma and tragedy, as also in 9/11 and in conventional wars, there will also be the serendipity of hope, as shown in Michael Ford's biography of Fr Mychal Judge, or in the witness of people like Eglantyne Jebb and Douglas Fox after the First World War, or Suzanne Kelly after the Omagh bomb. In good times as well as bad, in this peripheral vision of a university and on the peripheries of our society, there will always be inspiring people, communities, and ideas, sending out tiny ripples of hope.[39] Learning the art of serendipity, of sensing the tiniest of movements, drawing inferences from them, and acting accordingly to open up opportunities and promote justice, is the soul of a university education. In the words of an inspirational speech by Robert Kennedy to students at the University of Cape Town in South Africa on 6 June 1966:

> Each time you stand up for an ideal, or act to improve the lot of others, or strike out against injustice, you send forth a tiny ripple of hope and crossing each other from a million different centers of energy and daring, those ripples build a current that can sweep down the mightiest walls of oppression and resistance.[40]

Bibliography

Causley, Charles. *Collected Poems 1951–2000*. London: Picador, 2000.

D'Arcy, Úna. 'Lives Remembered: Teacher and Solicitor Bernadette Grant Was Omagh's First Female Councillor.' *Irish News*, 4 Feb. 2017. https://www.irishnews.com/notices/livesremembered/2017/02/04/news/outstanding-teacher-and-solicitor-and-omagh-s-first-female-councillor-916700/.

39. Sean Gallagher and I commissioned Oliver Sweeney to compose *Ripples of Hope* and to bring together a CD *Ripples of Hope across the Irish Sea*, including that original track but also music by another friend of (and visitor to) Hope, Julie Gold, *From a Distance*, and by others. As the notes to that CD make clear, my references to ripples are not only because of Hope on the waterfront but are inspired by Robert Kennedy's speech to South African students in 1966. We put this quote, as well as Cardinal Suenens' 'To hope is not to dream but to turn dreams into reality' and other sayings of hope, on cards and wrapping paper, samples of which I still have as further gifts of Hope.

40. Kennedy, 'Day of Affirmation Address.'

Elford, R. John, ed. *The Foundation of Hope: Turning Dreams into Reality*. Liverpool: Liverpool University Press, 2003.

———. *Pastoral Nature of Theology*. London: Cassell, 2008.

Ezhard, John. 'Serendipity Is Our Favourite Word.' *Guardian*, 19 Sept. 2000.

Foster, Brendan. 'Me and My Medals: Sir Brendan Foster.' *Times*, 31 Oct. 2020.

Gibbs, Susie, ed. *The Macmillan Treasury of Poetry for Children*. London: Macmillan, 1997.

Heaney, Seamus. 'The Skylight.' *Poetry Ireland Review* 29 (Spring 1990) 3. https://www.poetryireland.ie/publications/poetry-ireland-review/online-archive/view/the-skylight1.

Kennedy, Robert F. 'Day of Affirmation Address, University of Capetown, Capetown, South Africa, June 6, 1966.' John F. Kennedy Presidential Library and Museum, 1966. https://www.jfklibrary.org/learn/about-jfk/the-kennedy-family/robert-f-kennedy/robert-f-kennedy-speeches/day-of-affirmation-address-university-of-capetown-capetown-south-africa-june-6-1966.

Kitson, Robert. 'The Eyes Have It: England Vision Coach Calder Closing In on Unique Prize.' *Irish Times*, 30 Oct. 2019.

Lee, Simon. 'Open and Shut Cases.' Open University, Dec. 2020. https://www.open.ac.uk/blogs/50YearsOfLaw/wp-content/uploads/2020/12/Simon-Lee-Open-and-Shut-Cases.pdf.

———. 'Parables of University Life.' Foundation Day Homily. Liverpool Hope University, 25 Jan. 2016.

———. *Vincent's 1863–2013*. Oxford: Third Millennium, 2014.

Leff, Arthur Allen. 'Unspeakable Ethics, Unnatural Law.' *Duke Law Journal* (Dec. 1979) 1229–49. https://scholarship.law.duke.edu/cgi/viewcontent.cgi?article=2724&context=dlj.

Lipsett, Anthea. 'Leeds Met Tops Green University League Table.' *Guardian*, 15 June 2007.

MacLaverty, Bernard. Grace Notes. New York: Norton and Co., 1998.

Merton, Robert K., and Elinor Barber. *The Travels and Adventures of Serendipity*. Princeton, NJ: University of Princeton Press, 2011.

Millett, F. B. Review of *English Universities: University Grants Committee, Report for the Period 1929–30 to 1934–35 Including Returns from Universities and University College in Receipt of Treasury Grant for Academic Year 1934–35. The Journal of Higher Education* (Nov. 1937) 451–52. https://doi.org/10.2307/1973893.

Newman, John Henry. *The Idea of a University, Defined and Illustrated*. New ed. London: Longmans, Green and Co., 1893.

———. 'Lead, Kindly Light.' Hymnary, 1833. https://hymnary.org/text/lead_kindly_light_amid_the_encircling_gl.

———. 'The Prima Facie Idea of a University.' The Catholic University Gazette 2 (8 June 1854) 14.

Thorpe, Vanessa. 'Whatever "Quidditch" Is, We Love It.' *Guardian*, 10 Sept. 2000.

Torkington, Protasia, and Diana Neal. 'The Black Woman in Church and Society.' *Feminist Theology* 9 (1 Sept. 2000) 46–55.

Wilson, Andy. 'From Ivory Tower to Sporting Cathedral.' *Guardian*, 5 Apr. 2006.

DIVERSE STUDENT STORIES

A Welcoming, Stimulating, and Encouraging Environment

Editors' Introduction. *In the end the university experience is about the students. Although research, regional outreach, and the neighbourhood are all important, the central and constant core is the educational experience of the students. In the marketplace of higher education, Hope appealed to a certain type of student – students who often found Hope by accident but then thrived in the community. These three stories capture that reality very well.*

2

A Sri Lankan Student's Six Years of Studying at Hope

Suwani Gunawardena

I STUDIED AT LIVERPOOL HOPE from 1998 until 2004. I completed a BA (Hons) in sociology and history with an upper second and then completed a postgraduate certificate in ICT and a PGCE in ICT. I went on to get the first teaching position I interviewed for and am now the head of social sciences at Highams Park School in London.

I grew up in Sri Lanka and studied at university level in Delhi, India, before moving to Liverpool Hope on a partial scholarship to complete my first degree. I met Bernard Longden and Sean Gallagher who were then in charge of Hope Finance in Colombo, Sri Lanka. They were so welcoming and supportive and really wanted me to join Hope and offered me advice and help I needed to make such a significant move to a new country and a new university. I was really taken by how supportive, efficient, and friendly Hope staff were from day one. I was made to feel very welcome and was given excellent accommodation and the well-being support I needed to settle well and carry out my studies effectively. I felt a part of this close-knit community right from the outset. Hope is a small university, and I never just felt like a number and enjoyed the inclusive ethos of the place throughout my stay.

Hope has a huge international student community, including those who studied for full degree courses as well as many international exchange students who spent one, two, or three semesters at the university. I was involved in various activities and societies set up by and for international students as well as others which were open to all students. I played basketball and took part in international events, one of which was the regular 'bring-a-dish' parties that gave wonderful opportunities to celebrate various cultures under one roof. The teaching staff were also from varied and diverse backgrounds, which added to the welcome and inclusivity I felt at Hope. The friendships I built at Hope have outlasted my time there. Some of my very close friends are from my Hope days. I feel that they know me so well and vice versa, and our connections originated from Hope and the student support systems that enabled us to build them.

I also did lots of part-time jobs while I studied, varying from working in the canteen kitchen, to being a university library assistant and an accommodation office staff member, to tutoring at local libraries. All these jobs supported my financial ability to study at Hope as well as giving me a wide scope of experiences.

The lecturers and tutors at Hope that I studied under opened my mind to new possibilities and interests that I still pursue. Although I started my job teaching ICT, I changed to sociology a few years later because of my invaluable experiences in learning that subject at Hope. I especially want to mention two lecturers I had at the time, Dr Jayne Raisborough and Dr Julie Scott, who not only taught me feminism and other key aspects of social justice but also helped improve my academic ability to a very high level. I am grateful to them and all the others who were vital in helping me build knowledge and become who I am today.

The two people I am most grateful for during my time at Hope are Bernard Longden and Sean Gallagher. They not only recruited me to come to Hope but also provided continuous and invaluable support throughout my stay. As someone who had moved so far from home, without any family nearby, they became my family and looked after me and many other international students' well-being and welfare.

I enjoyed my time at Hope immensely. I am glad I went there, rather than perhaps to a more prestigious university, as I felt that the people I met were from such varied backgrounds and that this university allowed me to develop my personality and create and develop connections with a diverse group of people. It was welcoming, educative, and fun; everything I expected my university experience to be. The time I spent at Hope will always be etched in my mind with fond memories and gratitude.

3

Learning with Hope

An Autobiographical Learning Journey

Debbie Woolfe

WHEN I WAS APPROACHED to write this essay, I didn't know where to start; but I did know I wanted it to include aspects of hope, faith, and serendipity.

My life has been filled with these principles and they have influenced who I have become. For that reason, I have included not only aspects of my education and career but also aspects key to my personal journey.

> *The only person who is educated*
> *is the one who has learned how to learn . . .*
> *and change.*
> *—Carl Rogers*

Learning has always been central to my life, and for me, one of the things I have learnt is: there isn't much to separate learning in school and university, learning in my personal life, and learning in my career . . .

November 2020 – and I was recovering from long COVID. I had a challenging eight months (as many people had) since getting COVID in March 2020, when I received a text message from an unknown number. The message invited me to be part of a virtual conversation about Liverpool Hope University. Being more than a little sceptical, I replied to the message asking for some evidence that it wasn't a scam. I then received a response with a picture of a thank-you card that I had sent to Professor Simon Lee, who was the head of Liverpool Hope at the time I was there. I think that message would have made me emotional at any time, but after the year everyone had just had, it made me cry a lot. A dose of hope was most definitely appreciated and, although at the time I didn't realise it, very much needed. That virtual meeting has since opened some doors and led me to have an opportunity to share a little of my story and also to reflect on the serendipity and happy coincidences that have been part of my life.

I would have always described myself as a spiritual person. I'm not religious, but I have always had a strong sense of being guided by something higher and I've always had faith in that. When I was younger my mum had a New Age shop, so I was brought up learning about healing and different beliefs around spirituality. When I was about twenty-four, I had a spiritual experience that enabled me to see a wider perspective and remember what is important. I was driving and singing and feeling very joyful. I consciously surrendered to the moment and then had a sense of feeling out of my body. I remember being concerned but also knowing I was safe. I then felt as if a wise unhuman part of me – my higher self or spirit – was directly communicating with the human part of me, a human part untainted by life's experiences. I felt like there was nothing in between those two parts: no ego, and no human fears or knowledge.

The experience wasn't like a conversation between those two parts but, rather, an exchange of information. I learnt, felt, and experienced that everything was exactly perfect. Even the things that a human would think of as 'bad' were actually perfect, in terms of learning for the spirit. There was no such thing as good or bad – from a spiritual perspective – only the greatest learning. I felt that this life, and being in a body, was not real. What was real was the feeling of being connected to that wisdom and peace and total freedom, matched with complete security. What I experienced is what I believe we will feel when we are no longer on earth, and therefore there isn't anything to fear.

For a few days after that experience, I was left with the energy of it, and then the energy faded. However, I meditate every day and retune into that experience, to remind myself that none of this is real and that everything is perfect. No matter what is going on, the wisdom that I received from that experience has been with me every day since. Although I get caught up in the many mini-dramas of this life, every day I remember that experience and try to always see things from the perspective I gained during it.

Be kind whenever possible.
—Dalai Lama

Professor Lee asked me if I have always sent people thank-you cards, and I think I have, since the age of about eighteen. I've just always liked to say thank you when someone has had an impact on me. I never had any idea of the impact a thank-you could have on a person though, until Simon got in touch in November. It was a really wonderful feeling to know that the card I had sent around twenty years ago had had such an impact that lasted that length of time.

My parents and grandparents hadn't gone to university, and as the eldest child of a sister and two half-brothers, I was the first to go. I always knew I'd go, and both my parents spoke about it as if it had already happened, from as early as I can remember.

My parents divorced when I was two years old, but they were both supportive of my education. My mum had left school without qualifications, and she was always determined that my sister and I would have a good education. She would take us to Waterstones bookshop every weekend and let us explore the children's books for hours. I also remember her complaining to my secondary school, when I was in year nine, that I wasn't getting enough homework. The deputy head of the school told her I was doing fine and that I'd probably pass my GCSEs. She got really angry and told him that I was going to university and would get a first! That was really embarrassing at the time, but looking back, I know that not many people from that school went to university, and she was determined that whatever adversity I faced, my education would not suffer.

As a child, what I didn't know was the impact of a family environment that wasn't settled and wasn't safe. The best way to survive for me was to try to not be noticed. I have since become familiar with one of the studies on ACEs (Adverse Childhood Experiences). The study measured adverse experiences in childhood and compared scores with later health and well-being. People with an ACE score of 4 or more are more likely to engage in risky behaviours and experience health problems. A score of 4 or more is linked to being 12.2 times more likely to commit suicide, 9.7 times more likely to take drugs, 32 times more likely to have learning and behaviour problems in school, and 8.8 times more likely to have been in prison in the last year. Also, on average, people with a score of 6 or more on the ACE test die twenty years earlier than those with a score of 0. This is because the impact of chronic stress on children with high ACE scores impacts their brain development and, therefore, their health and well-being in later life. I scored 6 on the ACE test, along with 8 percent of participants who have a score of 4 or more.

To maintain my balance, school became my home. I loved my teachers and friends, and I was at school doing sport from eight every morning until nine every evening. My school had a bad reputation and was closed by Ofsted and then reopened with a different name. Again, I didn't know what that meant at the time – I just knew I felt safe there. I became head girl at the school and thrived with the feeling of belonging that I had when I was there. At the time I took my A-levels I was also just starting to remember some of the more traumatic events from my childhood. Coming to terms with that meant that I didn't do as well in my A-levels as I needed to. I got a D, an E, and a U. I had applied to Hope University with higher predicted grades, and luckily, and unexpectedly, I was still accepted.

Life is like riding a bicycle.
To keep your balance, you must keep moving.
—Albert Einstein

I had chosen Hope because of my newly found interest in psychology. A teacher who had helped me a lot at school had given me her old university psychology books, and it ignited my passion for the subject. I'd always wanted to be a physical education (PE) teacher, but the thought of being able to combine psychology and PE at Hope was very appealing. It is only at the recent reunion that I have discovered the spiritual and religious foundations Hope was based on and how well that matched my needs.

I visited Hope and felt instantly welcome. I loved the yellow brick road joining the campuses. I loved how nurturing it felt compared to some of the other universities I had visited. Leaving home is a big deal for anyone, but for me, with my insecurities, I needed to feel safe – which Hope offered.

I started at Liverpool Hope studying PE and psychology, working towards a BS Combined Hons. I'd love to say that it was an easy transition, but I, like many others, struggled for the first year. I made friends, but I didn't quite fit in with the 'partying' of the first year in halls. I enjoyed my lectures and loved learning about psychology though. I took an extra module in counselling psychology during my second year and needed encouragement from my tutor because I nearly gave it up. Then, it ended up being one of the grades that tipped my degree into the first class category.

I remember my personal tutor Keith Morgan very well. He was supportive with my dissertation and it became the second piece of work that helped tip my degree into first class. Years later, when I was working and wanting to do more research, I contacted him, and again, he offered to help with access to research. I often think of him and wonder what he is doing now, and wonder if he knew how helpful he was. Although I became a PE teacher to start with, I think my heart has always been with psychology and working with young people facing additional challenges. For this reason, I remember the psychology parts of the course more than the PE.

> *Do your little bit of good where you are;*
> *it's those little bits of good put together that overwhelm the world.*
> —Desmond Tutu

I loved the freedom of learning to live independently and relished the added freedom of being able to use the library, search for information, and study in a way that was so different from school. The library was always a bit awe inspiring to me, with its huge glass windows and little study rooms. It was a new experience to be so engaged in a subject and then have the information right there, to be able to explore for hours, following trails, just based on my interest, rather than a school curriculum. Looking back, I can see how much of a luxury it is to have the time and space to explore like that. I will always treasure those days.

However, I did also struggle that year. I always felt that I didn't quite fit in. I was homesick and had a couple of tough experiences that resulted in almost dropping out once or twice. It took a while for me to meet friends with whom I felt really comfortable. About halfway through the year, I made friends with some people on the floor below mine. Things changed from then on. I spent all my time with those friends, drinking tea and sharing stories. We all shared a house together for years two and three, and I am still friends with some of them today. Our house wasn't really a typical student house. It was freshly decorated and felt totally like home.

Over those two years I learnt it was okay to accept that I preferred to walk, talk, and drink hot chocolate whilst watching fireworks at the docks instead of drinking alcohol and having late nights. It was okay to spend time laughing with friends and learning about their hometowns and cities. It was fine to read and listen to music in our house and cook batches of spaghetti bolognaise that we could all share rather than going to the same number of nightclubs as everyone else. Those final two years were the two years when I learnt who I was, what I liked, and what I wanted. It was this time when I accepted that about myself and stopped trying so hard to fit in.

Those two years taught me what it was to have a stable life for the first time – to live in one safe place and wake up every day with a purpose. University was a forty-five-minute walk away, and we used to walk there and back, as a group, once or twice a day. I think I lost about two stone just from the regular walking! I remember feeling so grateful to have a spare fifty pence left at the end of the week to be able to get an extra chocolate bar. Living with best friends is the most fun thing and those days were a true blessing. I learnt how to appreciate the simple things in life and how to be independent, healthy, and safe. Those lessons have served me ever since.

The only way to have a friend is to be one.
—Ralph Waldo Emerson

During the first year of university someone from an organisation called BUNAC came to speak to students. They told us about Camp America, and although it was out of character, I decided to apply. I was offered a place at a camp for inner-city children from Chicago who were in foster care. I hadn't travelled much prior to that experience, so to go so far alone was daunting. I'm not too sure why I went. I guess I've always had a habit of forcing myself to do things that scare me. Part of me wanted to go, but another part was petrified of travelling so far, alone, and not really knowing what I was going to do. I've always felt quite guided, though, and something in me just knew that it was something that would work out for the best.

That trip was life changing. I remember the person from BUNAC telling everyone that we would fall in love. Everyone who does Camp America falls in love with either a person, the lifestyle, or the kids. I didn't really know what I was getting into. Ninety percent of the children at the camp were on medication for ADHD, and I remember being confused about why we were having restraint training during the induction. When the kids came, I understood. It was crazy! Looking back, I'm not sure how a load of relatively untrained eighteen- to twenty-five-year-olds managed to take care of some of the most challenging young people with whom

I have ever worked. The children had fights, sleeping problems, eating disorders. I don't think I slept more than four hours a night for the first month. It was probably the hardest thing I have ever done, and I have had bags under my eyes ever since!

The staff team became close, and we supported each other well. We had full timetables of camping, swimming in a lake, arts, campfires, hikes, and sports. There were many occasions when I laughed so hard that I cried. I did fall in love. I fell in love with the children, who after weeks of fighting, started to ask for hugs. I fell in love with weekends off and sitting in my friend's red pick-up truck, listening to the Dixie Chicks as we drove to Dairy Queen for ice cream. I fell in love with skinny dipping in the lake, under the moonlight, and getting a tattoo. I fell in love with friends and with travelling afterwards . . . sleeping on Greyhound buses and looking for rainbows in Niagara Falls. At the time, I thought it was the most amazing experience, and looking back I can see how much impact it had on my life. That opportunity was possible only because of being at Liverpool Hope.

There is beauty to be found in the changing of the earth's seasons,
and an inner grace in honouring the cycles of life.
—Jack Kornfield

I almost dropped out of university when I came back. Seeing those children and their trauma up close and feeling like I had made a difference to some of them made it really hard to come back. I felt selfish to be studying and being so free when I could've been there, working and making more of a difference. After a few weeks of it being really hard to settle back into the routine of lectures and essays, I decided to have some counselling at Hope.

At that stage, counselling was an easy decision although still quite scary. However, it was very organised, nurturing, and well worth overcoming my initial fear. The counsellor helped me see that by getting a degree, I would be able to help similar children even more. I've worked with children in care ever since, so I think she was right.

Reflecting on my time at Hope, I can see that I learnt how to take care of myself and be healthy. I learnt how to make very good friends and that it is okay to need help and be able to help others. I learnt what I liked and didn't like. I learnt what I wanted to do with the rest of my life. I learnt how to write essays and do well in exams, which was what I thought I'd learn. However, I think the life skills and experiences were the most valuable parts of my time at Hope.

I graduated from Hope with a first. When I found out, the first person I called was the teacher who had supported me so much at school. That teacher in an educational environment where I had felt most stable, safe, and cared for. The impact of this meant I knew what it was to feel free enough to learn, and to start to explore and develop as a person.

Graduation was the most wonderful day. All the Hope lecturers lined the steps of the cathedral and applauded all the students as we walked through them. I remember being filled with hope and inspiration and feeling proud – ready for the next step.

> *The more that you read, the more things you will know,*
> *the more that you learn, the more places you'll go.*
> —*Dr Seuss*

My next step was to do a PGCE at Exeter University. It was the only place that did a middle-years teaching course in PE. I hadn't planned to go so far away from home, but it just felt like the right place to go because of the course. I hadn't realised how far away it actually was until I got offered a place, but by that point, the distance was something I tried to forget about. Going to Exeter was another example of my habit of pushing myself to do things that felt hard, if they also felt right. It was far, but the course was right, and somewhere deep inside, even though I was terrified, I trusted that it was the right move. Whenever I have that feeling of knowing, even to this day, I tend to push myself into things.

The course covered all primary subjects, plus secondary PE. It has since been scrapped because the coursework was too much to cover in one year. It was a lot, but I felt well prepared from my time at Hope. I spent a term in halls and the remaining two terms on teaching practice in Mullion, a tiny village at the very edge of Cornwall. It has just one primary and one secondary school. It is about as far south as one can go in the country and was a seven-hour drive from home. It is the most beautiful coastal village, and I felt like I was on holiday for the whole year. Serendipity played a part in my time there. When I went for an induction visit, I met a teaching assistant from the primary school. Her daughter, who was my age, had just left home, and she had a spare room. I lived with her and her husband for my whole teaching practice. It was a very healing experience. They were so supportive, and I experienced a lot of stability with them. When some aspects of the teaching practice were hard, they were there to give me pep talks and encourage me to keep going.

Exeter was very different from Hope, too, though. First, I was only at the university for one short term. The lectures and support were great. It was a small campus, and it was a lot of fun to learn about how to teach all the primary subjects. We learnt how to make kites for DT, and the solar system for science. It was a little like reliving my own primary school years but in a calm, nurturing environment. After just one term, though, we went on teaching practice for the remaining two terms. In many ways teaching was probably the hardest profession I could've chosen to go into. I lacked confidence in a big way, and standing up in front of a class of children did not come easily. However, I had always known teaching was what I wanted to do, so it just got easier over time.

My primary teaching practice was wonderful. I had an amazing mentor, and I learnt so much from her. She was also called Debbie and was from Liverpool. These coincidences helped me feel more certain that things would work out fine. She was the most organised person I have ever met. She was always smiling and enthusiastic and had a way of making everything fun. I still remember the feeling of being left alone with a class for the first time. Suddenly, it was just thirty children and me. I remember looking round at them as they worked and wondering how they were all working. It was a magical moment. I found my secondary teaching practice harder. The students were equally well behaved, but I found it harder to feel part of the very well-established staff team. I remember being left alone with sixty year nine students and leading a warmup with them. I felt like I was before an army lined up and staring at me. Looking back, the teachers knew that the students were well behaved enough to be taught like that, but at the time I was petrified! The children in both the primary and the secondary school were very well behaved. This environment wasn't anything like inner-city teaching or teaching children with SEN, which is what I moved straight onto after I qualified. Over the two terms, I fell in love with teaching. Those two terms ignited my love of just being with students in a teaching role.

I learnt how important relationships are when teaching – and I gained the confidence, mainly due to how well behaved they all were – to be more creative in my lessons.

It was a good grounding in the basics, but to me, teaching is a lifetime of learning. I read a quotation by Louise Hay the year I completed the course, which read:

Most good teachers are continually working to release even more,
to remove even deeper layers of limitation.
This becomes a lifetime occupation.

I have tried to live by the quotation ever since, because being a good teacher is fundamental to me as a person. I now feel I am most connected to the best parts of myself when I'm teaching or training.

My first official job was at a special school for children with social, emotional, and mental health needs. I had known I would work with those students since my time at Camp America. However, I hadn't planned on it being my first job as an NQT. This position was the exact opposite to the perfectly behaved students I'd had on teaching practice. I had my own class of year five children and also taught PE across the whole school. That year was baptism by fire. I missed the sixty year nine students, all jogging on the spot, as my new year three PE class all ran out the fire exit with no shoes on. I wondered why I was trying to teach maths as chairs flew across the room, and I spent many hours of my first year teaching with my back against the door of the classroom to stop children from escaping. As the year went on, I learnt how key creativity is. If I had fun, then the children had fun. We learnt how to make challah (Jewish bread) in RE and learnt about solids, liquids, and gases via helium balloons. Even more key than creativity, though, was relationships. It took a full year to get to know all the children well enough, but I learnt that when I know them and they know I know them, they can learn. By some miracle, by the end of that year, I could teach PE to every child in that school, and none of them ran out the door or threw anything across the room or fought anyone else! They could set up the gymnastics equipment safely, play football without it escalating into a brawl, stop when I asked them to, and the boys even started to enjoy dancing. I know, now, the science behind why relationships are so important for children. At the time, however, I only knew that the better I knew them and they knew me, the safer and happier everyone was and the more opportunities for learning there were. The importance of relationship and creativity that year shaped me as a teacher, and those have been my priorities as a teacher ever since.

My next role was for a school sports partnership. This role was based in a specialsSchool while teaching PE across all the area's special schools and pupil referral units. I was lucky enough to have a manager who was even more creative than I, and to be part of a newly formed team who learnt together and became very good friends. Although we all worked across different schools so didn't see each other much, we came together in our little office and shared stories and plans. We developed competitions, leadership courses, and delivered training. Many teachers are not lucky enough to experience a time when funding is enough and when the only limit on what is possible, in terms of teaching, is your imagination.

As part of this role, my manager asked me to start some after school sports clubs for children in care, as well as travelling children, because they were the least likely to attend extracurricular activities. We had some interesting experiences. I remember on one occasion dropping a child at home early because he had refused to put his seatbelt on in the minibus. As we pulled up to his house, he jumped off the bus and ran off down the road. He was seven years old. I knocked on his door and explained the situation to his mum. While we both had the absolute best intentions and got along and were kind, neither of us could understand the other's perspective. She didn't understand why the lack of a seatbelt (and that her son had run off down the road) was any kind of issue for me – and I couldn't fully understand why it wasn't for her!

My passion for working with children in care was reignited again through these clubs and led me to put in a bid to start a Community Interest Company, so that we could run many more activities during the school holidays. The bid was successful for a few reasons. We were within the 5 percent most deprived area of the country and were going to be working in partnership with a local children's centre. Plus, thanks to my existing role, we already had relationships with all the special schools and PRUs, so we knew that demand for the scheme would be high. We gained £250,000 over a five-year period. I had written the bid naïvely, not really understanding the ramifications of it. I presume my manager had, but, being the awesome person that she was, she had just let me get on with it. The opportunity meant that our sports partnership would be unlikely to gain additional lottery funding for a while. The whole partnership would turn its focus to 'inclusion' in an even bigger way for the next five years.

I hadn't realised at the time what it would mean for my development. I was twenty-five and had no idea how to manage a budget like that. Until that point, the most money I had managed, in a work context, was the £150 that I had used to buy a volleyball net and balls for the first school I taught at! This was a steep learning curve. I learnt how to hire staff, write policies, buy a minibus, train staff and volunteers, process DBS checks, pay people's wages, risk assess, organise residential trips, and engage parents and carers. We gained two 'good with outstanding' ratings from Ofsted. The second evaluation missed out on 'outstanding' because one soap dispenser was empty! The other dispensers were full . . . not that I still think about that!

At its busiest, the scheme, called Especially Happy Holidays, worked with over one hundred children with additional needs or those who were in care. We mixed children who had attachment trauma, ADHD, autism, physical disabilities, and learning difficulties. The atmosphere of acceptance, safety, inclusion, and hope that was created meant that all our children and staff wanted to be there. We had minimal behaviour issues because everyone wanted to be a part of the scheme. The children were brave. One of our rules was to give everything a go. Bravery is a nine-year-old who is used to regularly being excluded at school building a strong relationship with a fourteen-year-old volunteer and then wanting to impress him. Bravery is a twelve-year-old visually impaired girl stepping onto a trampoline and trusting an instructor and her peers to jump freely and even start doing seat drops. Bravery is children, so used to failing or being left out or excluded, risking trying so many things they had never done before. They did activities such as drama, pottery, trampolining, swimming, cooking, basketball, music, drumming, orienteering, and climbing. We had visiting teachers and artists for more specialist sessions and had at least one theme day per holiday. Rainbow Day, Space Day, and World Day, each saw us dress up in costumes, build a ten-foot rocket, and learn Spanish.

One of my favourite times was at the end of a scheme when we each had a helium balloon. Each group had a different colour balloon so that when the groups stood in line, we created a balloon rainbow. Everyone wrote a wish on the balloons, and we released them at the same time. Seeing over one hundred balloons fly into the sky, with all the children's wishes on them, in a massive rainbow, was amazing! Nowadays, this activity would be different because more is known about balloons and the environment. However, back then, this was a pretty magical moment for everyone.

The absolute best part of the scheme for me in addition to the children and families, were our volunteers – recruited from local secondary schools. They were between the ages of fourteen and eighteen, and due to the area we were based in, many had also overcome various struggles to be able to take part. They came with the enthusiasm that only teenagers of that age have access to. They took part in our staff training sessions and were mentored by senior staff. With guidance, they learnt to lead their own sessions and completed training in lifeguarding, swimming, teaching, cooking, and trampolining. They each worked with a small group of children, who fell in love with them, and they were the heart of the whole programme. They were the first to arrive, the last to leave, and always ready and willing to try anything new with 100 percent effort. One day I came across about twenty of them dancing to the Hokey Cokey in the hall, long after they said goodbye to their children, cleaned their areas, and done their prep for the next day. About three years in, the volunteers won an award for their dedication, and I believe they were the main reason the scheme was so successful. As we had funding for five years, the children we worked with became teenagers and wanted to become volunteers, and the volunteers turned eighteen and became staff. I cannot entirely put into words how I felt being part of creating that growth. As I look back now, knowing that many of those volunteers have become teachers themselves, I cannot imagine any other experience as fulfilling as those days. If people are really lucky, we have the opportunity to help the world in the biggest way we can – the way that is unique to each person, the way that uses all the knowledge and wisdom that has been hard earned, and the way that makes each person unique. Especially Happy Holidays was this type of opportunity and experience for me. The programme helped numerous others, for sure, but having the opportunity to give to the world in the best way I could, with no obstacles in the way and all the support I needed, felt like true freedom. I will always be so thankful to have had that experience.

> *There can be no keener revelation of a society's soul*
> *than the way in which it treats its children.*
> —*Nelson Mandela*

Having had the experience of working with children who were looked after, my next role was a teacher advisor for these children within a virtual school – a totally different role. At the start, I worked a lot with young people in residential homes who were usually not attending school. I was able to start a small teaching session, which happened to be based at a racetrack. I was also required to undertake some postgraduate training. The training involved learning about trauma and the impact it had on a developing brain, as well as writing an intervention for traumatized young people.

At the time I was working with fourteen-year-old sisters. They didn't engage with any professionals. They hadn't been in school for at least four years. They were in trouble with the law and often ran away. At the time I met them, they had just moved to their fifth home that year, and education was the last thing on their minds. They spent a couple of sessions with me at the racetrack, and when I saw how much they loved watching the horses, I decided to base my intervention around the horses. I started to take them horseback riding every couple of weeks, and that was enough to make sure they stayed in the night before, kept the appointments, and started to engage a bit more. They became different people when they were in the lesson and with the horses. They were polite, friendly, keen to learn, and very excited to tell everyone about their experiences.

However, as time went on and management changed, my role changed to attending meetings and not being able to do much direct work with children or young people. My career seemed to involve finding out that lots of children were failing within education but not having the capacity or direction to do anything about it.

As my enthusiasm for the role waned, my desire to make a difference increased. I decided to became a foster carer. Fostering was another massive learning curve. As a single person, still working, I found it a challenge, even with everything I had already learnt and experienced, personally and professionally. The young person I fostered was nine years old and just about to change schools when they came to live with me. They had learning difficulties that had only just been officially diagnosed and led to a school move, which meant leaving a very supportive mainstream primary school in order to go to a special school, without good friends. In addition, the young person was also leaving siblings who they had always lived with, for the first time. It was a hugely challenging time for them. However, we had some very wonderful times together. They learnt how to eat healthily, develop self-care skills, dress well, and read! One of my favourite memories was watching them play on the beach with our dog. Seeing how happy and free they were in the moment made all the harder times seem very worth it.

When they left, I knew I needed to do something new. I needed to feel hopeful and excited again and see more beauty in the world rather than being caught in an endless loop of sadness and trauma. Without much thought at all, I resigned from my job and decided to start an alternative provision. Usually, I would think through a decision like that and speak with at least a few trusted people. On that occasion, though, I just knew it was the right thing to do, regardless of the consequences.

Serendipity played a large part in what unfolded next. I had good links with the riding centre that I had developed some work with from my previous job. Especially Happy Holidays had an underspend that had been used a year earlier to build a log cabin on the site of that equestrian centre. The agreement was that the equestrian centre could use the cabin, in return for giving free riding lessons to the young people who came to Especially Happy Holidays. While that happened for a while, things changed, and I moved into the cabin to set it up as a classroom. The business slowly grew. The intervention that had been written as part of my previous role had been named Stable Relationships by a previous manager who was a bit of a genius with words. That name fit the business well, and with the tagline of 'Building relationships to inspire learning', we started the most amazing journey.

Take a deep breath.
Keep your body fully in the present and your mind
in the recent future.
Don't let the past get in your way.
—Linda Kohanov

In the early days of 2014, I was offering a lot of different activities to a lot of different schools, organisations, and young people. As time went on, the equestrian work clearly was the most popular and helpful for children and young people who were in care. I hadn't known this, but the area we set up in had the highest number of children's homes in the country, and most of our students came from this area. A lot of these children's homes had schools for the children attached to them. In order to live in one of those particular homes, and therefore attend the school, the child had typically had more than two failed foster placements, as well as significant attachment trauma and the resulting behaviour and education challenges. These young people made up, and still make up, about 95 percent of the young people that used our services. As we learnt about how these children learn, and what they needed to learn, our body of work grew larger.

I had not planned to spend seven years working with horses. I didn't know much about them. As a child I had a toy riding centre with horses which I played with all the time instead of dolls, and I had loved horses and riding, but I had not been near one since. I was lucky enough to work with an amazing equestrian centre who said yes to a lot of crazy ideas, and they were initially as excited and hopeful as I was. Creativity was, once again, key in those early days.

I was able to connect the research on trauma and attachment to equine research. I learnt that horses are prey animals and process sensory information in a way that is like a person who is traumatized. The most important information was that 'fight, flight, or flee' is the first response for both traumatized humans and horses (although mainly flee or freeze for a horse). Further, horses are hyper-vigilant to stay safe and want to be part of a herd, which makes them skilled at picking up on human cues and at building connections with other beings. As time went on and we worked with more young people, we refined our original one-to-one intervention and now have a lot of evidence showing the positive impact on each young person. In addition, we developed training for adults and a way of teaching the brain to traumatized children, young people, and those who work with them. This trauma-informed method was adopted by many of the schools we worked with as the way they used to teach everything and manage behaviour.

We also had so much fun developing lessons that fit into the curriculum with horses. The students learnt to tell the time with horses, learnt about the digestive system and teeth with horses, poetry with horses, shapes with horses, the medieval times with horses. It was the most fun teaching I have ever experienced. We were working with the most challenging children and young people, but they were generally pretty perfectly behaved during their time with us. The staff of the children's homes were often in shock at the children's behaviour but eventually became accustomed to seeing them interact with us and the horses so positively. In addition, we would get the children's paperwork through with huge risk assessments. Whilst I had to read the risk assessments, and plan appropriately for them, I learnt that whoever I would meet was likely to be very different from who they were on paper. It taught me that so much in teaching can be prejudged, and if enough people prejudge, the child just becomes what is expected. Horses don't judge, though, and we followed their lead and didn't judge either. We saw the absolute best of those young people. We saw them sit in a classroom and write and work. We saw them help their friends and discuss challenges. We saw them fall in love with the horses and begin to trust their inner goodness, as people who could learn, and who had something amazing to give to the world. Many of them took part in leadership programmes with younger children and spent their weekends volunteering with the horses. Many of them now ride often and have hopes to become riding instructors or teachers.

After a couple of years, we decided to share what we had learnt with more children and young people. We hit the road with the horses and travelled around the country, setting up in school playgrounds and playing fields. We taught our brain-based model to hundreds of children and staff at mainstream schools as they learnt the importance of feeling calm to learn though grooming, walking, and playing games with the horses. We also made the news, and our work was featured in *The Times*, *Times Educational Supplement*, *The Mirror*, Channel 5 News, BBC radio, and numerous Special Educational Needs, equine, holistic, and teaching publications. The highlight for me (aside from seeing the amazing development in the young people every day) was being asked to speak at a conference at the Centre for Child Mental Health in London. The centre is run by Dr Margot Sunderland, a leading authority in the world of child mental health, attachment, and trauma. Sitting on a stage, next to her, as the audience asked questions about our equine programme, felt like I'd done what I was meant to do. I had given what I was most able to give, and anything after that would just be a bonus. Our main one-to-one programme is currently being run by another equine centre and is ready and waiting to be rolled out into others. The plan is to write a book outlining the programme and some of the stories behind it. However, I haven't quite got there yet.

The harder side of the learning involved in Stable Relationships was, ironically, the relationships within our team. I worked with some amazing and very talented equestrians and teachers. There were clashes between the world of education and the world of equestrians though. Some of these clashes were funny learning experiences, like the time I had to be told we couldn't play Duck, Duck, Goose with the horses, no matter how well behaved they were, because running behind a horse is never going to pass a risk assessment. Another time we pulled up to a jam-packed school car park in a massive horse lorry, and the equine instructor couldn't understand why all the teachers couldn't just move their cars. However, as time went on, the challenge became keeping our working relationships as stable as they needed to be in order to work as well as we could with the young people. Priorities changed, and different pressures meant that it just wasn't possible to keep working as we had been.

I decided that I would like to take all the learning from the last six years of Stable Relationships and get a more secure and 'normal' job in a virtual school where I could, hopefully, use that learning for good. I quickly got a job working for a virtual school near my home. The office was based in a massive park, and that was the one of the main reasons I took the job. I could see a waterfall from my office window and went walking every lunchtime. I couldn't believe I was lucky enough to work somewhere so beautiful, and after the amazing, but pressured, last few years of self-employment, I really relished being able to take a step back, ask my manager if anything got challenging, and just have a caseload of young people with very set tasks. It was a peaceful job. I knew I wasn't using all my abilities, or really being stretched, but it enabled me to buy my first home, feel settled, and enjoy life as peaceful and easy for a while. I had a stable job, great relationships with family and friends, a very full life filled with fun and much freedom. I remember thinking that it was the first time in my life that everything had felt just right – everything was good and there was no danger. I could start to relax into that. I was in the job for just over a year, and about two months into feeling settled and peaceful, and then COVID hit.

> *The secret of life, though,*
> *is to fall seven times and to get up eight times.*
> *—Paulo Coelho*

COVID has been tough for so many people for many different reasons. To me, this time has felt like the world was telling people to sort things out . . . to clear anything that needs to be cleared. I have sensed that anything people haven't consciously cleared up to this point, COVID, in one way or another, has forced it to be cleared. For me, the last year has been the deepest healing I have ever been through. I realised the pandemic was getting serious when schools were closed during the first lockdown. Education has always been stable in my life. No matter what else was going on, children go to school and teachers show up.

When schools closed, I realised the world had changed. I caught COVID in March 2020. My illness was in the very early days when the information stated that people either got very sick and ended up in hospital or got a bit sick and were better within a couple of weeks. I didn't get well for ten plus months and still have relapses at the time of writing this. The first few weeks were scary because I kept thinking that I'd suddenly get way worse and end up in a hospital. Long COVID was yet to be discovered or recognised. The fear made the illness harder, but I was more ill than I have ever previously experienced. Just when I thought I was getting better, I would be hit with another wave of new symptoms. COVID made it hard to trust my body. It took months and a lot of conscious lifestyle changes and a lot of working through past trauma, which I thought I'd already worked through, to get healthy again. Also, COVID ended up being the key to a much deeper level of healing, from my own trauma, than I would ever have dreamed possible. One of the first things I needed to do was learn to breathe again! I learnt that I had spent all my life, to that point, breathing through my mouth rather than my nose, and from my chest rather than my stomach. I'd often feel like I couldn't get enough air, so would take extra deep breaths to compensate. This is the way people breathe if they need more oxygen, quickly. Everyone breathes like this at times, especially during stress, before returning to stomach and nose breathing. However, for me (and many other people) it was the way I habitually breathed. I learnt to breathe in that way from being under constant stress when I was growing up, but in today's busy world, many people breathe like that as their usual way of breathing. I had some online sessions with a lung physiotherapist. As I learnt how to breathe in a healthier way, I started to feel my body in ways I had never previously felt. I hadn't realised that I felt disconnected from my body previously. It had always just been there, letting me do whatever I needed to do. I felt my body if it hurt, but otherwise, I didn't feel it.

As I started to feel more physically, I decided to start yoga to see if it could help me feel more comfortable with breathing and moving again. The yoga and breathing started to enable me to feel my body, fully, for the first time. I was reminded of the scene in the film *Men in Black* when the alien takes over the farmer's body. The alien squashes into his body and looks so uncomfortable. He doesn't quite fit, and he finds it hard to breathe and talk and walk. That was how I felt for the first few months. Trying to coordinate calm breathing with walking, or even moving, was so hard. It took a few months of very conscious focus on it for it to finally start to feel a little more natural.

I had bad fatigue for about eight months and started a yoga class for people with chronic fatigue or related illness. During this class the focus was always on relaxation, calming the nervous system, and gentle movement coordinated with breath.[1] I slowly became more comfortable with breathing and moving, and I started to feel good in my body for the first time. It was such an awesome experience. Doing the yoga tree pose,

---

1. See Agombar, *Yoga Therapy for Stress.*

for example, and feeling it throughout my body, was amazing. I finally understood why a person would want to be in their body.

I also started having one-to-one yoga sessions. The sessions have taught me so much about feeling previous trauma, being with emotions, being present, and having compassion. I'm writing about yoga here because it has had a huge impact on how I have changed as a person through COVID, and it is the link between my previous job and the new job, which I got just as I started to recover properly from COVID.

I've been in my current job for just three months – a role in another virtual school. I'm managing a small team of staff, and we are responsible for monitoring and improving the educational outcomes of the 350 secondary-aged, looked-after children in an area of the Midlands. Since I started, one person has left and another has recently come back after being off with stress. The team is used to frequent changes during usual times, never mind COVID times when schools are stretched to their limits and exclusions are way higher than usual due to many staffing and logistic challenges.

I believe passionately that children and young people can feel only as secure as the adults around them, so I'm concentrating on helping the adults I'm working with feel safe and stable. For looked-after children, feeling secure is a challenge at the best of times, but after a year of COVID it currently feels like spinning plates. If one thing is temporarily stable, another comes crashing down. For me, this job feels like the perfect opportunity to put into practice everything I have learnt over a varied career, but more specifically everything that healing from COVID, and yoga, has taught me.

I had learnt all the theory behind working with trauma and traumatized young people and had been lucky enough to gain a wealth of experience in working with these young people who continue to constantly teach me the importance of creativity and relationship. Over the last year, COVID gave me the opportunity to feel what it is like to be on the receiving end of truly feeling and embodying trauma while also working and being with people who are present and compassionate in relationship, through yoga.

My new job can be stressful and challenging. My personal role is to take responsibility for managing my stress by using all the techniques I have learnt as a result of COVID, and healing from it. I have much greater capacity to be compassionate and stable for my team than I would have had pre-COVID. I am very protective of them, and I know that the more supported and safe they feel, the better job they will be able to do with their young people and schools. I'm excited to improve things within the team and, as a result, for the young people we work with.

Looking back at my time since Liverpool Hope, I have had a blessed career. I have had the most amazing opportunities, and Hope opened doors for me, even after a start in life that meant I probably should never have made it to university in the first place. I have learnt that it isn't really what you do that makes a difference, it's who you are. This year, and all its challenges, have brought that a lot more sharply into focus for me. The more I have been able to let people really see me, and the more I have been able to really see them, the more difference I've been able to make. Often, we don't know the difference this makes – I think this is especially true in teaching and in education.

My time at Hope shaped who I became. It helped me learn how to build relationships filled with safety, support, and fun. It unlocked my love of learning and showed me the freedom that is possible when there is an absence of fear, both physically and emotionally. These lessons had a massive impact on the rest of my life, and I very much hope that I have been, and will continue to be, able to share them as I move forward into the next stage of my life.

The act of writing this has led to me to explore the more positive side of life . . . the magical coincidences, the positive experiences, the feeling of knowing when something is meant to be exactly the way it is. Looking back at my life through these processes, I can see there is great balance and harmony. I'm not sure that the magical parts would have been possible without the harder parts, so I've come to realise the value of hope and faith in knowing that no experience will be wasted in terms of learning, and being able to make a positive difference in the world, no matter what challenges we face.

Our deepest fear is not that we are inadequate.
Our deepest fear is that we are powerful beyond measure.
It is our light, not our darkness that most frightens us.
And as we let our own light shine,
we unconsciously give other people permission to do the same.
As we are liberated from our own fear,
our presence automatically liberates others.
—Marianne Williamson

Bibliography

Agombar, Fiona. *Yoga Therapy for Stress, Burnout and Chronic Fatigue Syndrome.* Philadelphia: Singing Dragon, 2020.

Coelho, Paulo. *The Alchemist.* New York: HarperOne, 2015.

Hay, Louise L. *You Can Heal Your Life.* Carlsbad, CA: Hay, 1999.

Kohanov, Linda. *The Tao of Equus: A Woman's Journey of Healing and Transformation Through the Way of the Horse.* Novato, CA: New World Library, 2007.

Rogers, Carl. *Freedom to Learn in the 80s.* Columbus: Merrill, 1983.

Seuss, Dr. *I Can Read with My Eyes Shut.* Sydney: HaperCollinsChild, 2017.

Sonnenfeld, Barry, dir. *Men in Black.* Culver City, CA: Sony, 1997.

Williamson, Marianne. *A Return to Love: Reflections on the Principles of 'A Course in Miracles.'* London: HarperCollins, 1996.

4

The Brazilian Variant of Hope

PAULA BARROS AND LESSANDRO RODRIGUES

TALKING ABOUT HOPE IS the same as thinking about a promising future. The meaning of this magic word transports people to a world where dreams come true. Where there is hope, goodness is present.

Some may think of hope as passive. However, what is often perceived is that having hope without working for the desired dream to happen is the path to disillusionment. Thus, it is possible to argue that hope is linked to the construction of a better future, something that is done in an active and intentional manner.

A beautiful example is recorded in the city of Liverpool, Hope Street. That street's name is full of meanings. At one end of Hope Street and at the other end are two cathedrals, two beliefs, and the hope of peace that was hard built (and still is) by the hands of many women and men, anonymous and not.

Consequently, hope can be said to be the construction of bridges. They are bridges that lend themselves to connect the present time to a future of full, or possible, happiness. Thus, in order to have hope, it is necessary to have energy and a willingness to work and build good day after day.

Studying at Liverpool Hope University (at that time, 2001–2003, still 'College') was part of building a dream, so it was an act full of hope. Hope was a calculated adventure in search of a better future in two dimensions: personal and collective. Both dimensions are equally valuable for students who are aware of their role in society.

Choices Full of Dreams and Challenges

Back in 2000, when we were still architects recently graduated from the Universidade Federal de Minas Gerais, we were at a crossroads. The options were to continue with our activities in the architecture office (which Paula coordinated and expanded at that time), invest in the public career that I started (in 1999 I had assumed the post of head of the municipal Department of Culture in Betim), or invest in academic performance (which was a possible dream to be turned into reality). We made the decision to dream, and for that we went to study and deepen our knowledge for a few more years on the school benches, hence the decision to take the master's degree. We imagined that new knowledge, if it did not open doors for academic performance, would serve to enrich our repertoire and professional career already underway.

Once this first choice was made, we went on to another: Where to look for new knowledge?

We were living in a time when the world was getting smaller and smaller, where people and job opportunities were moving to circulate freely between countries. We had a great deficiency to overcome in order to face this new reality – the lack of international experience, which became an aggregate objective for academic development, was central. Consequently, we decided to study abroad, but not just anywhere, because we dreamed of something that would put us in contact with different cultures and that would give us the opportunity to experience the world.

England became an almost natural option to carry out our desires. First, the history of the country is mixed up with that of the development and formation of the Western world in several aspects, among which science, education, urban development, culture, economy, architecture, arts, and others were on the list of our concerns and possible study objects. Second, the relationship with people from different nations is part of the local culture, perhaps a consequence of the period in which the empire covered lands from the east to the west of the globe. Finally, the fact that England is part of Europe allowed us easy access to other countries with different languages and culture than those with which we would establish contact while on English soil.

Once the country was chosen, the next step was to define the university, which we based on the offer of master's programmes that met our expectations. We were looking for a reliable source that could present us with the best and, therefore, that would later be recognised in Brazil, so we found the British Council on the internet.[1] It was there that we learnt about the existence of the MA degree in contemporary urban renaissance, offered by Liverpool Hope University College, under the coordination of its Department of Geography.

The modules that were offered had total adherence to what we were looking for, as well as the focus of the course, which sought to train students to act in processes of urban revitalization. This field of study and professional activity takes place in a multidisciplinary environment where there is dialogue and interaction between professionals from different backgrounds, such as architects, urban planners, geographers, engineers, sociologists, economists, biologists, and others dedicated to thinking about the development of urban space in the contemporary world. The opportunity to learn in a universe like the one presented to us by the information materials accessed via the internet and later received by mail helped us to make the final choice.

Another important factor to be considered in this process was the existence of an English school devoted to training international students within Hope itself. Our master's course would start in September 2001, but we moved to Liverpool in January of that year to improve our English language skills. That, in itself, was a lot. For six months we had English classes Monday to Friday, nine a.m. to four p.m., in a class made up of Brazilians, Chinese, Japanese, Turks, Koreans, Argentines, and Palestinians.

There, we started to become citizens of the world. This has been fundamental for building our understanding of life, the relationship of respect and tolerance that must exist between people of different cultures, and also our role in a globalized world.

Finally, it is relevant to say that the choice of MA programme and university were also influenced by the city where all this would happen, Liverpool. At that time, we knew very little about the local reality beyond what was presented to us in Hope's own promotional material. The Beatles and Liverpool Football Club were our only references before choosing the university, but the reality of a city that was going through a culture-led urban regeneration process delighted us. Liverpool, according to the information we accessed, seemed to be the perfect laboratory (certainly one of the best in Europe at that time) to study our object of interest and what the MA in contemporary urban

---

1. See https://www.britishcouncil.org.

renaissance proposed to offer – knowledge related to cities undergoing urban revitalization processes.

Transforming Hope into Reality by Work

Liverpool was reborn from the ashes of previous years in which economic, social, and urban degradation had lowered its reputation as one of the UK's leading urban centres. The quest to be recognised as a European Capital of Culture and World Heritage Site meant that there was an integrated movement of the local community with its public and private institutions in the same direction. The atmosphere was of great euphoria, and it seemed to influence the decisions, the projects, and the resurrection of a time of glory that seemed to be left behind.

Today we realise that during those years the certainty that it was possible to aspire to bigger flights was reborn in Liverpool.

Therefore, we say that our choice was very correct and can be understood by us as a gift. We felt that Liverpool welcomed us. It certainly existed because the university had become our new home. At Hope we learnt a lot, but something infinitely higher than that was built in the relationship with our classmates, teachers, employees of Hope, and friends that we met in various social activities. One of the highlights was the Foundation Hour and the football matches on Tuesday evenings in the company of university employees, including the vice-chancellor, Prof. Simon Lee. He was a man who had certain skills on the football pitches, but he was infinitely better directing Hope, where he was Bobby Charlton, with his brain vision of the entire space from where he worked and coordinated his team.

This gift from Hope's former rector is essential for the strengthening and maintenance of our relationship to this day, and this gift enabled us to get to this very moment when we are writing this report. The ability to see someone's competencies and to value them is something that helps people to transform their hopes and dreams into reality.

With that, we can say that Hope fed our spirit, body, and mind, and we are very grateful for that. Our original dream was turned into reality. However, the reality far surpassed what we had hoped would happen.

The fact that we felt at home gave us the confidence to explore other possibilities besides those that we were initially looking for. We found in Liverpool the chance to exercise our professional skills in another country, which also qualified us enormously. Paula was hired as an architect by a design practice that worked in a city that was being transformed with full European investments aimed at revitalizing the local urban space. She was linked to Austin-Smith: Lord for a few years and was involved in the elaboration of various projects that are now built spaces in the city.

In parallel, I had the chance to take part in the work that used to be developed by a nongovernmental organisation dedicated to the valorization of local architecture and built heritage, Liverpool Architecture and Design Trust (LADT). There, while still a master's student and with the support of Hope University, we created, organised, and coordinated, in 2002, an international conference aimed at presenting experiences of urban revitalization underway in the English Northwest, in Barcelona, and in Brazil. For that event we involved institutions based in three countries: the Centro Iberoamericano de Desenvolvimento Estratégico Urbano (CIDEU), based in Barcelona, Spain; the Northwest Development Agency, an English regional development agency that was still in operation at the time and headquartered in Manchester; the Belo Horizonte City Hall, capital city of the state of Minas Gerais; the Escola de Arquitetura da Universidade Federal de Minas Gerais, headquarters of the event that took place in Belo Horizonte; the Instituto de Arquitetos do Brasil, Minas Gerais section; and Liverpool Hope University. Those were intense days of much learning and discussion, fuelled by the presentation of different views on the experiences of urban intervention underway at that time in the cities and countries represented in the conference.

It is important to recognise the role of that event as a catalyst to enable the construction of a continuous participation of Hope University in Brazil. We took that opportunity to establish a first bridge between Hope and our country and envisioned the possibility of extending it and perpetuating it over time. Hope's envoy to that conference visited Betim, a city where we had deep roots, to get to know two institutions that could potentially accommodate an arm in Brazil, which originated as Hope One World and is now Global Hope. That gesture allowed us, and the institutions visited, to dream it would be possible to have an international partner dedicated to its continuous development.

Almost twenty years have passed since then, and we realised that Hope also took its roots in Betim by believing in the dreams of Missão Ramacrisna, an entity that still hosts in Betim, annually, teachers and university students linked to Liverpool Hope University.

Hope for the Future

We imagined that returning to Brazil with a master's degree earned at an English university would be a passport for professional success. At the same time, we thought that returning to Brazil having established privileged contacts with people and institutions could help us to influence the improvement of life in the community that we had left behind. Two decades after that period, it is possible to say that hope was transformed into reality through the hard work and dreams of many people.

From a personal perspective, returning with a master of arts from England opened several doors. Since 2003, the academic exercise as a university professor has brought a lot of satisfaction, new learning, and the establishment of new friendships and working relationships with former students who are now professional colleagues. In parallel, the academic trajectory started in those years made us understand that studying is something for life, and now, as doctors, we continue to study, teach, and learn in the daily toil of the classroom.

On the other hand, the collective dimension resulting from that individual act full of hope fills us with joy and pride. Since 2003, Liverpool Hope University has been part of a community close to us in Betim. The decision to explore possibilities in a country where the language is not English and in a socially and economically disadvantaged community can be considered an act of courage, but mainly one of hope to build a better world for everyone. Some educational institutions are run by people who believe they train not only professionals, but also citizens. This is the case with Hope and its former and current administrators.

Those who ran the university at the time had the belief it was possible to give hope not only to their students and the community where it is located, but also to extend it to places other than those traditionally served by the institution. They dared to create bridges with an institution that is dedicated to the care of children in situations of social risk, Missão Ramacrisna. Through education, professional training, and the arts, this organisation has been doing exemplary work for decades in a local poor community.

To the excellence of the work carried out by Missão, the expertise of a university that operates in the field of visual and performing arts was added. It has been twenty years since Hope came to Betim to build hope day after day with teaching, exchange of experiences, and friendship. The presence of Hope University has helped to elevate the aspirations of many children and adolescents who come to be sure of the value of what they produce, which is fundamental for the personal success of each one of them and of Missão itself.

We believe that, in addition to the many and varied benefits generated in Betim, Hope University's activities in Brazil provide an expansion of the repertoire and worldview of its students and teachers. Immersion in a reality different from the one we are used to awakens other interests than those we have. Certainly, the many Hope students and teachers who were in Betim went through this process when they learnt about the difficulties faced by the people with whom they spent time in Brazil, as well as the strategies used by them to overcome the challenges of their daily lives.

Those who participate in a project like the one developed by Missão Ramacrisna do so only because they are sure that hope and work can together transform people's lives. This belief moves individuals with varying capacities, as well as institutions, in the same direction. Certainly, Hope University decided to participate in this process because it believed that something there had adherence to its purposes and beliefs.

Today, almost two decades after the arrival of the first students and teachers in Betim, what was strange is part of the repertoire. The novelties from the past have already been incorporated by the institution and its representatives who arrive in Betim every year. So, we can imagine, the maintenance of this project occurs because nowadays there are people at Hope who still believe there is space for positive change ahead and that the university can play a helpful role.

The bridge that was dreamed of in the past is well established today, but not completed. We think it will never be, because there will always be a new goal to be achieved, as happiness is a moving target. So, as long as there is hope, there must be work and dreams of better days, which will continue to move people and institutions, such as Missão Ramacrisna and Liverpool Hope University.

Personally, we can say that our current hope is that here there is always room for dreams. With the dream, there will be work and its realisation will be possible with the participation of many. Among the many will be the university that welcomed us, that decided to be part of the life of our community, and that has been helping (during the last two decades) to positively transform the lives of many people as strongly as it has helped to transform our personal lives.

May we continue to have hope, energy, and a desire to transform people's lives for the better. Let´s keep in touch with Hope! Nowadays, more than in any time of our lives, hope is necessary to fight against all challenges we have been facing in the world, in our countries, cities, local communities, and personal lives.

Thanks to Hope and hope.

5

This Researching Life
A Personal Odyssey

MICHAEL FORD

TEN MONTHS AFTER THE ATROCITIES of 9/11, I found myself sitting at the end of a row in a hushed cathedral that doubled that day as a university graduation arena. The organisation was second to none. The atmosphere electric. My ever-supportive family and friends were out there somewhere in the auditorium, but, as the first to be summoned to receive my doctorate in philosophy, my mind was on someone else.

Ascending from my seat in my red-and-black gown, the mortarboard a little too low on the forehead, I moved as elegantly as I dared toward the beaming vice-chancellor in conscious memory of one person – my father.

Dad had been a lecturer at the UK's first tertiary (post-sixteen) college. One recurring image I have of him is marking mathematics examination papers – reading them again and again to try to push borderline candidates over the pass mark. He was professionally scrupulous and fair, but always on the side of students, especially if they had worked industriously. Before my father's unexpected death at age of forty-nine, he had tried to persuade me as much he could to have a university education. I resisted time and again because I was determined to go to journalism school. Dad understood, though, and lived just long enough to witness my early newspaper reportage. He had, in fact, been an electrical engineer who had moved into teaching at thirty-six and never regretted it.

He had always recommended the world of higher education as a fruitful career pathway.

So that afternoon, in the modern cathedral building affectionately known as 'Paddy's Wigwam', I was doing it for Dad and thinking of him. The experience remains one of the most moving of my life, thanks largely to the creative vision of the then rector and chief executive, Professor Simon Lee, whose artistic flair and eye for detail made the day so memorable. Although I was officially a University of Liverpool graduate, Hope was instrumental in championing my research interests and offering a context where I could flourish – spiritually as well as intellectually.

In this personal account of a journey before, during, and after my time at Liverpool Hope, I write as someone with a dual appetite for journalism and theology, which, like embryonic twins, began to form during my teenage years, then gave birth to a distinct, if atypical, vocation. What kept both robust was a fervent love of research, which my years at Liverpool Hope synthesized and consolidated.

In this chapter, I aim to commentate on 'the beautiful game' of research and the unexpected goals it can lead to, especially for someone who was shaped by two passions simultaneously, preoccupations that some people might judge contradictory. The first part will try to give a sense of how my interest in research evolved, the second will explain how I drew from both disciplines for my PhD and how Liverpool Hope supported me unfailingly, while the final section will illustrate how studying there changed me for life. By the end of the essay, I hope to have shown how seemingly opposing drives within one person can create a harmony and result in human growth, especially when the fruitfulness of each is dependent on rigourous research.

The Origins of a Binary Research Temperament

By the age of fifteen, my predilection for both theology and journalism was gradually becoming evident. After my confirmation, I would visit the parish priest every month for a private discussion. What he would allude to as 'Michael's list' was an inventory of wide-ranging questions about the Christian religion. He did his best to satisfy the insatiable, if nascent, theological curiosity. I just wanted to find out more and more.

The same was true of the journalistic side but not in a conventional way. With *This Is Your Life* becoming one of the most popular shows on television, I embarked on my first serious research project: secretly digging out the lives of seven family members, eliciting tributes from relatives, friends, and colleagues, and then, at Christmas, surprising the unsuspecting subjects with their life stories (Dad and Mum included). I learnt so much about the nature of research during those months. While trying to uncover the date of a show on which my mother had appeared, the producer suddenly remembered that, when he had been writing the words for the posters two decades before, he had pressed too hard on a table that had since been polished many times. However, when he reached for a large magnifying glass and went forensically over the surface, he located the very date in the wood. As an aspiring researcher, to me that was an illustration of what persistence could achieve.

A couple of years later, I took the project a step further by researching the lives of two members of the local community, arranging this time for dozens of people to travel to my hometown for the surprise tributes. By the age of twenty-one, I was working on the actual television programme itself. As a young man, then, I was obsessed with research into other people's lives, piecing together their stories and energised by the way the biographical jigsaws fitted together. Experience as a newspaper feature writer, profiling anyone from a politician to a professor, fed the enthusiasm.

Although Dad wasn't to know it, sadly, I eventually weened myself off the addictive nature of journalism and went to the University of Bristol as a young mature student, reading theology and religious studies. In my third year, I researched the life and spirituality of Thomas Merton, with a framed monochromatic picture of the American contemplative perched on my bureau. I bought every book of Merton's I could afford and spent hours in the library discovering more about him. He was breathtakingly prolific, and any reader of his books, poems, or correspondence cannot fail to be struck by the breadth of his knowledge. His inspiring zeal for research and the scope of it are evident in a letter to Dom Jean Leclercq in October 1950:

> In Daniélou's Platonisme et T.M. on pages 7 and 211 there are references to St. Bernard's dependence(?) on St. Gregory of Nyssa. The opening of St. Bernard's series of Sermons obviously reflects the idea of Origen and Gregory of Nyssa that the Canticle of Canticles was for the formation of mystics while Proverbs and Ecclesiastes applied to the beginners and progressives. I find Bernard's echo of this point an interesting piece of evidence that

he considered the monastic vocation a remote call to mystical
union—if not a proximate one. Then, too, Gregory's homilies on
the Canticle of Canticles are full of a tripartite division of souls
into slaves, mercenaries and spouses. Gregory's apophatism is
not found in St. Bernard, but in his positive treatment of theology Bernard follows Origen. I think Fr. Daniélou also told me
that Bernard's attitude toward the Incarnate Word is founded
on Origen—I mean his thoughts on *amor carnalis Christi* [car-
nal love of Christ] in relation to mystical experience. I may be
wrong.[1]

While unravelling Merton, it was my experience of journalism that
came into play as I worked swiftly and thoroughly, checked the quotations, and wrote concisely. Likewise, when interviewing religious figures
for the city radio station down the road, I would draw from my knowledge of theology and ethics to prepare some questions they might not be
expecting. Journalistic copywriting and academic prose are not, however,
the same. The reporter summarises, simplifies, and offers an unbiased
account, whereas the research theologian analyses, homes in on, dissects,
and argues. I had, then, always to be careful that my broadcasts did not
sound too theologically complex or one-sided, for I was starting to learn
the academic skills of constructing my own case and that was against the
journalistic grain.

In later years, I managed to secure an ideal post for me as a producer
in the Religion and Ethics Department of the BBC, which was divided
between worship programmes and news/documentaries, but I maintained a foothold in both by taking my theology into the journalistic area
and my journalism into the world of faith. The famous poem of Dietrich
Bonhoeffer often hovered overhead:

> Who am I? This or the other?
> Am I one person today, and tomorrow another?
> Am I both at once?[2]

With journalism and theology firmly established as a dual professional identity, I travelled widely at home and abroad, meeting people
from all walks of life, from the Rev. Jesse Jackson to Archbishop Des-
mond Tutu, from the Dalai Lama to Dame Vera Lynn. Likewise, each
assignment provided the means to tether my theological and journalistic

1. Merton, *School for Charity*, 24–25.
2. Bonhoeffer, *Letters and Papers*, 131.

experience, whether it was the Dunblane Massacre in Scotland; the assassination of the Israeli prime minister, Yitzhak Rabin; the upsurgence of Islamic fundamentalism in Turkey; or the handover of Hong Kong. Many of the issues I covered had ethical implications such as racial and social justice, poverty, the place of women in the church, homosexuality, transgenderism, abortion, and ecological awareness.

Nonetheless, much as I valued this work at the cutting edge of current affairs, I missed academia and began to toy with the idea of a postgraduate research degree. I loved the in-depth world. But the practicalities of returning to university while continuing to lead a full-time life in the media appeared complex. It took some years to make the move and face the sacrifices. There would also be the transition from balanced, opinionless reporting to a more critical style, even about figures whose work I admired.

There was one person, in particular, whom I was keen to research – and he happened to have been the first person I had interviewed for BBC Radio 4, the main UK network. Henri J. M. Nouwen was a pastoral theologian and prolific author of international renown whose books I knew well. Moreover, he had been strongly influenced by Thomas Merton. With his gift for accessible spiritual writing, Nouwen brought the transcendent back into people's lives at a time when therapy seemed to have become more popular than religion. Nouwen was said to have reinvented the Christian spiritual tradition in a culturally pertinent way. He also needed a double harness. A clinical psychologist as well as a Roman Catholic priest, he was noted for finding the right words to bring hope to people, whether through paperbacks, lectures, homilies, or pastoral encounters. He always distinguished between optimism and hope, showing how joy was a fruit of hope.[3] It was no surprise that an anthology of his writings was titled *Seeds of Hope*.

After Nouwen's sudden death in 1996, I felt drawn to retrace the steps of his extraordinary life. There was a paucity of publications about this multi-gifted man who had been plagued by self-doubt and anxiety. What were the roots of that insecurity? Was this why his work was so appealing? There was much to investigate. I had two potential objectives in mind: to write the first book about him after his death or to produce a doctoral thesis on him. I reasoned that if the book did not come off, the doctorate might; or if I were not accepted for doctoral research, I might

---

3. Nouwen, *Here and Now*, 19.

eventually secure a publishing deal. To my surprise, both projects materialized and instantly plunged me into a dilemma: how could I manage
both while continuing at the BBC in a pressurised and peripatetic role?

In the end, I took an unpaid sabbatical to commence the research,
knowing the long flights between destinations would provide time to reflect on my future. My job was put on hold, but eventually I decided to re-
linquish my post and begin a new life as an author/academic researcher,
still working as a regular freelancer at the BBC but without the pension. It
was a step into the unknown but, after all, most likely a vocation, because
it was so crazy.

Transatlantic Investigation

Producing a psychological profile of a psychologist-priest proved a major
exercise over six years across continents. Plotted with military precision,
it would also be the first time that the personal struggles of a Roman
Catholic prelate had been scrutinized in this way. This was necessary
because Nouwen had written openly about his emotional pain but had
not always been transparent about its sources. His semi-confessional
style prompted many questions for a researcher. My methodology would
merge interview praxis in Europe and North America with theoretical
and psychological investigation in universities and colleges.

Research, while always hopeful, can be a lonely, isolating activity.
Perhaps only those who have confronted its relentless demands can fully
appreciate what is involved. I began by rereading all Nouwen's books and
then devising a card index to file all his key themes. I moved on to study
the little that had been published on him and made a few preliminary
telephone calls. Gradually I drew up a list of potential interviewees, an
inventory that grew longer and longer. The acknowledgements in Nouwen's books were a useful starting point, and the Henri Nouwen Literary Centre near Toronto supplied me with a number of key names with
addresses and telephone numbers. Over the course of a year, I travelled
across Northern Europe and North America to meet Nouwen's friends,
colleagues, rivals, and family members. There were some email and
telephone conversations, including one from Peru with the father of lib-
eration theology, Gustavo Gutiérrez, who had known Nouwen in South
America. This was a breakthrough in terms of original research. The
initial fax read, 'It is with great pleasure that I will cooperate with your

work concerning Henri. He was a good friend (I remember him very well) and Henri was also an exceptional person.' This was the academic equivalent of a journalistic scoop. I felt that my theology and journalism were synchronized as never before.

I interviewed a total of 125 people. Eighty percent were male. Most were aged over fifty. A fifth were Roman Catholic priests, Anglican priests, and Protestant ministers. The majority of the 20 percent female interviewees comprised religious sisters or women who had spent some time living in community. Most interviewees were practising Roman Catholics. Others represented Orthodox, Episcopal, and Baptist traditions. A few were Jewish. All represented key areas of Nouwen's life and ministry. I travelled to the communities where Nouwen had lived, worked, and visited – or to the places where his associates now resided. The research was indubitably coloured by my own journalistic experience, which I regarded as a legitimate form of inquiry for a theological subject. Reliable reporters leave no stone unturned, and this doggedness characterized the academic side too. I remember the first interview taking place by chance at the University of Oxford where I had just interviewed an American bishop for the BBC. It was pure serendipity. I reasoned there was a chance he had met Nouwen, and so I asked him. 'Oh yes,' he said, 'I certainly have.' I switched the recorder back on and heard how Nouwen's texts had helped seminarians in the bishop's diocese. The research was underway.

From Britain, I travelled to Rotterdam to meet Nouwen's family, followed by a visit to the University of Nijmegen scouring noticeboards and administrative records to try to track down Nouwen's former professors. I did not know if they were even still alive. I knocked on almost every door in one department to see if the current staff remembered anything about Nouwen's studying there forty years before. Few seemed to know anything about him. But I persisted. Behind the final door I tried was a lecturer who had not only heard of Nouwen but also gave me the names of two of his teachers. Within an hour, one of them was eagerly cycling to meet me, and by dusk I was having tea in the home of the other.

In Berlin I interviewed a pastor whom Nouwen had helped through a family suicide; in Brussels I quizzed Nouwen's Flemish publisher; in Trosly, Northern France, I stayed at L'Arche community where Nouwen had learnt to be a pastor for women and men with developmental disabilities. After each encounter, I felt the research crystalising. However, there were still many puzzles and evasions as to the nature of my subject's complex personality and struggles. Like journalism itself, academic research is about asking questions from many different angles. Determination to discover the truth, however, does not have to be accompanied by insensitivity.

From Europe I headed across the Atlantic to Boston. At Harvard I questioned Nouwen's former teaching staff; in New York more publishers and friends offered insights; in Nashville, Tennessee, a former teaching assistant from Yale shared his memories; in New Mexico, I joined a conference honouring Nouwen's memory. Each location yielded more information, more contacts, more acuity into a multilayered personality. Interviewing in those days on cassette, I was filling more and more each day. A mistake I made, however, was not writing up the material as I went along. Laptops were yet to make their mark, and I did not have much time to listen back to the interviews. Like a film, the chronology of Nouwen's life was recorded out of sequence.

At Yale Divinity School, Connecticut, where the Nouwen archives were then located, I spent days in an academic Aladdin's cave expanding my knowledge. It was here that I came across Nouwen's honorary doctorate in 1980 from Virginia Theological Seminary (where Professor Markham is now dean and president). Drawing at times from the author's own book titles, this citation gave me a sense of Nouwen's stature as a pastoral theologian:

> For a generation of Christians in search of their lost humanity and a forgotten spirituality, you have found a way out of solitude into creative discipleship and ministry. Few of your contemporaries have managed with such grace and clarity to combine the insights of modern psychology with the ancient truths of biblical religion. As a pastoral theologian your own vital priesthood serves as a living reminder to your colleagues in ministry of the need to help each new generation hear and understand the loving compassion of the Word of God. Through your books and essays, your published meditations and reflections, you have become one of the most widely read interpreters of the Christian way for seekers and followers in our time. And when you preach and teach the Gospel of God's renewing love in Christ, your hearers know the power of prophecy, evangelism, and the priestly cure of souls. . . . Baptized and ordained by the Catholic Church, you are now at home in many traditions and communities of the Christian family. Though a university scholar and

professor, you have discovered the secret of teaching all sorts and conditions of searching souls.[4]

Nouwen was an original and creative teacher. As I researched further at Yale, I found myself making new discoveries about his countercultural approach to theological education and chaplaincy:

> A university is not only a place for intellectual pursuits but also for a good amount of intellectualization: not only a place for rational behavior but also for elaborate rationalization. It is probably not only the most verbal place but also the most wordy and talkative place. Religion is not exempt from this phenomenon. The campus minister is exposed to a nearly unbelievable amount of words, arguments, ideas, concepts, and abstractions. . . . Often the drama of the campus minister is that, trapped by the need to understand and be understandable, he loses communication with the realities which, as he himself knows, are transcendent to his mind, In this context the campus minister needs silence. . . . Silence is that moment in which we not only stop the discussion with others but also the inner discussions with ourselves in which we can breathe freely and accept our identity as a gift. . . . Without silence we will lose our center and become victims of the many who constantly demand our attention.[5]

It was perhaps not surprising to read of Nouwen's identification with silence, for he tested his vocation in a Trappist monastery during several sabbaticals. It was at the Abbey of the Genesee in Piffard that Abbot John Eudes Bamberger, a medical doctor who had previously lived in the same community as Merton, contributed perceptions that enhanced my understanding of Nouwen immensely. After his death, Nouwen was even described as having been the Merton of his age. Bamberger corrected this perception:

> Anybody who thinks Nouwen was the Merton of his generation either didn't know Henri or didn't know Merton. They were very different types of people and they wrote to a different audience from different levels of experience. Henri was basically a teacher and a communicator on the popular level, whereas Merton wrote for a more specialized group in terms of his personal experience. . . . I think Merton was an unusual type of person; I don't think Henri was. He was not gifted in at all the same way

4. Quoted in Bergin et al., *Claiming God's Gifts*, page number unavailable.
5. Nouwen, 'Training for Campus Ministry', 32–33.

Merton was. Merton had a terrific amount of energy and also an unusual kind of intelligence. Henri was very devoted and reasonably intelligent, but he wasn't extraordinarily intelligent like Merton.[6]

Following my weekend with the Cistercians in upstate New York, I travelled by bus over the border into Canada to meet old friends of Nouwen and into Toronto to talk to academics at Regis College where he had also taught. For several days, I stayed in Nouwen's room at L'Arche Daybreak community at Richmond Hill where the writer had been pastor for nearly a decade. From Canada, my investigation took me back to the United States and to South Bend, Indiana, where Nouwen's teaching career had begun at the University of Notre Dame. Next on the itinerary was California where I discovered Nouwen had supported an HIV/AIDS ministry in the Bay area of San Francisco.

After six weeks on the road, I returned to England to transcribe some tapes before flying off again to Germany to join a flying trapeze troupe with whom Nouwen had spent some of his later years and among whom he had devised some highly original theology. The following month I was in Surrey speaking with a British couple who had guided him through his emotional breakdown, staying in the very cottage where Nouwen had authored some of his books. A few weeks later I returned to the US (Washington, DC, and Allentown) to meet more of Nouwen's friends and then returned to Liverpool for an Ash Wednesday interview with a Jesuit peace activist who had read Nouwen's work in jail. Later in the year I had to return to New York and Toronto for further conversations.

The empirical research, then, was extensive, as breathless as it reads, perhaps even excessive, but I wanted to do it as thoroughly as I could. The costs were covered by my book advances and additional expenses for travel.

Modus Operandi

Although I had questions in mind for each interviewee, I did not have a specific list in front of me; therefore, I did not disclose my questions beforehand. I shaped my work from a predominantly psycho-spiritual dynamic, which enabled me to address and examine equivocal statements that recur in Nouwen's writings on the themes of anxiety, loneliness, and

6. Ford, *Wounded Prophet*, 131–32.

the search for love. At the same time, this method allowed me to put to the test rumours about the precise nature and intensity of my subject's emotional struggles.

As I was working towards a thesis as well as a book, it seemed that such an open-ended style of methodology and the direct involvement of people from so many contrasting worlds would provide me with a certain academic equilibrium, from which I would be able to extricate fact from fantasy and make more informed and balanced judgements. My Poirot-like approach seemed germane to the investigation: the role of the detective is akin to the work of both a journalist and a theological researcher.

Later, as I reflected on what I had heard, I became convinced that Nouwen's remarkable books could not be fully understood in isolation from the emotional vicissitudes of his own life. I maintained that the study of a particular set of spiritual writings could never be separated from what was known – or could be known – about the life of their author. The connection was indissoluble, too valuable to be overlooked. As my approach to Nouwen owed as much to my journalistic training as it did to my theological formation and psychological interests, it seemed appropriate I should filter his life and work through those lenses.

My modus operandi was in the spirit of British author Richard Holmes for whom biography is 'a kind of pursuit, a tracking of the physical trail of someone's path through the past, a following of footsteps. You would never quite catch them; no, you would never quite catch them. But maybe, if you were lucky, you might write about the pursuit of that fleeting figure in such a way as to bring it alive in the present.'[7] For Holmes, the essential process of biography has two main elements or 'closely entwined strands'. The first is the gathering of the factual materials; the second is the creation of a fictional or imaginary relationship between the biographer and his subject, an ongoing dialogue between the two as they move over the same historical ground and trail of events. Holmes states, 'There is between them a ceaseless discussion, a reviewing and questioning of motives and actions and consequences, a steady if subliminal exchange of attitudes, judgements and conclusions.'[8]

But it was not always easy to stand back objectively. My relationship with Nouwen was not so different from Nouwen's own association with Merton about whom he writes, 'I met him only once. . . . Yet thereafter, his

7. Holmes, *Footsteps*, 27.
8. Holmes, *Footsteps*, 66.

person and work had such an impact on me, that his sudden death stirred me as if it were the death of one of my closest friends. It therefore seems natural for me to write for others about the man who has inspired me most in recent years.'[9] As Holmes notes, hero worship can develop into a love affair as one, more or less, consciously identifies with the subject:

> If you are not in love with them you will not follow them—not very far, anyway. But the true biographic process begins precisely at the moment, at the places, where this naïve form of love and identification breaks down. The moment of personal disillusion is the moment of impersonal, objective re-creation.[10]

This was certainly true for me as I took on board some less than flattering stories about an author who had, in fact, become a transatlantic friend. Was it possible to separate the 'Henri' who had been a personal inspiration from the 'Nouwen' who was now the subject of a critical biography and thesis? Would the two ever marry – and would it matter if there was a divorce? Nouwen was not the author I thought I knew, although eventually it became obvious to me that certain overreactions on his part had been dramatic expressions of a hidden, suppressed suffering. It was essential to dig, to detect, as Holmes puts it, 'a more complicated and subtle pattern'. Through its uncovering of personal pain, biography can find creative force and human nobility.[11] Because Nouwen had never written an autobiography and there were no detailed accounts of him as a person (a word derived from the Latin, *personare*, 'to sound through'), I found myself working with a tabula rasa, without any powerfully received images of Nouwen's character or inner identity, except through his own pen.

Something else intrigued me. A number of those who had already written about Nouwen seemed to warn others against delving too deeply, as though researchers should not ask too many questions. Academically, as well as journalistically, this only made me more curious. In perhaps an overprotectiveness towards Nouwen, these other writers had argued along the lines that the mystery of one man was too immense and too profound to be explained by another, and they warned of the need not to violate any secrets. What were they hinting at, and moreover, why were they so fearful? While, as I have intimated, sensitivity towards another's

9. Nouwen, *Thomas Merton*, 3.

10. Holmes, *Footsteps*, 63.

11. Holmes, *Footsteps*, 130.

life, especially so soon after a death, is not an inappropriate stance for a writer or academic, researchers should surely not be inhibited from asking questions or following leads especially where, in Nouwen's case, his own ambiguous writing impels a serious researcher to find out more. Although he was honest about the deep veins of his vulnerability, Nouwen was not an open book. He did appear to invite his followers to read between the lines – if they so wished.

A particular difficulty for other associates of Nouwen was that, even though they discerned him to be an authentic spiritual guide, they tended to overlook or deliberately ignore his human weaknesses because they felt obliged – or needed – to keep him on a pedestal. This might have caused them to spiritualize him to such an extent that they would never criticize him to his face or take issue with him. And yet, paradoxically, Nouwen was never a proud or conceited priest, and often displayed moving traits of humility; moreover, he was never slow to acknowledge his faults or ask forgiveness. Some people were, therefore, more cautious about what they were prepared to share, and there were attempts to control the public perception of Nouwen.

It is not unusual for doctoral students to produce a monograph of their work after graduating. In my own case, though, my biography *Wounded Prophet* was published while I was still working on the thesis, so I had to ensure that my PhD had a different focus. During this time, I received encouragement from an academic interviewee who said, 'I read your book with real gratitude for your research.' This made me realise that a painstaking research project was not a thankless task but something worthwhile in itself.

I had, in fact, previously signed on for an MPhil at another university, but my supervisor had unexpectedly moved back to North America two years later and I decided not to continue electronically. The University of Liverpool accepted my transition without any major issues. I was registered under its philosophy department but, as the university did not have a theology staff of its own, I would study spirituality at what was then Liverpool Hope University College. I was placed with two excellent supervisors, Ian Markham – Hope's first professor of theology and public life – and his colleague, Dr David Torevell. I could not have been more warmly welcomed. Much like my father's attitude towards his students, their eagerness to do all they could to support me made such a difference. Furthermore, I felt at home within the ecumenical ethos of Hope.

Within a few weeks, I had a short viva voce in the philosophy department of the University of Liverpool to upgrade my MPhil work into a PhD pathway. I still remember being questioned by Dr Michael McGhee and Professor Markham who made such percipient points that I really felt my research was being taken seriously – and valued. Professor Lee himself took a consistent interest and Pro-Rector Emeritus Dr R. John Elford took me to lunch at the Athenaeum Liverpool to discuss my work – all of this made me feel part of the Hope community. The staff could not have been more hospitable. Hope grounded the restless reporter – at least for a while.

But, as most research students would probably concur, one can pass through some unending tunnels when on track for a PhD. During the darker periods of bringing the research together, Ian and David were calm and proficient in rebooting my confidence and guiding me forward. The psychological drawback of researching one individual is that there can be a lingering fear, even peril, that the subject of your research will start to inhabit you. This did happen on one or two occasions, and I had to learn distance the hard way.

The time also came when I had become so close to my thesis that it appeared to make no sense and I could not see how to take it forward. I did not quite feel like throwing my work over a bridge in a time-honoured doctoral style, but I certainly felt overwhelmed at one stage. In my frustration one afternoon, I took myself off to the Odeon, Marble Arch, to turn my jaded mind to something else. It happened to be Anthony Minghella's *The Talented Mr Ripley*. In the middle of the screening, with widening eyes, I sat up straight in the stalls, exclaiming to myself, 'This film about identity is disclosing precisely what I should be writing about in my thesis. Eureka!' There and then, all the ideas started flowing again. I left the cinema, walked the length of Oxford Street to attend a Mass, and came out without remembering the Eucharist at all, so overpowering an effect had had Minghella's work on the shape of my PhD. Minghella had saved the day. Later, I had an opportunity to tell him in person that his movie had transformed my thesis. ('I'm so sorry,' he joked). It was a lesson in always remaining positive about research, never yielding to despair, and ultimately believing in the serendipity of hope.

By the time it came to my doctoral viva, I felt calm about facing the examining panel and was aided in this by Father Mike Thompson who offered moral support in the student's union beforehand (and later did a master's in theology at Hope). The late Catholic educationist Father

Michael Hayes was the meticulous chief inquisitor, with Hope's ever-perceptive Dr Jan Jobling acting as internal examiner. As I emerged with a positive outcome, I remember a smiling Professor Kenneth Newport making the one-time news reporter from the wilds of the West Country feel part of an academic community on the edge of a northern city. It wasn't that the PhD went to my head exactly, but, in the elated weeks after the viva, a strange thing happened: I found that I couldn't stop calling other people *Doctor* instead of their usual title – including the British Foreign Secretary live on global television! This was evidently some form of hysteria, now that the six-year ordeal was finally at an end.

But I could not afford to rest on my laurels.

While feverishly writing up my dissertation in the months after 9/11, I received a telephone call from New York to inform me that a copy of *Wounded Prophet* had been uncovered in the room of the atrocity's first official victim, Father Mychal Judge. The Franciscan fire chaplain and legendary Manhattan pastor who had faced similar struggles to Nouwen had died in the Twin Towers while ministering to fire crews. Friends told me it was possible he had been reading the book on Nouwen only hours before his death. This was serendipitous enough, but then, in the final stages of preparing my thesis for examination, a publisher asked me to write a biography of Mychal Judge to be published on the first anniversary of 9/11. I submitted the thesis in February 2002, flew to New York to interview fifty or so people for the Mychal Judge book, and got back just in time for my *viva* in April.

When I returned to America to promote the book, the scent of serendipity was still in the air as I found myself speaking at St Bonaventure University in upstate New York. This was where none other than Thomas Merton had been employed as an assistant professor of English between June 1940 and December 1941 when the seat of learning was known as St Bonaventure College. But I was not there only as an author that day – I remember conveying to the audience special greetings from Liverpool Hope, so the two places of learning were somehow connected by my visit. There was also another, little-known, connection: Merton's sister-in-law, Margaret, lived at Camden Street, Birkenhead, not far from Liverpool. Research is full of surprises.

A Current Flowing through a University

Research, both academic and journalistic, is essentially about breaking new ground by making connections for the first time. The word derives from the French *recherche* and means literally 'to search closely or investigate thoroughly'. Words of the Swiss theologian Hans Küng should invigorate any researcher:

> I have an infinite intellectual curiosity. I am never satisfied. I must always know more about everything so I can detect just what are the problems. I do not have many prejudices before starting, as I do not fear the outcome.[12]

In terms of the wider community, university research should be seen not as a hidden stream, occasionally nourishing academic life on the surface, but as a visible current, flowing through the heart of the institution. Research should always aim to underpin the teaching life of a university and the vocational preparation of its students. It is vital that up-to-date thinking in any discipline should directly lead to rigour and quality in all its courses. Research should expose students to the enthusiasm and passion which scholars have for their subject. It should always have implications for the curriculum, creating new courses as well as enriching existing modules.

Never an esoteric exercise taking place in the secret confines of an ivory tower, in the manner of the masters of *The Glass Bead Game* in Herman Hesse's famous novel, research should always be a vibrant, interdisciplinary activity, infusing and informing every aspect of university life. The cross-fertilization of ideas and expertise serves only to enrich a university's research culture. It helps create a particular atmosphere within the teaching environment, produces a strong intellectual consciousness, and, in a practical sense, ensures that students receive the best possible professional guidance before entering their chosen field. Research should involve partnership at regional, national, and international levels in a spirit of shared knowledge and innovation. It should be the policy of any university department to encourage all its staff to become research active. Research is a university's red carpet, not only in the sense that it can bring awards, but also because it creates hope and joy in an academic context.

When I began studying spirituality at Hope at the turn of the century in one of the early doctoral cohorts, the research culture was just

12. Hans Küng, in Lefevere, "Hans Küng."

developing. In 2021, the university submitted to the Research Excellence Framework thirteen units of assessment involving 177 staff, which essentially means that all these lecturers now have significant publications, which in turn will affect the university's funding and international reputation. The submission was hailed as the result of 'the incredibly hard work' of all Hope's researchers and those who support research activities. In just two decades, research has made its indelible mark at Liverpool Hope.

Reading for a research degree unquestionably changes a person. As you are handed your scroll, you are not the same person who filled out the application form. In fact, you should allow a doctorate to change you. It is a developmental process and always leads to personal growth. My time as a postgraduate student at Liverpool gave me the courage be different and to own that uniqueness, to take it back into the world, especially in terms of the psychology I had learnt through my research. The most noticeable refinement emerged in my writing which became tighter and more focused. That was on the journalistic front. Theologically I noticed improvements too. While making a radio programme in Kentucky and New York city for the fortieth anniversary of Merton's death, I had to script 'on the hoof' and found I was able to sum up spiritual concepts swiftly and with more theological coherence than I had ever managed before. On this assignment, I came face-to-face with monks who had actually lived with Merton.

With a longer-term research plan in mind, I made sure that I asked more questions of them than was necessary for the broadcast. Then, when I got back to England, I transcribed all this original material for my next book, *Spiritual Masters for All Seasons*. It was a distinct exercise in creating a spirituality of journalism, combining a journalistic interview methodology with theological research. It was appropriate that I should dedicate the book to one husband and wife couple with whom I had worked closely in journalism, and another who were theologians and had supported me spiritually. One reviewer, a theologian, emphasised the journalistic impetus of a spiritual book. This underlined the potential of a theology of journalism that had been evolving since Hope. In an official sense at last, journalism and theology seemed much less like opposites and more like complementary disciplines.

During my freelance journalistic days, I would occasionally interview people for longer than was customary. While this technique was sometimes necessary for the integrity of the story – to secure a better line or more substance that I detected was there but that needed careful extrication – I also felt that an interviewee's more complex responses, unsuitable for a crisp radio report, could be saved for future research purposes with the subject's permission. Clearly, I still yearned for the academic life, but I also realised it would be virtually impossible to find another context where I could couple both journalism and theology.

But serendipity was not far away again.

After speaking to the Institute of Communication Ethics in London, I was unexpectedly offered a visiting fellowship in spirituality and journalism at the University of Lincoln in the east of England. For some years, this invitation permitted me to develop both my research interests without feeling the need to justify anything. During this time, I came across the work of the American communication theorist James Carey (1934–2006). In one of his speeches, the Columbia University professor explained how the 'rough-hewn craft' of journalism had 'never been very comfortable in the overstuffed chairs of the faculty commons upholstered for professors of the liberal arts and the traditional professions of theology, law and medicine.' Here, then, he was clearly distinguishing between journalism and theology. However, he went on to point out that the natural academic home of journalism was under the humanities and humanistic social sciences, including philosophy, from which it could clarify its own moral foundations.[13]

Ethics has always been part of philosophy, and there are now a number of key texts on the ethics of journalism. When I was reading for my first degree in theology and religious studies, I was taught ethics as part of a philosophy programme and, at the BBC, I was employed, not in religious broadcasting as such, but in the Religion and Ethics Department where my work as a journalist and as a theologian were not in fact in conflict because they found a common haven in the world of ethics. In academia, also, journalism and theology should not be deemed in contradistinction, because they do, in fact, inhabit a mutually shared space under the umbrella of ethics and philosophy.

Even today, a column I continue to write on journalism and spirituality in *Today's American Catholic*, published in Connecticut, allows me to develop this understanding further, while during the pandemic lockdowns I undertook two research projects on the lives of British film directors Anthony Minghella and Alfred Hitchcock, and the influence of Roman Catholicism on their work. Retreats and other presentations,

---

13. Carey, 'Where Journalism Education.'

at home and abroad, provide other opportunities. One weekend, while I was preparing a retreat on Nouwen and needed some audio material to illustrate one of the sessions, I came across the interviews that, largely for reasons of space, had not been used in *Wounded Prophet* or the doctorate. Rather than keep the material in plastic boxes under the rafters, I felt it could form the basis for a new study on Nouwen, *Lonely Mystic.* I included sequences from my thesis that had never been published.

A difficult issue was whether or not to include private correspondence between Nouwen and his part-time secretary at Harvard, copies of which I had been given in Oakland two decades before but had kept confidential as it had seemed too premature to make them public. I realised, however, that the content, while not censorious, might unsettle some devotees of Nouwen. But following a conversation with one of my doctoral supervisors, I concluded that, from a research perspective, the publication of the postcards would make a further contribution to knowledge in terms of Nouwen's anguish at the time of his emotional breakdown. Future researchers might reap the benefits, and it was therefore perfectly reasonable to publish them twenty years on. Research can blossom many years after its initial collation.

In my experience, it is crucial that a researcher maintains strict independence over the research assignment, be it for a thesis or book. There is always the risk that some people who generously open doors also try to exert pressure on the course they believe the project should take. This must be politely but firmly resisted. It is solely the researcher's prerogative and responsibility all the way through.

Despite inevitable brushes with resentment and suspicion, which can dog any postdoctoral researcher (as well as media person), much continues to flower from the Liverpool Hope experience. The secret, perhaps, is not to become emotionally affected by those who may be envious or fearful but to work quietly on, bearing in mind the advice of Merton to a correspondent about not relying on the hope of results but on the truth of the work itself.[14] That was certainly the spirit that permeated Liverpool Metropolitan Cathedral that day when I shook hands with a vice-chancellor and heard these words:

'By virtue of the authority invested in me, I admit you to the degree of doctor in philosophy in this university.'

14. Forest, 'Thomas Merton's Letter.'

Thanks to everyone who had supported me along the way, not least the guiding lights of Hope, I really did sense that what took place that afternoon was a profound rite of passage. My life had always felt more like a vocation than a career, so it could not have been more fitting to have been officially installed as a doctor in that spiritual edifice. Looking again at the souvenir film of that afternoon, I am not sure the colour of my tie quite matched the gown, and I wish I had worn a flashier pair of shoes, but when all is said and done, the outer accoutrements were not really that important, and neither were the letters after my name.

It was the inner journey that mattered more.

Bibliography

Bonhoeffer, Dietrich. *Letters and Papers from Prison*. Translated by John Bowden. New introduction by Samuel Wells. London: SCM, 2017.

Bergin, Katherine T., et al. *Claiming God's Gifts: Trusting in the Power of Love and Acting in Faith*. [Introduction to the writings of Henri Nouwen.] South Bend, IN: University of Notre Dame Center for Social Concerns, 1997.

Carey, James W. 'Where Journalism Education Went Wrong.' Middle Tennessee State University, n.d. http://frank.mtsu.edu/~masscomm/seig96/carey/carey.htm. Site discontinued.

Durback, Robert. *Seeds of Hope: A Henri Nouwen Reader*. London: Darton, Longman & Todd, 1998.

Ford, Michael Andrew. *Father Mychal Judge: An Authentic American Hero*. Mahwah, NJ: Paulist, 2002.

———. *Lonely Mystic: A New Portrait of Henri J. M. Nouwen*. Mahwah, NJ: Paulist, 2018.

———. *Spiritual Masters for All Seasons*. Mahwah, NJ: HiddenSpring, 2009.

———. *Wounded Prophet: A Portrait of Henri J. M. Nouwen*. London: Darton, Longman & Todd, 2006.

Forest, Jim. 'Thomas Merton's Letter to a Young Activist.' Jim and Nancy Forest, 18 Oct. 2014. https://jimandnancyforest.com/2014/10/mertons-letter-to-a-young-activist.

Holmes, Richard. *Footsteps: Adventures of a Romantic Biographer*. London: Penguin, 1986.

Lefevere, Patricia. 'Hans Küng, Celebrated and Controversial Swiss Theologian, Has Died.' *National Catholic Reporter*, 6. Apr. 2021. https://www.ncronline.org/news/people/hans-k-ng-celebrated-and-controversial-swiss-theologian-has-died.

Merton, Thomas. *The School for Charity: Letters on Religious Renewal and Spiritual Direction*. Edited by Patrick Hart. New York: Farrar, Straus, Giroux, 1990.

Minghella, Anthony. *The Talented Mr. Ripley*. Los Angeles: Mirage, 1999.

Nouwen, Henri J. M. *Here and Now: Life in the Spirit*. London: Darton, Longman & Todd, 1994.

———. *Thomas Merton: Contemplative Critic*. New York: Triumph, 1991.

————. 'Training for the Campus Ministry.' *Pastoral Psychology* 20 (Mar. 1969) 27–38. As reproduced in *Inclusion and Embrace* for the 1997 Tipple-Vosburgh Lectures and Alumni/AE Reunion.

Shannon, William H. *The Hidden Ground of Love: Letters by Thomas Merton.* New York: Farrar, Straus, Giroux, 1985.

6

The Pedagogy of Hope
Organisational Strategy and Student Experience

Sanjee Perera

Canon Dr Sanjee Perera is the archbishops' advisor on minority ethnic An-glican concerns in the Church of England. She is a cognitive ecclesiologist specializing in ethnocentric identity in Anglican ecclesiology. Sanjee is an honorary research fellow at the University of Durham; research fellow at William Temple Foundation; associate fellow at the Open University School of Law; visiting fellow at the Centre for Trust, Peace and Social Relations, Coventry University; and honorary research fellow in Theology and Reli-gious Studies at the University of Chester. She is also a trustee of various Christian missional organisations including World Friendship and SPCK. She is an avid gardener, choral singer, and a church crawler with a pas-sion for stained glass and lives in community with ordinands at Queens foundation.

Go and open the door.
Maybe outside there's
a tree, or a wood,
a garden,
or a magic city.
Go and open the door.
Maybe a dog's rummaging.
Maybe you'll see a face,
or an eye,
or the picture

of a picture.
Go and open the door.
If there's a fog
it will clear.
Go and open the door.
Even if there's only
the darkness ticking,
even if there's only
the hollow wind,
even if
nothing
is there,
go and open the door.
At least
there'll be
a draught.

—MIROSLAV HOLUB

CZECH POET MIROSLAV HOLUB, author of these words, was no mere dreamer; he was a pathologist and immunologist who didn't live to see the turn of this millennium but was a prophet for this pestilence we are drowning in, who saw the hollow bones of time, and in it found grace beyond measure. His were among the hastily written words a friend sent to me recently, in the midst of this pandemic, at a time I was numb with grief. The nostalgic in me opened a long-forgotten scrapbook, the scrapbook my friends made me as I left for university at the turn of the century, and added the poem for posterity, to remind me that the world was kind too. It was a scrapbook saturated in that calling, cajoling, anxious love, made by friends who knew I was frozen in grief by the death of my best friend in the late 90s. He had happened to be on a train that held the fatal toxic despair of a suicide bomber on his way back home to Sri Lanka – a journey I should have taken with him. We had dreamed of university together, he and I. And here I was, alone in Liverpool, a foreign city, abandoned to live out a long existence without him. The scrapbook brought back the memory of ancient scars bereft of hope, and the rich pedagogy of an extraordinary institution I blew into rather by chance, because of the whimsical philosophy of my father, who hoped I might return to the land of the living in the soft wet earth and warm hospitality of this bustling city of migrants.

Hope, by definition, is always a serendipitous find, and elsewhere in this book I know Prof. Simon Lee has written about my father's encounter with Sean Gallagher, the Liverpool Hope finance director who inspired him to move me across to this maritime city, that called out to the trader and adventurer alike. My father had seen something rare when he encountered Sean, a staunch and gentle Irishhman who is a second father to me to this day, serving coffee at Hope on the Waterfront, the university's internet café in Albert Dock. Later, Dad said, if Sean was the typical senior administrator at this university, he felt I was in safe hands. More importantly he felt that there was something I could learn from this unique wellspring that I might not find in the grand institutions I aspired to, or the musty libraries I had spent my young years hiding in. For me, university was about learning why great atrocities happen, and a place to make sense of an existentialist crisis that had come too early. When my father suggested I transfer from university in Western Australia, I was confused at best, and for months vociferously annoyed. He relented, and suggested I try it out for six months and return to Australia if it didn't suit. We were a family that rarely verbalized emotion, but in a rare moment of deep candid wisdom, he said, 'Of course I care about your qualifications, but more importantly I want you to live, and love life!' Perhaps, my near escape from sharing my best friend's fate had shaken him more than I had given him credit for. In the horrors of a civil war we lived in the shadow of, I had escaped with my life more times than he was comfortable with. Near-death encounters make philosophers of us all, but for him university was clearly more about self-discovery and life skills than academic qualification. More than two decades later, I have acquired those various qualifications and honorary fellowships and titles I aspired to. I have devoured libraries and reveled in the company of great thinkers and woven rich patterns into the fabric of knowledge in pioneering research. But the quality that has seen me through the furnace of life, that has kept me alive and even flourishing, despite much, is that often disparaged quality *hope*.

Hope is an integral part of the human condition, and its significance for higher education has been widely noted. Nevertheless, it is also a complex and dynamic metaphysical category of human experience, and getting to grips with its characteristics and dynamics is a contested controversy. As most psychologists might, I understood it as an undifferentiated experience within the frameworks of socially mediated human capacity with varying affective, cognitive, and behavioural dimensions.

Among the various paradigms posited within cognitive and affective domains, the work of social psychologist Charles Snyder[1] shaped the affective domain of my own work on moral development, pro-social behaviours, and group processes, even when the neo-Kohlbergian schools of neurocognition dominated the thesis. Alternatively, pedagogical strategies of hope draw on philosophy and theology instead of sociobiology or cognitive psychology and are often based on the modes of (a) patient, (b) critical, (c) sound, (d) resolute, and (e) transformative models, which are associated with different pedagogical strategies, including the works of Paulo Freire, Henry Giroux, or bell hooks.[2]

Typically categorized as a positive emotion, hope often occurs in the midst of negative or uncertain circumstances. It is decidedly cognitive, yet we suppress the emotion for fear we will be disappointed if the hoped-for outcome is not realised. At the same time it is a state we intentionally experience or maintain. We decide to hope or refuse to give up hope for fear of actual, psychological, or even moral consequences that may occur if we do not hope. And the types of outcomes we hope for are as varied as the emotion is complex. They range from hopes of this world such as getting a promotion or recovering from an illness to the divine hope rooted in God's promise.

Seeds of Hope

Liverpool, in hindsight, was an unlikely place to look for the subversive pedagogy of grand metaphysical realities. The first impression I had of the city was the rubble. It was my first encounter with European war damage. The bare shells of row upon rows of condemned Victorian and Georgian buildings awaited their fate, like an effigy of the generations of desperate refugees that had arrived at its ports. At the close of the century, this city founded on the lifeblood of slavery was still rebuilding from war damage, sectarian tensions, and race riots.

The violence erupted in April of 1981 in Brixton as a result of Operation Swamp, which reached Moss Side and elsewhere due to oppressive racialized discrimination,[3] spilling over to Liverpool by that July and fusing the brimming racial tension in Toxteth. More than 486 police

---

1. See, e.g., Snyder, *Psychology of Hope.*
2. Webb, 'Pedagogies of Hope.'
3. Grover, *Crime and Inequality.*

officers were injured, seventy buildings were burnt down, and the damage caused to the city's fabric came to an estimated value of £7.5 million. The city was shaken to the core as more than five hundred people were arrested and one was killed.[4] Tear gas (CS gas) had been deployed for the first time in Britain.[5] Bishop David Sheppard and Archbishop Derek Worlock, alongside local churches and their leaders, such as Fr Austin Smith, stepped in to mediate and develop a dialogue with the leaders of the Black community to calm the tension.[6] The *Scarman Report* identified racial discrimination in its 1981 account, but not institutional racism,[7] and in 1989 a hard-hitting report commissioned by Liverpool City Council, chaired by Lord Gifford QC with Wally Brown and Ruth Bundey, addressed racism and the legacy of slavery, including in the allusion of its title, *Loosen the Shackles*; but it was not until 1999 that the *Macpherson Report*'s use of the telling phrase of 'institutional racism' cut through indifferent or ineffectual media reporting to resonate with the wider public.[8] This led to a further dislocation from systems solutions in the city, challenging the legitimacy and moral authority permeating from virtue-based institutions.[9]

Starved out by economic estrangement in national politics, and struggling under the yoke of urban poverty, the city distrusted the establishment and was wary of organisational interventions. No city in the country was as desperate for *hope* to be more than a fluffy metaphysical idea. Social mobility and higher education were beyond the hopes of many of its working-class inhabitants, who were increasingly frustrated at being locked out of the nation's prosperity and sustained employment. And in strange serendipity, the new rector, Prof. Simon Lee, envisioned a pedagogy requisite for the time, the place, the century; set to work with a group of like-minded visionaries; and renamed the institution Liverpool Hope.

Born out of the ecumenical practical theology of two bishops of the city – the Anglican bishop of Liverpool, David Sheppard, and the Roman Catholic archbishop of Liverpool, Derek Worlock – Liverpool Hope

---

4. *Liverpool Echo*, 'Leroy Cooper.'
5. John, 'Legacy of Brixton Riots.'
6. Worlock and Sheppard, *Better Together*, 75.
7. Scarman, *Brixton Disorders*.
8. Home Affairs Committee, *Macpherson Report*.
9. Hansard, *Scarman Report*.

aspired to embody this much-abused Christian virtue. Maria Power, expert in Catholic social thought, exploring how Sheppard and Worlock fused Anglican and Roman Catholic theology in their promotion of the Common Good argues that

> with its emphasis on the achievement of human potential, [it] became an umbrella term under which they placed a number of concepts that were central to their partnership. The most important of these focused upon the poor or disadvantaged of the city and manifested itself in the practice of what is now known in the Catholic Church as the 'preferential option for the poor' or as Sheppard preferred 'bias to the poor'. It was from a belief in this concept and its rootedness in the Gospel that all of the practical applications of their work emerged.[10]

She suggests that confronted with a city in decline and crisis so dire, 'set to become the Jarrow of the 1980s,'[11] Sheppard and Worlock conceived their bishopric ministry and theology attuned to this context. Driven by the gospel and believing that they had to do so in a way relevant to the city rather than remaining within a suburban or middle-class silo, they wove an ecumenical theology that would transform a city.[12] Liverpool Hope adopted this ecumenical theology, and the words and ambitions of this remarkable partnership.

Building on the work of three indomitable Anglican and Roman Catholic battleships against poverty and despair – St Katharine's, Notre Dame, and Christ's Colleges – and the vision, innovation, and enterprising creativity of their religious sisters who were the lifeblood of Hope in the city, Liverpool Hope seemed to set about in an implausible adventure of a glorious ecumenical fellowship. The cynical of the city, who often had more trust in the charity of these sisters than in grand theology, watched closely as the name Hope was adopted from Hope Street, which links both cathedrals, a living parable of its ecumenical aspirations, in a city rife with sectarian tension. Reflecting on the name and revitalized vision, Revd Dr John Elford argues that Hope was *'one of the most mission-explicit Christian institutions in British higher education'*.[13] This city mired in poverty and cynicism and fatigued by false promises was no place for

---

10. Power, 'Reconciling State and Society?', 553.
11. Power, 'Reconciling State and Society?', 552.
12. Sheppard and Worlock, *With Hope*.
13. Elford, *Foundation of Hope* (emphasis original).

nostalgic churchy virtue ethics that held no substance, and Liverpool Hope set to work to prove to the city and to the world the tangible actions and dynamic substance of this pedagogy of hope.

Like the city, I arrived a resentful, juvenile combination of cynicism and naïveté, bruised by violent ethnic conflict, distrustful of structural redemption, and sceptical of the claims of glossy institutional PR exercises. My father, in his wisdom, had seen that the scars of the city would match my own. The institution met my naïve cynicism with characteristic tender hospitality. When I first arrived at the airport in the late 90s in Liverpool, I was met by Sean Gallagher and Anne Wade, a friend of my parents with whom I would live and who would serve as my guardian. Being singularly naïve and entitled, it didn't occur to me how peculiar it was to have a personal welcome committee of the university senior administration, which would not have happened anywhere else, in any other university in the country.

Hope against Hope

In a letter to the American philosopher Jesse Glenn Gray, Hannah Arendt wrote that the only reading she recommends to all her students is *Hope against Hope* by Nadezhda Mandelstam.[14] Written by a Russian Jewish writer and educator, and the wife of the poet Osip Mandelstam, the work details life under Stalin's regime and the struggle to survive at the centre of the liberal resistance, and of the terrible final years of persecution and torment before the author's husband is murdered. The sequel, *Hope Abandoned*, is about horror as a way of life than as an anomaly. Clive James calls these two books 'key chapters in the new bible that the twentieth century had written for us'.[15] Arendt called it 'one of the real documents' of the twentieth century.[16] They grasped the hard logic and resilience I had awoken to at the time.

Arendt scholar Samantha Rose Hill, from the Hannah Arendt Center for Politics and Humanities, argues:

> Many discussions of hope veer toward the saccharine, and speak to a desire for catharsis. Even the most jaded observers of world affairs can find it difficult not to catch their breath at

14. In Russian, *nadezhda* means 'hope'.

15. James, *Cultural Amnesia*, 414–15.

16. Hill, 'When Hope Is Hindrance.'

the moment of suspense, hoping for good to triumph over evil and deliver a happy ending. For some, discussions of hope are attached to notions of a radical political vision for the future, while for others hope is a political slogan used to motivate the masses. Some people uphold hope as a form of liberal faith in progress, while for others still hope expresses faith in God and life after death.[17]

Hill explores Arendt's condemnation of hope as a dangerous barrier to acting courageously in dark times and suggests that the discourse of hope is often a distraction from realism and action, 'to escape into some fool's paradise of firmly held ideological convictions when confronted with facts.'[18] As a teenager cossetted by extraordinary privilege and then faced with extreme realities, this was a congruent worldview to settle on. Having aspired to study theology for most of my teenage years, I dropped it halfway through my degree for two more pragmatic 'ologies', namely psychology and sociology. I wanted to attribute causality to the atrocities of the world, and theodicy afforded little microanalysis on this, I thought at the time. *My best friend died because Eve made Adam a fruit salad* was less satisfying than the promise of complex systems solutions and big data analysis of political ideologies, pro-social behaviours, group dynamics, and socioeconomic models.

Hospitality as Strategy

In sharp dissonance to my intellectual pursuits, my first week on campus was much like that first day when I arrived in the city. The long-suffering Isabelle O'Reilly, the then Registrar Mary Ford's personal assistant, was tasked with babysitting me. She took me from lecture to lecture. When I said I'd like to join the choir, she dutifully took me across to Dr Ian Sharp who welcomed me to the S Katharines Choir, which I sang in for years to follow. When I said I'd like to join the Student Union and the student newspaper, she introduced me to the Student Union sabbatical team and the Derwent, and I immediately found myself appointed as a subeditor and running for SU exec elections that were scheduled a few weeks after I had arrived. And this charmed extraordinary experience rolled on, seeming implausible even to me, as I narrated the hospitality

17. Hill, 'When Hope Is Hindrance.'
18. Arendt, *Human Condition*, 72.

and opportunity at the institution to friends in other higher education institutions. When I was looking for a student job as a bartender, I found myself swiftly employed as a finance assistant and personal assistant to the finance director, managing everything from Sean's towers of records of the institutional bids to the dead files room. I rarely appreciated the various finance sector staff development training programmes I was packed off to, but two decades later, I must confess they added a value to my career that I couldn't have imagined then. A year later, senior management deployed me to the marketing department, confident that the talented Sharon Bassett, the then director of marketing, might serve as an excellent mentor to my nascent ambitions. Again, it equipped me with skills and experiences that I draw from deeply to this day.

This curated mentoring continued in a satellite of scholars and activists, including exceptional pioneers like Professor Protasia Torkington. A racial justice activist and sociologist, who in the early to mid-90s was one of the handful of female Black professors in the country, Pro is one of the unsung heroes of Liverpool's racial justice legacy in the wake of the Toxteth riots. Deeply involved in rebuilding trust in the city with her community reconciliation work in the aftermath of the violence, Pro was made the director of the Applied Research Centre and Liverpool Hope's public engagement work to enhance her work in with the city's Black communities. Hope in the Community gave her the freedom to do what she loved best, while still teaching, researching, and mentoring. Later, her Black Science Summer Schools transformed a generation of Black aspirations into reality, and I count it a privilege to have seen this incredible work firsthand.

Another of my lecturers who had a significant impact on me was American theologian and housing justice activist Canon Dr Shannon Ledbetter who was a former Bond girl turned clergy woman,[19] when ordaining women was a novelty. Her dedication to the gospel and to urban housing projects in Granby Toxteth on fallow church land, partnering first with Habitat for Humanity, then setting up her own charity – Housing People, Building Communities – filled me with a confidence that these directives of the gospel to feed the hungry and give shelter to the homeless were possible with perseverance, creativity, and vision. I learnt as much about myself and my calling and vocation, talking to atheist students and homeless volunteers, as I did the skills of an adept

19. With apologies to Canon Dr Ledbetter who is often embarrassed at being framed thus.

roofer and construction worker. While I have always been confident in my intellectual, academic, and analytical skills, years of dance class and deportment lessons hadn't confronted my acute dyspraxia. I have always been terrified of strenuous physical chores, and construction work was probably the last place one would expect to find me. Handling a drill while balanced precariously on a scaffold on a roof edge gave me a confidence and perspective I hadn't expected to find at university. I continued to take student teams to volunteer years after I had graduated, when I was employed as a psychology lecturer and senior resident tutor, hoping it would give my students what it gave me, a confidence in the impossible.

I am grateful that none of my lecturers and tutors were mere armchair academics locked away in an ivory tower. Both vice-chancellors I was privileged to serve under were adamant that academia must be a fresh spring, and tutors, lecturers, and educators must engage in primary research, public or industry engagement, and community activism. Liverpool Hope was no stale, out-of-touch Camelot; it was a fresh spring that wove an enchantment on all its students, an enigma that captivated the listening, learning soul into an active agent of what Hans Urs von Balthasar might call the archetypes of the *dramatis personae* in the 'theo-dramatic horizon', the culmination of the action and passion of God and man.[20] The institution was clear: the pedagogy of Hope wasn't contained to curriculum and classroom. It was a place that immersed and stimulated in you a lifelong lesson that continues to unravel in captivating revelation. It is here that I started to listen, almost unconsciously, to the inner workings of a university, curious to unravel this enigma and heard the echoes of a pedagogy that I hadn't quite found in the Sheppard-Worlock library.

Strategic Social Mobility

Quite often, early in the morning, just before nine a.m., the senior management team – Prof. Lee, Sean Gallagher, Bill Chambers, Alan Catterson, Bernard Longden, Keith Alcock, Tony Grayson, and Rob Page – would all gather in a huddle in our big open-plan finance office and talk through the serious business of the day. And there I was, a mere fresher, a fly on the wall, quietly getting on with work, listening into the careful strategies of Hope. Again and again, I saw a careful weaving of words from inspirational social justice activists; Liverpool Hope publications were

---

20. Balthasar, *Dramatis Personae*.

brimful of these. Robert Kennedy's speech to students in South Africa on standing up for justice emblazoned our prospectus:

> Each time a person stands up for an ideal, or acts to improve the lot of others, or strikes out against injustice, they send forth a tiny ripple of hope, and crossing each other from a million different centers of energy and daring, those ripples build a current which can sweep down the mightiest walls of oppression and resistance.[21]

Another favourite was Cardinal Suenens's famous words on Hope:

> To hope is a duty, not a luxury. To hope is not to dream but to turn dreams into reality. Happy are those who have the courage to dream dreams and who are ready to pay the price so that dreams take shape in other people's lives.[22]

A catalogue of iridescent and evocative words borne of great tempest, courage, and sacrifice infused every print and painting, crack and crevice, brick and mortar across the campus. And this is when I began to realise that what may have seemed like cheesy quotations to social science academics and the various unions, including the Students' Union, whose executive I was a part of, were the earnest hopes of these sober senior administrators.

I was fascinated; given the revolutionary politics of the 90s, they were the *Man*. And this was a time of union uprisings due to restructures – restructures in which much of our domestic and service staff were made redundant. Staff were redeployed to different positions based on the evolving needs of students.[23] As the invisible, insignificant student staffer I was, few noticed me in the room as I eavesdropped on the power dynamics while taking minutes or administering secretarial duties. I

---

21. Kennedy, 'Day of Affirmation Address.'

22. Suenens, *New Pentecost*, viii.

23. The governing body, strongly influenced by the four bishops and two sisters of Notre Dame among its members, exercised a policy of no compulsory redundancies. This meant that, unless a staff member wanted to leave, redeployment was necessary to adjust to changing circumstances. For instance, there were staff preparing three meals a day for students living in halls of residence, but the days were coming when students and their families wanted a self-catering option. Many students did not wish to be woken up early so that domestic staff could clean their rooms, but they did want the library to be kept open through the night, not least to use the computers there before the era in which students had their own laptops. This led to staffing redeployment to adapt to the changing needs of students.

prepared to take a Marxist view on the proceedings, unquestionably on the side of the unions, one of which I was an executive officer of. I often listened in scorn as redundance numbers escalated as the nature of universities changed. Suddenly, students were expected to clean their own rooms and do their own laundry, significantly changing the privileged life of undergraduate scholars and university expense on domestic services, leaving an entire sector of higher education service staff in vulnerable employment conditions.

I had spent most arguments with my father in my teenage years accusing his network of Rotary clubs for being conspiring capitalist ventures that kept the poor and the underprivileged in their place in our small poverty-stricken nation. I took a similar view of the institution in an easy transfer between authority figures. And then, I heard some unexpected and often uncomfortable truths. Service and domestic staff were retrained as receptionists and in pastoral, finance, and marketing roles, encouraged to engage in degree programmes which a staff development fund paid for. Often, older union members resisted, unable to trust such extraordinary change to the university sector or their life's work and left in disgruntled dissatisfaction. But many, if not most, stayed on and were part of the extraordinary transformation that changed the lives of many for the better, and this obscure ivory tower quietly subverted and unclogged the social mobility of a city, one domestic staff member at a time.

That was my first lesson of the pedagogy of hope: hope required a social relation of trust. A trust that must reach out from all parties concerned in a natural recognition of the innate goodness of human beings. Theologians might attribute this to humans being made in the image of God. The more cynical social sciences might attribute it to the evolutionary pedagogy of necessary pro-social behaviours written into our genetic code over time. The difficulty with achieving this condition is, of course, that human beings are socialized into dynamic systems of power from their first breath. In psychology, most theories of power predict that power reduces empathy and perspective-taking.[24] And, more often than not, institutionalized power is often where empathy is disoriented, and sanitized, structural policies reduce human interactions into professional currencies devoid of the three great Christian virtues – faith, hope, and love. In short, I was ready to believe the senior administration was the status quo that would commercialize the ivory towers of academe, and

24. Lammers et al., 'Looking through the Eyes.'

bleed out the beauty and joy from learning, and manipulate the greatest of human virtues in marketing logos. My barely concealed disdain may have been self-evident at the time as a member of the editorial team of the student newspaper and Student Union executive. And yet, the administration continued in the grand discourse of high ideals, conflicting my narrative, weaving in beauty, joy, daring, and adventure into the pedagogy, curriculum, and infrastructure. The longer I was a part of the institution, the more unsure I was of my binary assessment, and the more I realised the caveat to my Arendtian dilemma;[25] pedagogies of hope can serve to reproduce social relations as well as to transform them.

To better understand this dynamic condition, I turned first my undergraduate dissertation, and then later, my doctoral study, to moral development and social identity and tied myself in the theoretical knots of Kant, Hume, Rousseau, Heidegger, Habermas, Dewey, Piaget, and Kohlberg. To momentarily return to Arendt, whom I eventually purged from the thesis, the most heartening thesis of *The Human Condition* is its framing of 'human natality' and the miracle of beginning. In sharp contrast to Heidegger's stress on our mortality, Arendt argues that faith and hope in human affairs come from the wellspring of human progeny, each a unique miracle of chance and agency that is capable of new initiatives that can create catalyst change.[26] But such catalyst change requires great cost, daring and risk, extraordinary and imaginative vision, and a significant confidence, not just in the strategy that might deliver the imagined vision, but in the tender sensitivity and constructive, collaborative trust of the stakeholders of that ecology, and the landscape of impact.

An Ape Out of Water

Glenn Geher and Nicole Wedberg, in their exploration of Darwinian psychology, suggest our hope or despair or disproportionate perceptions of opportunity, threat, value, and risk are due to an evolutionary mismatch between the conditions that surrounded our nomadic ancestors, which we adapted to in our early evolution, and currently more technologically enhanced and differentiated environments.[27] Our phobias

---

25. That Hope merely serves to reproduce the same power structures of oppression and paralyses real transformation and catalyst action.

26. Arendt, *Human Condition.*

27. Geher and Wedberg, 'Ape Out of Water.'

and sense of proportion and impact are often steered by these ancient imperatives, and our resilience and stress reactions are a product of experiences that have washed over our genetic weave over many millennia in a long evolutionary journey.[28] Trust comes with caveats in our species, and group processes are often survival strategies with positive or negative consequences.

The social sciences, particularly psychology as a discipline, have spent nearly two centuries conducting experimental interventions on trying to better understand group behaviours and their consequences. And even more importantly, exploring organisational insights in weaving these pro-social behaviours into institutional structures, civil society, and the public square. In the wake of two world wars and innumerable ethnic and civil conflicts around the planet, one can forgive the discipline's suspicious framing of group dynamics and collective action, despite its countercultural achievements. And yet the redemptive quality of the species and one of the significant species markers that has enhanced our place on the food chain, and for better or worse, the colonization of the planet, is this capacity for creativity, constructionism, cultivation, compassion, communication, responsibility, empathy, and faith – in short, *hope*. Various organisational psychologists, sociologists, and political scientists have posited a plethora of models of human cooperation, creativity, and constructivism. For example, Ostrom's core design principles posit that cooperation is part of the human potential, but argues it needs a specific social context to avoid more self-interested behaviour appropriating the social paradigm.[29] In effect, Ostrom's design principles describe how groups culturally maintain practices that manage self-interested behaviours that are detrimental to the group or species. There exists a catalogue of such models and paradigms that attempt to describe pro-social behaviours.[30] But the social sciences in their instrumentalist frameworks fail to capture the transcendent quality of hope, because at the heart of hope lies significant risk. Too often, both risk and hope are

28. Remarkably, genes such as the arginine vasopressin receptor, 1A gene (AVPR1A), and the oxytocin receptor contribute to social behaviour in a broad range of species. Other polymorphic genes constituting those encoding for dopamine reward pathways, serotonergic emotional regulation, or sex hormones – further enable elaborate social behaviours – are built into our genetic make-up. See Ebstein et al., 'Genetics.'

29. Ostrom, *Governing the Common*.

30. See Wilson and Wilson, 'Rethinking the Theoretical Foundation.'

quantities we cannot grasp within the quagmire of big data we have sunk into. All our complex technological advances that have progressed from artificial intelligence to machine learning and deep learning cannot isolate or identify the DNA of hope, though we try.

In the here and now, as I inhabit the role of archbishops' advisor on minority ethnic Anglican concerns, risk is all I see in all the recommendations and policies that fall under my care. I worry about risking the infrastructure of the Church, of the faith landscape and the ecclesia, as they face up to the grotesque sins of slavery and its consequences, of racism and all the intersectional prejudices that distort and damage the Church. In this secular age, where many people go to church as a 'feel- good activity', populist liturgy and theology increasingly avoid facing up to the brokenness and sinfulness of human nature that was the staple of once-traditional prayer book liturgy. As many of the aggrieved emails I receive might suggest, people don't want to face up to the sins of our ancestors. Making the church face up to our colonial past and the atrocities of slavery and empire risks estranging the state and the mostly secular nation.

But most of all, I worry about risking the earnest and naïve agency and vulnerable hope of the minority ethnic communities as they look for a transcendent intervention in transforming the Church of England, a Church, I can say with some confidence, based on the significant findings of my last large-scale primary research study of the subject,[31] is a place that is psychologically damaging to their well-being. All the data driven logical, rational, intellectual calculations of the tides and turns in the Church of England tells me that despite all that is being done, despite the exhausting amount of work I am putting into this work, not enough will change in our lifetime to find the healing, acceptance, and opportunity we yearn for in this Mother Church.

A Theology of Risk

Many of us working for the church who see ourselves as civil servants of the faith find it easy to lose sight of the fact that we are practical theologians called to risk much for the fruits of faith, hope, and love. The Gospels

31. The Minority Anglicanism Project carried out six primary research studies across theology, sociology, and psychology, investigating experiences of marginalization and disenfranchisement. The final large-scale study, which compared the forty-two dioceses of the Church of England sample to other denominational samples, found acute indicators of compartmentalization, deindividuation, disassociation, and identity distress in ecclesial contexts within the Church of England.

are, the entire Bible is, a flagrant and absurd study of risk. Free will was a risk; letting us out of Eden was a risk; almost every chosen prophet, each a walking, talking testament of human error and lack of judgement, was a risk. The divine intervention was risk; the Christ child born in the body of a fragile, vulnerable, young, human woman of a nomadic tribe in the power of a historically brutal empire was a risk. Our faith is all about risk; it is a study in risk. When hope is sanitized from the costs and risks of love, it remains an untouched icon framed outside the discourse of what theologians might call realised ecclesiology. Without a theology of risk, without sacrifice and surrender that embody the true value of love, hope veers to the saccharine and is reduced to an implausible optimism.

It is impossible to consider this theology of risk and its place in the pedagogy of hope without describing the impact of two notable scholars, both editors of this book, Professors Ian Markham and Simon Lee. I was privileged to have been taught by Prof. Markham in my first year in theology. To have been schooled in the theology of risk and the pedagogy of hope so early in my career by scholar-activists like Ian Markham seems a particular advantage in my current role.

Prof. Markham's careful strategy, nuanced deliberation, and fearless reparation work at Virginia Theological Seminary continue to inspire and inform my own deliberations on risk. The VTS website describes the work thus:

> In September 2019, VTS announced the creation of an endowment dedicated to the payment of reparations, and the intent to research, uncover, and recognize Black people who laboured on-campus during slavery, Reconstruction, and segregation under Jim Crow laws. The endowment is a part of the Seminary's commitment to recognizing its participation in oppression in the past and commitment to healing and making amends in the future. Additional funds have been allocated to support the work of Black congregations that have historical ties to the Seminary; to create programs that promote justice and inclusion; and to elevate the work and voices of Black alumni and clergy within The Episcopal Church.[32]

The sheer daring and fragile hope of this work caught in my throat. Of course, slavery can never be compensated, but this work was more than a token of White guilt; it added a grand brushstroke to our practical theology and 'realised ecclesiology' that created a catalyst moment. The

---

32. Virginia Theological Seminary, 'Virginia Theological Seminary.'

drive, imagination, vision, and courage required to achieve that moment was a work of art. I wrote to Professor Ian Markham in the spring of 2021 and requested access to restricted documents that narrate this journey. Two decades beyond my theological instruction under his tutelage, I sought instruction again to better understand this audacious venture. As then, twenty years later, this scholar-activist and dean of the prestigious Virginia Theological Seminary, who probably didn't remember who I was, took time to write back, and more importantly to instruct and model that primordial pedagogy of hope that has been the axis of civilizations.

Professor Simon Lee often says Liverpool Hope was an institution that keeps in touch and continues to teach beyond convocation. And much like some of the scholars I have mentioned above, this has been particularly true of him. He has been proactively in touch, often sending books, articles, journal papers, and even tweets he feels I should read, respond to, or be instructed by. These last couple of years, some of the darkest of my life, he has been more present than usual. When my research funding at Birmingham University fell through in the midst of COVID-19 chaos, he intervened in finding job opportunities and encouraged me to apply to the Open University Law School to develop pedagogical- and justice-related work in various projects. But his greatest contribution to my life has been in helping me grasp the hard mettle and steely confidence of this elusive pedagogy.

When life has been at its darkest, Simon has never allowed me to curl up in despair or dwell unnecessarily on the damages of time or the dark crises that are inevitable to the human condition. He has been relentless, like a personal trainer of the mind, demanding excellence, engagement, and courage when I wanted to slow down, stop, or take cover. His emails often narrate the hidden struggles and challenges of what others see as achievement and the steely determination required in the vision and architecture of hope. He describes his early career in Belfast at Queen's University, during the Troubles, as steeped in risk, never having been to Northern Ireland before his appointment, and yet deeply invested in its solutions. His appointment as vice-chancellor to Liverpool Hope at the age of thirty-eight called to the rubble and despair of a sceptical city; he was as a wild card candidate compared to the traditional appointments to this former teacher training college. He describes the sisters and the bishops who appointed him as experts in the theology of risk, who overturned the tables of the staid, careerist risk aversion that is common to so many in the church and in higher education. His pedagogy and vision of hope, and the change of name, were as audacious as his battle with the government over the institutional title or the transformation of what was a modest teacher training college to a daring beacon to the city and the nation. His commitment to this shared vision was relentless, and his capacity to transmit that confidence was infectious. No student was beyond the best efforts of every scholar and service staff member they came into contact with, and the collegiate community had a responsibility to bring out the best in every student. While student-centered pedagogies were becoming common in universities around the country, particularly in the cathedrals group universities, no HEI deployed this overt pedagogy of Hope with such constructivist zeal as Liverpool Hope.

Accessible Pedagogy

Having had three years as an undergraduate immersed in the discourse and dissension on how best to strategize and operationalize this pedagogy, I found myself given charge of a small part of its sacral duties. At the dawn of the millennium, within months of having graduated from my undergraduate studies, I found myself pursuing a PhD and employed as a tutor and, swiftly afterwards, an hourly paid lecturer, in the Department of Psychology. I was also appointed to a residential tutorship, given charge of a women's hall dedicated to Angela of Merici, the founder of the Ursuline order and a pioneer in Italian women's education in late medieval Venice. Here I began to intuitively apply some of that hospitality, generosity, and unrelenting hope I had soaked up in those first three years.

It was an experiment rich in its own challenging learning curves; the first came early in my teaching career. I was given charge of a Unique Learning[33] module for AL students who had not achieved the required grades to take on the degree course of their choice, who were required to do an extra credit foundation course to prepare them to join their peers on the psychology course. Many students who apply to do psychology are often unprepared for the demanding numerical skills and basic biology required of them in the first year; many struggle to engage their latent numerical competence due to a debilitating fear that often blocks true engagement with introductory modules.

In these Unique Learning modules I was often faced with a defeated group of students who were crushed by what had clearly been damaging

---

33. Elford, *Foundation of Hope*, ch. 4.

secondary education experiences. And of course, there were also those who struggled to cope with our introductory first-year modules and failed the first semester or year. Faced with statistics and biology, instead of Freud, Jung, and analyzing dreams, many were angry that their distorted populist expectations of the psychology curriculum were not met. Many were more than happy to take out their disgruntled anger on the young, naïve, green tutor who had only just graduated herself. Almost all these modules began with students challenging curriculum content, which is of course set by BPS, the British Psychological Society, our national accreditation and licensing body governing the discipline. Behind the anger and frustration was a paralyzing fear of inadequacy. The particular despair that is the result of seeing your academic and career dreams subverted because of your incapacity to grasp a particular skill or keep up with the pack is acutely damaging. The shame of failing one's first year and being culled from the herd left wounds that required a particular healing pedagogy. Others had burdens caring for family, crippling financial challenges, life-altering traumatic events, or undiagnosed learning disabilities, which were just beginning to be formally recognised and catered for in the early 2000s. Like my lecturers and tutors before me, my first task was to listen and learn who they were and what they were passionate about and take an interest in what they contributed to our Deweyan ecology. My second was to find their strengths and sensitivities, their wounds and wonders, and build a fellowship of each of these small tutorial groups, not letting one or a few needs or personalities appropriate the complex pedagogical dynamic. The teaching had to be immersive, not just instructional; the content had to be more than mere transmission of knowledge; it had to advance, electrify, and engage. Knowledge had to photosynthesize in collegiate socialisation, in debate and discourse, and I had to give them the confidence to emerge into the sunlight of collegiate fora. In those early days, I felt my age, gender, and race were limitations as I aspired to become a wise sage that my students might find great wisdom from. I soon learnt I was enough, as I was. The pedagogy of hope required I was authentic and true to myself. And as I faced my own fears and inadequacies, my students confronted their own. My calling was to be a healing constant in their life, unrelentingly patient, using my intellectual acuities to identify the gaps of knowledge or understanding. All I was required to do was to see through the rubble of their circumstances and broken potential, imbuing the redemptive capacities that all collegial contexts used to once possess. The Deweyan pedagogy of the institution took over and did the rest.

I had not set out to become an academic, though I had discovered an insatiable love of research, but the deep magic of teaching, mentoring, and tenderly nurturing young (and not so young) minds was captivating. I learnt the secret many teachers hold dear; unlocking human potential is incredibly rewarding. Of course, I enjoyed lecturing in broadcast mode, narrating knowledge in new and dynamic ways that capture curiosity and imagination. I loved taking complex ideas and paradigms and describing them in simple, quirky, and relatable metaphors, in a way that is accessible and memorable. I loved leaving a lecture theatre of students hungry for more, puzzling over a concept that was purposefully left at the edge of a description so that they might follow up a bread crumb trail of ideas in the reading list, which I promised was where the real magic happens. But, the real joy of teaching happened in the smaller tutorial groups, and my love of teaching research methods and statistics left me with a heavy teaching load. One of the greatest joys of my teaching career is seeing these particular tutorial groups achieve first class degrees or upper seconds three years later, as they graduated with honours. Some have embraced their various challenges and gone on to do doctoral study in these, be that dyslexia and other learning difficulties, or the impact of urban poverty on access to higher education.

Inebriated by benchmarking exercises and measurable change, it would be easy to delude myself into the conceits of impact on student life, but that would rob me of the sacral gifts of the classroom. With each debate, discussion, and question, each lecture, each tutorial, the content knowledge which we engaged in fused my own synaptic weave into a new and richer tapestry. Each and every student, however amicable or difficult, has added shade and nuance to my own perspectives, conclusions, capacities, and competences. As Liverpool Hope's glossy prospectuses claimed in its desire to educate the mind, body, and spirit, adopting and adapting John Henry Newman's ideals of a 'wholeness of vision' and 'enlargement of the mind,'[34] it sought authenticity and evolution in its pursuit of truth.[35] Its combined honours programmes sought the richness found in the fusion and friction of subjects, between the classroom and the nightclubs, in organic conversations students had with lecturers,

---

34. Newman, *Idea of a University.*
35. Gruenwald, 'University as Quest.'

domestic staff, and barkeeps. This Deweyan ecology was the rich soil, the sunlight, and the rain, giving opportunity for students to flourish, flower, languish, or shrivel as they chose. Its invitation was to make that choice; free will was the catalyst component. And the culminating truth of our pedagogy was the relationship between hope and free will.

Organisational Transformation and Impact

The impact of Liverpool Hope on the city is another volume, yet to be written. In the time of the two vice-chancellors I was privileged to serve under, I saw them risk the currency of the modest university's expansion and developmental plans in the decaying and disused Angel Field Farm, which became Hope at Everton. I remember the university buying the place for one pound. When I saw it for the first time, I thought it was a terrible idea. I couldn't imagine beauty or hope in such an ignominious, rough, dilapidated urban space. Now, every time I see it, not just its physical and material beauty but all the joy of its collegiate life, I remember that smug cynic who thought it was a lost cause, and the lack of faith and imagination to grasp the vision of that disparaged few. The evolving campus is a dynamic illustration of why we must lift our heads beyond the grim mundane to look to the compelling imaginaries of humanity if we are to flourish as a city or civilization. There is an artist in every bureaucrat waiting to engineer a fusion of infrastructure and virtue aesthetics, to create beauty and joy that can be measured only by human experience in the slow metrics of time.

The Deweyan pedagogy I saw slowly emerging on our beautiful campus, painted into its sunlit stained glass, teased by the scent of David Austin roses, fringed by aromatic rosemary hedges and lavender scallops that a new generation of students take for granted, remind me all that the institution stands for. In the late 1990s and 2000s, an era when many institutions were cutting arts and humanities budgets, it was one that invested in drama and theatre and high culture, but also a place where the hard questions about justice, equality, reconciliation, and peace were confronted. I spent more time attending marches and parades, in immersed research, than I spent in the lecture theatre. Post-Good Friday agreement, swept up in the elation of the social justice issues around the Northern Ireland peace process, hope as a catalyst reactive element of the zeitgeist had become tangible.

Liverpool Hope was a living example; it wasn't an ivory tower, but a place that practiced what it preached, and engaged with the local community and gave opportunity and access to those less likely to enter academia, a place where the first minority ethnic vice-chancellor in the country could thrive, living up to the ideals of its suffragist founders. Working with Prof. Lee recently, disagreeing about privilege or toppling statues, at the Open University and in blogs for the William Temple Foundation, I am reminded that education is not a training for the production of capital, but a north star to navigate the storm.

There are many stories I could share about that golden age, born in the rubble of our cynical city, but instead, let me leave you with my gratitude for this extraordinary and idealistic group of educators, who attempted to live out a purposeful ethos borne of dazzling imagination, unrelenting courage, and translate it to possibility and policy, strategy and curriculum, and an extraordinary pedagogy of hope.

Bibliography

Arendt, Hannah. *The Human Condition*. 2nd ed. Chicago: University of Chicago Press, 1998.

Balthasar, Hans Urs von. *Dramatis Personae: Persons in Christ*. Vol. 3 of *Theo-Drama-Theological Dramatic Theory*. London: Ignatius, 1978.

Ebstein, Richard P., et al. 'Genetics of Human Social Behavior.' *Neuron* 65 (25 Mar. 2010) 831–44. https://doi.org/10.1016/j.neuron.2010.02.020.

Elford, R. John, ed. *The Foundation of Hope: Turning Dreams into Reality*. Liverpool: Liverpool University Press, 2003.

Geher, Glenn, and Nicole Wedberg. 'Ape Out of Water: Evolutionary Mismatch and the Nature of Who We Are.' In *Positive Evolutionary Psychology: Darwin's Guide to Living a Richer Life*, 26–38. Oxford: Oxford University Press, 2019. https://doi.org/10.1093/oso/9780190647124.003.0003.

Gifford, Tony, et al. *Loosen The Shackles: First Report of the Liverpool 8 Inquiry into Race Relations in Liverpool*. London: Karia, 1989.

Grover, Chris. *Crime and Inequality*. New York: Routledge, 2013.

Gruenwald, Oskar. 'The University as Quest for Truth.' *Journal of Interdisciplinary Studies* 23 (2011) 1–18.

Hansard. *The Scarman Report*. Vol. 425: debated on 25 Nov. 1981. https://hansard.parliament.uk/Lords/1981-11-25/debates/008514e8-e688-4dfe-ba60-777fee95e3e5/TheScarmanReport.

Hill, Samantha Rose. 'When Hope Is a Hindrance.' Edited by Nigel Warburton. Aeon, 4 Oct. 2021. https://aeon.co/essays/for-arendt-hope-in-dark-times-is-no-match-for-action.

Home Affairs Committee. *The Macpherson Report*. UK Parliament, 30 July 2021. https://publications.parliament.uk/pa/cm5802/cmselect/cmhaff/139/13902.htm.

James, Clive. *Cultural Amnesia*. New York: Norton & Company, 2007.

John, Cindi. 'The Legacy of the Brixton Riots.' *BBC News*, updated 5 Apr. 2006. http://news.bbc.co.uk/2/hi/uk_news/4854556.stm.

Kennedy, Robert F. 'Day of Affirmation Address, University of Capetown, Capetown, South Africa, June 6, 1966.' John F. Kennedy Presidential Library and Museum, 1966. https://www.jfklibrary.org/learn/about-jfk/the-kennedy-family/robert-f-kennedy/robert-f-kennedy-speeches/day-of-affirmation-address-university-of-capetown-capetown-south-africa-june-6-1966.

Lammers, Joris, et al. 'Looking through the Eyes of the Powerful.' *Journal of Experimental Social Psychology* 44 (2008). doi:10.1016/j.jesp.2008.03.015.

Liverpool Echo. 'Leroy Cooper: The Toxteth Riots Were a Wake-Up Call and Did Some Good.' *Liverpool Echo*, 4 July 2011; updated 7 May 2013. https://www.liverpoolecho.co.uk/news/liverpool-news/leroy-cooper-toxteth-riots-were-3369244.

Power, Maria. 'Reconciling State and Society? The Practice of the Common Good in the Partnership of Bishop David Sheppard and Archbishop Derek Worlock.' *Journal of Religious History* 40 (Dec. 2015) 545–64. https://doi.org/10.1111/1467-9809.12328.

Newman, John Henry. *The Idea of a University*. London: Aeterna, 1852.

Ostrom, Elinor. *Governing the Commons: the Evolution of Institutions for Collective Action*. Cambridge: Cambridge University Press, 1990

Scarman, L. *Brixton Disorders: The Scarman Report*. Parliament, 4 Feb. 1982. https://api.parliament.uk/historic-hansard/lords/1982/feb/04/brixton-disorders-the-scarman-report.

Snyder, C. R. *The Psychology of Hope: You Can Get There From Here*. New York: Free, 1994.

Snyder, C. R., and Carol Ford. *Coping with Negative Life Events*. New York: Plenum, 1988

Snyder, C. R., et al. *Excuses: Masquerades in Search of Grace*. New York: Percheron, 2005.

Suenens, Leo Joseph. *A New Pentecost?* Translated by Francis Martin. New York: Seabury, 1975.

Virginia Theological Seminary. 'Virginia Theological Seminary Designated $1.7 Million as a Reparations Endowment Fund.' Virginia Theological Seminary, n.d. https://vts.edu/mission/multicultural-ministries/reparations/.

Webb, Darren. 'Pedagogies of Hope.' *Studies in Philosophy and Education* 32 (2013) 397–414. doi:10.1007/s11217-012-9336-1.

Wilson, David Sloan, and Edward O. Wilson. 'Rethinking the Theoretical Foundation of Sociobiology.' *Quarterly Review of Biology* 82 (2007) 327–348. https://doi.org/10.1086/522809.

Worlock, Derek, and David Sheppard. *Better Together: Christian Partnership in a Hurt City*. London: Hodder & Stoughton, 1988

———. *With Hope in Our Hearts: God's Reconciling Love Reflected in a Unique Partnership*. London: Hodder & Stoughton, 1994.

PARITY OF ESTEEM

Inclusivity and Change

7

The Black Science Summer School

Pro Torkington

WHEN I LIVED IN South Africa I believed that the reason there were no black doctors was because of the apartheid regime, which prevented black young people's entrance into science based education. However, when I got to Alder Hey Children's Hospital in Liverpool, there were no black doctors from the local community. The School of Tropical Medicine in Liverpool had black doctors, but they came already qualified, to do postgraduate courses.

Some years later, whilst having lunch with colleagues at Hope University College, a black woman I hadn't seen before joined us. She was not a member of staff. Her name was Doris, and she was a teacher in one of the schools in Liverpool. She also ran an after-school class, teaching science to black school children. That, she said, will encourage them to do science subjects in senior schools, which will enable them to study medicine and other science-based subjects in the university. She knew of a project run by the Sisters of the Blessed Sacrament in New Orleans, USA, where this approach had opened opportunities for many black children to qualify as doctors. I shared this information with Professor Simon Lee and wondered if we could learn something from the USA practice. 'You won't know unless you go and find out,' was his response. Doris and I went to New Orleans to gather more information.

The success of the nuns' project depended on the link they made between families, the boarding school that they ran, and medical universities. The boarding school provided not only teaching but also an ambience that encouraged learning. To familiarize children with higher education at an early age, partner universities ran science summer school sessions, which gave pupils the confidence and the belief that they, too, could successfully study science-based subjects like medicine. Many of the black doctors in different parts of America, the nuns told us, went through their system.

Doris and I came back to the UK excited but also deflated. The nuns had a lot of money from American trusts and well-moneyed parents, which enabled them to take in pupils from poor families. We did not have access to that kind of money at Hope. But maybe we could have the science summer school, to give black young pupils a taste of college life and a feel of independent living? We put this to Professor Simon Lee. He was very supportive of the idea. But it would need some money, and for that I had to talk to my fellow deans for financial support. The following week, at the deans' meeting, I brought up the subject. They each offered one hundred pounds towards the project to pay for accommodation, food, tuition fees, and various activities. This did not ring any alarm bells, since I, too, expected no more than ten pupils to come on the first visit.

At the time I was a trustee of the Catholic Association for Racial Justice (CARJ), based in London. All the trustees were Catholics, and they had links with Catholic schools and the nuns who ran them. Some trustees had actually taught in some of the schools. That made it easy to spread the word about the project and adding a plea for funding. The response was amazing. CARJ immediately donated two thousand pounds, and more funds came from schools that intended to send pupils to the summer school. Other donors did so, however, because they liked the project and were willing it to succeed. Instead of the ten pupils that we expected on the first visit, fifty-six year-ten pupils from across the country came in 1999. We were lucky to have the full support of Professor Simon Lee who ensured financial support whilst we waited for the funds promised by many donors.

To my knowledge there had never been that many black children, or adults for that matter, staying in the college. Some people found it challenging and unacceptable? However, many welcomed the opportunity to contribute to the programmes at different levels.

My involvement remained basic. My presence assured the parents, who knew my link with CARJ, that their children would be safe in Liverpool. I was the mother figure that the kids met at Euston station at eight a.m. when their parents brought them. If they needed anything – to iron their clothes or pain killers or just to share something they were not comfortable about – they knocked on my door. The people who organised and ran the course were Emanuel Mufti, the organiser, and Lynn McCabe, the secretary to the project. The leaflet by Emmanuel Mufti provides information on the aims and activities of the project.

Many years after I left Hope, I received an email from someone calling himself Rex. Rex was in the first group of year-ten pupils who came to Hope in 1999. He was now getting married to Anita, a girl he had met on that visit. He was inviting me to their wedding – a special surprise for his wife. I went and met many more of their friends who came to Hope at the same time. They all had good jobs in which they thrived. Anita did law and was then a legal advisor, and Rex was in IT. Others were in pharmacy, IT, and international organisations. They were all convinced that the Black Science Summer School at Hope was the greatest impetus in their success.

It is with sadness that programmes like the Black Science Summer School, which gave confidence and self-esteem to black children at an early age, were not adopted by educational establishments. Even Hope, the first educational establishment to set up such a programme and that had staff with magnificent plans for future developments, failed to continue the project.

8

The Art of Change in Hope and Liverpool
Space . . . the Final Frontier

ALAN WHITTAKER

Antecedents

I STUDIED CERAMICS AT Cardiff College of Art (1971–1974) and the Royal College of Art (1974–1977) and worked in industry for Rosenthal Studio Linie Porcelain in Selb, Germany. I was appointed as a lecturer in ceramics at Liverpool Institute of Higher Education (which was to become Liverpool Hope University) in 1988 and as head of art and design in 1998. I retired from full-time academia in 2019. When I arrived, the world of education and art and design was undergoing a fundamental change, and this change continued throughout my time at Hope. In terms of education, the college changed from being a small, teaching-focused, church teacher training college mainly for women, offering teacher certificates and Liverpool University-accredited bachelor of education qualifications, to one that was a university with its own degree-awarding powers, offering research-informed bachelor-, master-, and PhD-level qualifications.

The art and design sector nationally was large, and competition was great, especially in the northwest of England where Liverpool John Moores, Manchester Metropolitan University, and the University of

Central Lancashire (UCLAN) at Preston offered similar courses. In addition, student numbers applying for bachelor of design degree courses continued to grow, especially at universities where courses offered a new approach to design incorporating new digital technologies. To compete with other universities, it was imperative that art and design at Hope made the transition from a teacher training college to a high-tech digitally based institution. When I arrived at Hope in 1988 the purpose-built Benedict Arts Centre had been home to the subjects of fine art and design, and music and drama, since 1964 when Christ's College had been constructed. In 1990, music and drama had moved to the main campus across the road to allow for these subjects to grow, breathe, and expand their horizons. However, the developments described above meant that it was crucial to the subject that the university was able to financially support the development of a new approach to design and be at the forefront, regionally and nationally, of this exciting new approach to the design degree. With regard to fine art, student numbers were also growing, offering a combined BA subjects degree, but primarily with teacher training as part of a BEd degree. Fine art was proposing to develop a single honours degree course.

The Cornerstone Campus

These developments in the world of art and design coincided with the drive for widening participation in higher education and developments in urban renewal in deprived regions of the UK, of which inner-city Liverpool was a prime candidate. Urban Splash was a key player in this regeneration. Significant funding was available from the Higher Education Funding Council for England (HEFCE) for widening participation and from the North West Development Agency, the European Regional Development Fund (ERDF), and the European Social Fund (ESF) for urban regeneration.

In order to achieve this development and to raise the profile of Hope's creative subjects in Liverpool, Hope proposed that a new campus be created in the Everton ward of Liverpool on the outskirts of the city centre. This was one of the most deprived areas in the city and nationally, and had many derelict sites, one of which was the St Francis Xavier's Roman Catholic school (SFX) that had moved several years earlier to a new site in Woolton, one of the wealthiest suburbs of south Liverpool.

This move to Everton enabled an enormous space to be created, which, initially, was home to the deanery of Hope in the Community as well as art and design with its massive investment in high-technology equipment. In order to compete with other universities, Hope invested in a wide range of new technology, computer-aided design, and computer-aided machinery. As part of the fine art and design degree, the material areas of ceramics, metal, wood, painting, printmaking, and sculpture and new facilities for computer-aided design and computer-aided machinery (CADCAM) were developed in what was initially called the Cornerstone Building as part of the Hope at Everton Campus. This extremely ambitious proposal was, not surprisingly, enthusiastically supported by fine art and design, whivh was the first academic subject to move. The Cornerstone was initially incomplete and needed further investment to eventually house other creative subjects, including music, drama, and dance, and their specialist space and facility requirements. These developments lead to its renaming as the Creative Campus.

Prior to the move to the new campus, discussions between the subjects of music, art and design, and drama had taken place, and a new creative and performing arts degree (CPA) had been proposed, developed, and accredited. This new degree was in addition to the single honours degrees of music, fine art and design, and drama.

Links and Networks

HRH Prince Charles: The Catalyst?

HRH Prince Charles opened the Cornerstone Building and viewed the new development prior to completion. He was able to spend most of the day in fine art and design experiencing the new technologies available to the students. He was also able to draw on a computer and understand and personally experience a totally innovative way to draw and design. HRH is a painter himself and appreciated the way a computer could enrich the creative process. At that time the world-renowned artist David Hockney was working on a large series of paintings that he was developing on a computer tablet. These were to be exhibited in 2009 at the Royal Academy in Piccadilly, London, where HRH Prince Charles was patron. This visit contributed to raising the profile of Liverpool Hope within the creative community of Liverpool.

International Links

Hope was increasingly an international university, which was developed through the university's charity Hope One World, founded in 1982 (now Global Hope), and the European Capital of Culture of 2008. The university had already established Hope One World, which had a portfolio of international charitable aid projects. One project was proposed by two Brazilian graduate architects, Paula Baros and Llessandro Rodrigues, whilst studying for masters degrees in urban regeneration at Liverpool Hope. They proposed that Misao Ramacrisna, Betim, Belo Horizonte, in the Minas Gerais area of Brazil should be chosen for an art and design project. Misao operates in parallel with conventional school systems, and children attend school in the mornings and Misao in the afternoon or vice versa. Art and design run alongside other subjects such as language, numeracy, IT, biology, and geography. Adults work in various productive activities from furniture making to textile construction and ceramic manufacture. The Arts Co-operative at Misao sells their work through local, national, and international trade fairs. Income generated from these sales helps finance activities in the school. Liverpool Hope staff and students (normally two staff members and up to four students) have visited Brazil each year in August for the last twenty years for up to one month and worked in the school and Arts Co-operative at Misao developing new ranges of work and teaching the children.

Another major international influence was the awarding of the European Capital of Culture designation to Liverpool for 2008. This had varying impacts. Without doubt, it restored confidence and fostered resurgence in the fortunes of Liverpool as a truly great international city. Liverpool again become an international city and attracted and stimulated tourism, education, culture, media, and sport. It became internationally recognised and the place to visit, form partnerships with, and work.

Liverpool Hope's contribution to the Capital of Culture was the Big Hope. This was a week-long international youth congress attended by over six hundred young people from sixty plus countries and addressed by internationally famous presidents, politicians, religious leaders, artists, environmentalists, and charity workers. The main aim of the Big Hope was to foster leadership and citizenship. As part of the Big Hope, we sponsored attendance by many of our Global Hope partners, including two staff and two students from our Brazilian project in Misao

Ramacrisna. They visited Hope to further develop their creative skills by working alongside staff and students in the Cornerstone.

Another highly significant development preceding and resulting from the Capital of Culture years was the initiating and strengthening of many partnerships between the city council, arts organisations, and the universities. These have continued to the present time. For Hope at Everton, highlights include mutually beneficial projects, staff links, joint degree programmes, awards, honorary degrees, and sponsorships with the following:

- National museums and galleries of Merseyside
- Bluecoat gallery (Central Liverpool's oldest building c. 1716)
- Bluecoat Display Centre
- Tate Liverpool gallery
- FACT (Film, Art and Creative Technology)
- Royal Liverpool Philharmonic
- Playhouse and Everyman Theatres
- Open Eye Gallery
- European Opera Centre based in the Cornerstone
- Carter Preston Foundation Trust
- MA by creative practice (a practical-based MA course)
- Cornerstone Gallery[1]

Concluding Comments

Hope, to me, brings vision, ambition, drive, and the opportunity for change in a global society. It is about growing and developing together to enrich life. In retirement, I chair the Art, Design and Architecture Committee at Liverpool Metropolitan Cathedral, and I also chair the trustees of the Bluecoat Display Centre and remain a trustee of the Carter Preston Foundation.

---

1. Following my visit to the Getty Museum in Los Angeles to attend the European League of Institutes of the Arts (ELIA) annual conference, it was apparent that universities should exhibit artistic achievements. The Cornerstone Gallery became Hope's exhibition venue.

I and fellow colleagues were able to develop links, collaborate with, learn from, and influence organisations, charities, and universities in many countries around the world for the mutual benefit of ourselves, our students, our communities, and our university.

Finally, it is salutary to reflect that had we not moved to the Creative Campus, fine art and design would not have survived and prospered. The Benedict Arts Centre, the campus's predecessor, with its outdated resources, would not have been able to compete within the university sector nor satisfy the requirements of the Quality Assurance Agency.

There is hope in dreams, imagination, and in the courage of those who wish to make those dreams a reality.

—JONAS SALK, VIROLOGIST

9

Camino of Hope

SEAN GALLAGHER

After climbing a great hill, one only finds that there are many more hills to climb. I have taken a moment here to rest, to steal a view of the glorious vista that surrounds me, to look back on the distance I have come. But I can rest only for a moment, for with freedom come responsibilities, and I dare not linger, for my long walk is not ended.

—THE CONCLUDING WORDS OF NELSON MANDELA'S AUTOBIOGRA-PHY, *LONG WALK TO FREEDOM*, OFTEN QUOTED BY SIMON LEE AT HOPE GRADUATIONS

My Long Walking

WALKING FROM WINDERMERE, MAKING our way up to the forested slopes of Helvellyn, in the summer of 1967 while waiting for A-level results, was a life-changing experience for me, falling in love with the Lake District and with walking the fells.

It was my first holiday with my school friends, rather than with my family. I have been walking ever since. Around the time I came to work at what is now Liverpool Hope University, a couple of decades later, we went walking as an extended family each year. My parents, four siblings, and our families spent Easter week from 1989 for ten years in the Lake District, at Castlerigg, outside Keswick. We went walking each day, and the highlight was the whole family annual walk up Cat Bells. Over this ten-year period, we completed all twenty-nine fells in Wainwright's *The North Western Fells*. In 1993, when I was forty-four, I did my first long-distance walk from St Bees on the Cumbrian coast to Robin Hood's Bay on the North Yorkshire coast. This coast-to-coast walk of about two hundred miles took over two weeks. My friend Eddie and I took eight children with us: Eddie's two children and my two sons, Matthew (sixteen) and Danny (eleven); two nephews, Sean (fourteen) and Joe (eleven); and two of their friends, while my two daughters were in Malta on a school trip.

I wanted to do more long-distance walking, and the opportunity came with my fiftieth birthday in 1999, when I was director of finance and resources at Liverpool Hope University College. I came across the Camino Frances across Northern Spain, five hundred miles from a small-town St-Jean-Pied-de-Port on the French side of the Pyrenees to Santiago de Compostela in northwest Spain. The chief executive of Hope, Simon Lee, allowed me to take four weeks of leave either side of Easter. My brother-in-law, Graham, and my two sons, Matthew and Danny, came with me for the first two weeks and celebrated my fiftieth birthday with me in the square outside Burgos Cathedral. I then continued by myself for two weeks, and a friend, Keith, joined me for the final week into Santiago de Compostela. The camino was a great opportunity to reflect on what was important to me. I didn't watch any TV or read any newspapers. I didn't have any contact with work and phoned home only once each day.

Turning fifty with four children, I did have the usual worries about the children and money. Fortunately, I didn't have any work stress. Whilst the job, and the boss, could be demanding, I had a good relationship with Simon, who was always supportive. I worked with competent, supportive staff and without the office politics that I had experienced in earlier and later jobs.

The camino is a very special experience and does change your life. People on the camino are not interested in what you do at home. The talk is always about places on the camino, how many miles you are walking, where you are stopping. People introduce themselves by their first name and the conversation is always about the walk, always supportive.

I'm always conscious that the camino paths I'm walking have been walked over the centuries, since the middle of the ninth century, by pilgrims making their way to the tomb of one of the closest friends of Jesus, St James. The numbers walking into Santiago have gone up massively since the 1980s. Only 690 pilgrims walked into Santiago in 1985, increasing to 55,000 in the year 2000; 215,879 in 2013; and 347,578 in 2019.

I've been walking the camino routes for over twenty years and have walked into Santiago on four occasions. Modern day pilgrims make the journey for many different reasons. For me, on my first walk to Santiago, it was not a pilgrimage. It was an adventure, based on this love of long-distance walking, not for religious reasons. Now I say that I am a pilgrim and enjoy the simplicity and peace of the Ccmino. People walk for many reasons: religious, spiritual, to have an adventure and a physical challenge, and to come to terms, as best we can, with bereavement or retirement.

So, walking is a way of life for me, predates my time at Hope and extends beyond my time there. Undoubtedly, though, Hope gave my walking a boost, encouraged me to think of the wider world, and helped me put my walking and my life in a rounded perspective. As the mission statement put it, Hope was about 'educating the whole person, in mind, body and spirit'.

I mention all this because it would have been easy to have given 'Walk on, with Hope in your Heart' as the title of this essay, but I think that the reality for me, and for other staff and for all our students, is that Hope is part of a longer journey. 'Journey' itself has become a cliché in talking about education or self-awareness, as has another obvious expression to describe the experience I am about to address of working at Hope, 'walking the talk.' For me, though, walking really is a way of life and was a part of our management at Hope. My aim in this essay is to capture as best I can what it was like for me to be a part of Hope twenty to twenty-five years ago and how Hope is still a part of me now. In books about universities and theology, I imagine that the perspectives of a director of finance and resources are rarely found. So, walk with me through these pages and see if the way of the camino might be good for you.

Managing Change: Master's Classes

Before I had those four weeks of leave in one block to walk the camino for the first time, there was another significant aspect of this time at Hope for me. In appraisal, Simon had suggested that I should think about a part-time MBA. I liked the idea of further study, but not for a MBA, which I suspected would be full of business school jargon (like 'walk the talk'). I got to choose any postgraduate degree at any university and chose the opportunity to study part-time for an MSc in managing change at Sheffield Hallam University. There were only sixteen people on the course, and we worked in sets of four. All sixteen were in senior positions in their workplaces. The majority were very focused managers/leaders who believed in changing the staff if staff didn't change. A couple of us had a more developmental approach, believing more in people. This approach fit with Simon's, who did promote internally, giving staff every opportunity to progress. I realised that maybe accountancy wasn't the appropriate career choice. I did enjoy working in and leading teams with the opportunity to develop people and give them the opportunity to take on more responsibly without being micromanaged.

Simon didn't distinguish between academic and administrative staff. He was very much focused on student experience and listened to people's contributions. What I don't think some other leaders in higher education understand is that almost all the support staff were also committed to the student experience at Hope once we were allowed to be let into the real work of encouraging students on what I would call their camino. For me, this was what marked the years with Simon at Hope. Dr Burke perhaps had to concentrate on merging the colleges and the survival of the institution. Prof. Pillay wanted to boost research and Hope's credentials or reputation as a university by concentrating on appointing fellow academics, again understandably, and was very good himself at making the grounds beautiful on both campuses. However, Simon's way was to walk with the students and support staff along the Pathway of Hope, to go around less privileged parts of Liverpool and the Network of Hope throughout Lancashire, to revisit with communities he knew across the Irish Sea, to encourage us to take our own first steps into new areas of recruitment or new ways of supporting students who were with us, and to let us have a go. All this struck a chord with me. I enjoyed being out and about, listening to students and staff, whether they were praising one another or criticizing us.

For example, in that earlier book, *The Foundation of Hope*, Simon told the story of how I was involved in the recruitment of our first student from Sri Lanka, Sanjee Perera, and she herself spoke when we marked the twenty-fifth anniversary of the name change to Hope. It's a bit embarrassing but, to make sense of what I am about to explain, please bear with me quoting from Simon's account:

> Sean Gallagher regularly gave up his weekends to clean tables and serve customers in Hope on the Waterfront. Few universities or colleges have such senior members of staff who would show this commitment to teamwork, but it is part of the success

of Hope that senior colleagues are so involved in the front line of customer care. It was not surprising, therefore, that Sean should be on duty when a Sri Lankan businessman was looking for something to do one Sunday in a windswept and largely closed Liverpool. He came into Hope on the Waterfront and struck up a conversation with Sean. He was so impressed that he sent his daughter across the world to study with us. She took an undergraduate degree, then a master's and is now pursuing her doctorate while working as a resident tutor. Meanwhile, her positive experiences of Hope have led to more than twenty other Sri Lankan students joining the Hope community.

My point is that we were then trusted to help Sanjee, and, more unusual in higher education, Bernard Longden and I were trusted to go out to Sri Lanka to see if more students with the same values wanted to come. Sanjee understood the ethos of Hope and had a real work ethic. We found many like-minded students and families. They were a bit sceptical of the way university education was going in England, preferring the style of teaching we had experienced in school decades earlier. Therefore, Bernard and I asked academics such as Sally Edmondson, Liz Gayton, Penny Haughan, and Janet Speake to go out there and give lectures, to show the students they really knew their subjects, and to use modern teaching methods to help the students become more independent learners.

We would see our Sri Lankan students all the time around Hope and, over time, students from many other countries. We now know, twenty years later, how much this meant to the students themselves. I am still in touch with many of them, mostly through Facebook.

My seventeen years working at what is now Liverpool Hope University included six with Dr Jim Burke as rector, eight with Prof. Simon Lee, and three with Prof. Gerald Pillay. I came from local government, where a job I enjoyed was ended by Prime Minister Margaret Thatcher's government abolishing the Greater Manchester Authority in 1986. Then the stock market crash, known as Black Monday, in 1987 wiped out a significant part of the pension fund we were administering in Tameside. I was interviewed via a headhunter by one of the pro-rectors, Mgr Bernard Bickers, and worked closely as director of finance with Dr Burke from 1989 in the era of the Liverpool Institute of Higher Education (LIHE), with its merged colleges, pro-rectors, and governing bodies. I was the first finance director as Jim Burke replaced generalist managers from military backgrounds with people from professionally qualified HR, estates, administrative, and finance backgrounds. Jim won the battle with the colleges and left LIHE in a position to move forward. He had a good grasp of finance, was cautious, and had a deep respect for the University of Liverpool, where he and I had studied in different generations and where he had worked. He was also deferential to government and the quangos, over our lack of the word 'university' in our title. Although he was a successful academic, he was comfortable with administrators and appreciative of our roles. Perhaps he was comfortable also with Catholic men, like himself, me, and the other senior officers he appointed.

Simon Lee was appointed to succeed him in 1994, to start in 1995, and appreciated the qualities of all staff. He did not distinguish between 'academic' and 'nonacademic' staff. He inherited the senior officers who had served with Jim Burke. It is important to name some of the characters who served in the administration of Liverpool Hope in this era of radical change. Too often, explanations of what a university was like in this or that time ignore altogether the contributions of staff other than the lecturers and professors. Most of the staff were, of course, in other roles.

When the registrar, John Clarke, retired, an open competition was held internally, which led to Mary Ford succeeding him, and when she retired, the same process led to Joy Mills succeeding her. They were all absolutely meticulous, hard working, and committed to the values of Hope. The university secretary, Tony Grayson, and I were most supportive and loyal, seeing that Simon could take Hope forward. Staff were proud to say they worked at Hope. We welcomed the changes needed to survive. Alongside Simon Lee, Tony fought a long and ultimately successful battle with the government over the title of our University College. Tony had enormous respect for Bishop David Sheppard and Archbishop Derek Worlock, and the feeling was mutual, so the governance of Hope worked well with the bishops alternating as the chair of the governing body and Tony acting as the clerk. Tony sadly died prematurely. Rob Page, our personnel director, retired early and enjoyed being outdoors. As that had been his personal aim, it made sense that he was concerned to help all staff have a decent pension. I gradually took on more and more of the overseeing of support roles and was eventually director of finance and resources and then deputy chief executive. Within that role, I had been responsible for separating the roles of Paul Capewell for library and IT on his retirement and overseeing the appointment of a new director of IT services, Joy Kumar, who had been the deputy director of IT for Lancashire Police. It was good to have someone with experience in an important outside organisation where IT was crucial. The library team also did a good job in their new set-up, by this stage, led by Linda Taylor, who was in turn supported by Susan Murray. The personnel team was now led by Helen Klepper, reporting to me, with good support from Pam Donohoe. Alan Catterson was director of estates, and Doug Wood was head of accommodation. They used to travel to and from work together, from Sefton, but didn't always seem to clear up overlapping responsibilities on their journeys. Bernard Longden had been a lecturer and deputy registrar who became director of strategy and planning, working very closely with me. Tony Grayson's equally efficient deputy, Graham Donelan, took over his role. Three associate registrars also worked closely with us: Catherine Harvey, Jean Bates, and Nicola Roberts, as did the Hope across the Irish Sea team, led by Paul Rafferty and then by Gillian Atkinson. The senior administrators had become a more diverse team. It was fun to work with these colleagues. Hope encouraged us all to pursue degrees or other forms of continuing professional development. The finance team – especially Keith Alcock, Lynn Jones, Claudia McLean, and Ann Rimmer – took on more responsibility as I was diverted into other matters. This was a strong team who worked hard and would go the extra mile for students, for staff, and for other communities. For example, they acted as the accountable body for community groups in receipt of European Union (EU) grants. For example, if the EU decision-makers could see a need but wanted to be sure the funds would be properly applied, they would be in touch with the finance team. This was tough work. The way the EU financial year worked, the decision-makers in Merseyside had to commit their budgets by 31 December or else they lost that funding. I know Simon was impressed and grateful that this finance team would work with one of our deans of Hope in the Community, Martin Carey, between Boxing Day and New Year's Eve each year to make sure not just Hope but our community partners mopped up any spare funding to support projects that made a difference in disadvantaged communities.

We constantly discussed how all these good people could be supported to take on more enjoyable, stimulating, and challenging responsibilities. Sharon Bassett, initially Simon's executive assistant, and Helen O'Sullivan, initially a lecturer, are cases in point. We could see their potential and wanted them to have a go at ever more challenging jobs ranging from quality assurance to marketing to directing student services, where they excelled. There were no limits. I had a lot to do with Rita Lewis, who ran the domestic services, and Colin Littler, who ran the catering. Rita set very high standards and cared about all her team. Colin's deputy, Dave Cropper, was another colleague who died prematurely. Keith and I went round to see his wife, Sally, who also worked for us as one of our cleaning team. With Rob Page, we would check whether the finances were sorted out for the family in these sad circumstances and if there was anything else Hope could do. Sally wanted to be kept busy, out of the house, and to see if she could move on from her role. So, she was one of the keenest volunteers to help at Hope on the Waterfront, and eventually became a receptionist in Hope Park as roles evolved into staffing Hope Zones to help students and welcome visitors.

Although students might not notice most of us in university administration, a happy and committed team who understand the vision and the special character of a place like Hope can make a significant difference to the student experience. Anyone employed in that time will tell you that Simon Lee knew every member of staff by name and face. The senior officers also knew everyone, and this was a great strength. There were some 700 members of staff as the student numbers doubled from 3,500 to 7,000.

Some of the same people also played a part behind the scenes in bringing church colleges closer together even though they were competitive with one another. For instance, Keith Alcock and I encouraged other church colleges to join a benchmarking group, which eventually was supported by the funding council, and this helped us, and our governors, understand our comparative strengths and weaknesses. You could call it a strength or a weakness, but our staffing costs were relatively high, for example, principally because Archbishop Derek Worlock and Bishop David Sheppard were very sympathetic to the trade unions, had a no compulsory redundancy policy, and paid generous overtime if, for instance, the catering staff were asked to stay late for a special event.

There were challenges, not least because the institution had become more staff-focused than student-focused over the years, and so there was some friction. For example, it was the era when supermarkets were experimenting with twenty-four-hour opening, but our library was shut in the evenings. The students, backed by Simon and me, among others, wanted round-the-clock opening, and we made that happen. It wasn't the full service with librarians, but computers, as well as books and journals, were available in a comfortable space all night, with security, which many students appreciated. The evening meal, included as the third meal of a day in the price of accommodation on campus, was taken incredibly early, from four p.m., to enable members of our catering team to get home for their family meals at teatime. We did not want staff to miss time with their own families, but we were working to serve our students, who were paying for accommodation with three meals a day, so we had to change. Little things happened just because they always had, but we changed them. For instance, instead of just getting the refectory table and chairs refurbished every year, we replaced them, introducing some round tables. Simon Lee, Pro-Rector Dr John Elford, and many of us came to lunch in the refectory every day, eating alongside staff and students, not in a reserved dining room. Therefore, everyone could see how to raise issues with the leadership of the institution – just catch people on their way into lunch or around Hope Park. Later, when she became the chair of governors, Sr Eileen Kelleher was in that refectory also in the mornings and afternoons, available to listen to anyone. Not only at Hope on the Waterfront but in Hope Park we added a new café, called Fresh Hope, as students and staff were more inclined to want to step out of their rooms or offices to walk across campus and chat over coffee. You could usually find Sr Eileen in one of these spaces, listening to students.

In these years, there was a focus on the name change, integrating the campus, becoming more student centered, raising our profile, finding a temporary outlet in the centre of Liverpool, finding a permanent second campus in a regeneration area within Liverpool, supporting community action, developing partnerships around the Northwest, especially with church connections, recruiting from across the Irish Sea and internationally, and improving student accommodation. All these were activities where the administrators could play a significant role, often leading the implementation of ideas suggested by Simon Lee in response to concerns raised by staff and students. Sometimes, Simon proposed something because he had wider experience of different types of universities, colleges, schools, and communities in different parts of the country. For instance, he knew lots of schools in Northern Ireland where he thought their students would enjoy life on our campus, connected to home by easyJet. So, we created Hope across the Irish Sea, and I really enjoyed working in Ireland, North and South, with Paul Rafferty, Gillian Atkinson (now Dyche), Sr Eileen Kelleher, and Eddie and Chris Ferguson.

At the same time, though, we had to grapple with financial challenges and questions of status. The governments of both political parties did not seem keen on recognising church colleges as universities. The VC and senior staff of the University of Liverpool could not have been more helpful, but the VC of Liverpool John Moores University and his main adviser, Stuart, saw Hope's rise as a threat. We were small compared to them, so it didn't make sense, but it was a sign of the impact Hope was making.

Governors varied in the time they could give and the amount they understood but were in general very supportive indeed of Simon's leadership. Nigel Bromage, John Kellaway, and the bishops of Warrington were especially sharp on finances. Cash was tight in this era, before student fees, so Keith Alcock and I had to manage the cash flow carefully. Staff understandably wanted kit, such as computers, to start every new academic year, but the funds came only in monthly tranches from HEFCE and the TTA and were contingent on attracting and retaining students. Dr Burke was right to build up reserves, as he was not sure about major investments until his last year, when he was keen to see a new library project start. That was only just affordable. We then had to get Poor Estate funding from HEFCE for any further developments. It gave everyone a boost when such a group of financially astute governors agreed with the strategy Simon and I put to them of improving the estate, switching from a mindset of struggling to keep the institution solvent to one of ensuring that our students had really good campuses, which would in turn attract more students and make Hope viable in the long run.

With hindsight we could have been even more supportive of some of Simon's ideas – for instance, improving our halls of residence, starting new subjects such as medicine and physiotherapy (Edge Hill and UCLAN), giving students laptop computers with courses preprogrammed, as he told us was happening in the USA, but we did have a go at lots of initiatives and enjoyed them. For instance, Tony Grayson was a very gifted university secretary but was not that interested in formal occasions, and neither was I. We were not at first as keen as Simon Lee was to make graduations such special days. We soon cottoned on and could see that graduating students and their families loved these ceremonies and that they were also a great way of spreading goodwill and attracting other students, as families went home full of enthusiasm for Hope. So, we encouraged all staff to play their parts, to prepare carefully and to attend wherever possible. Tony became known as the Enforcer for the way in which he personally made sure people didn't interrupt the graduations by coming in late to the cathedral. The marketing and communications team were first class, working closely with Simon but also very good with the IT technicians, and together made the ceremonies run well before turning the days into fabulous special magazines, called *Hope Direct*, with photos and stories of happy graduates and their families. Staff could be proud of all this, and it helped recruit students from Ireland to Sri Lanka when we could show the atmosphere of our graduation days in good materials and in DVDs.

As the campus became integrated, Simon and I would walk along the pathway, for instance, to the refectory, and I would be back and forth as more teams reported to me, so we would always be having chats with students and staff. This was much better than being stuck in our offices. As Sanjee Perera noted in her talk at our reunion, we began the day in discussions there (where she was working part-time), but once others were out and about, the pathway was the place to be. Dr Burke's secretary, Audrey Plevin, had been at school with Dr Burke's wife, Doreen, but when Audrey retired, we recruited young graduates to run Simon's office as his executive assistants – first Rosemary Waite and then Sharon Bassett. You could always drop into their office and ask if you could have an extra few minutes to talk something over with Simon by walking along the pathway to his next meeting.

The pathway was Simon's idea, but Alan Catterson executed it quickly and brilliantly, and it somehow transformed the campus, the atmosphere, and perceptions of the estates team. Until then, people just crossed the road, Taggart Avenue, wherever it suited them and made their way through buildings by back entrances, as the two campuses of the old colleges had not been integrated. In Simon's first few weeks, Alan realised he was going to be central to changing the campus, but he knew we didn't have much spare money to invest. Simon said it was important to have a common pathway through the campus, and it wouldn't cost much to knock down some buildings, and that would open up the campus. Alan did that straightaway, and sure enough, people started to follow a set path. Then Alan made it into a proper, bold pathway, uniform, much wider and distinctive in a new yellow material, with brick edging and plants to the side. This was good for disabled access and also for everyone to chat as they walked side by side. As people were funneled to cross the road at a particular point, the planners finally agreed that we could have a pelican crossing there, which made it all safer. Encouraged by the reaction to this, we then knocked down the houses in which the pro-rectors had been living. In one space, right on the pathway, we built a new state-of-the-art nursery, which we could afford in partnership with Busy Bees because they were professionals who would run it well and there was an income stream associated with it. In the other space, we just left it open with a better view of the main building and the new library, begun by Dr Burke.

Then Simon and I toured round Liverpool, looking for places where we could establish a temporary, and eventually a permanent, second presence in Liverpool. Mgr Michael McKenna, Archbishop Derek Worlock's finance director, and the developers Urban Splash were very helpful. We settled on the Albert Dock for the temporary home from home (a base that would need to function as a home), and the SFX school and church in Everton for the permanent campus. Simon let people he trusted get on with their work, and he had confidence, for example, that Dr John Elford and I would work in our different ways to make the Everton development happen. It was important that the funding council and the Objective One decision-makers would support the project. Simon was challenging the government and the funding body on issues, such as the name, so he was happy for me to make sure that we secured the Poor Estates funding for Everton by working with the regional adviser for the funding council. Where Keith and I needed his support, however, he got involved. For example, although we had an excellent relationship with the bank, NatWest, even our supportive manager could not persuade head office to give us a mortgage for the hall of residence in such a rundown part of Liverpool, although they would have done so readily if it had been another building for us in Childwall or Aigburth. So, Simon led our pitch to the senior managers in London, explaining that this would help regenerate the area because PGCE students would then look to live nearby as they started their careers in teaching, and they backed us at Everton. We had no problem filling the spaces there, closer to the centre of the city, and also because the trend was away from catered to self-catering, and this student accommodation was designed for that new era.

As the Network of Hope developed, I also travelled around the Northwest. I was very involved with Hope across the Irish Sea and with our international students, but I suppose there were others who also had strong links in those directions. In the Northwest, though, I was really at home. I have lived in Bolton all my life except when I was an undergraduate in Liverpool, and I was educated by the Salesians in Bolton, so I guess I had a particularly good understanding of the issues facing the principals of our Catholic sixth form college partners in Blackburn, Bury, Preston, and Wigan. These were good people, and it was a pleasure to work with them, their students, staff, and governors, and to give their colleges some of our confidence. I've gone walking with John Crowley, and it was always good to be at St Mary's or Holy Cross. It really meant something to the students that staff enjoyed coming out from Liverpool.

The cliché now heard all the time, about people being on a 'journey', was true for me, both literally and metaphorically. Hope was changing, Liverpool was changing (Claudia and team helping with Objective One accountable body work), our engagement in Lancashire was changing, our involvement in the world was changing, and I was changing. In fact, I decided to take that part-time master's in managing change.

I also took the journey a 'step' further in real life by spending four weeks around my fiftieth birthday walking the camino for the first time. I've done that every year since.

Simon later told me that a favourite passage of his from the New Testament is the road to Emmaus, that walking along together, bewildered, and welcoming people who join you, breaking bread with them, all lifts the scales from your eyes, and you begin to see what's really going on around you and who it really is accompanying you. I told Simon and his wife, Patricia, when they joined my family and friends for a day of one of our walking holidays, from Viterbo to Rome, that when you are walking in a group like that you get the chance to chat to everyone over a few hours. In a way, that has been an extension of the best part of our time together at Hope.

I am still involved in the life journeys of former students and colleagues, even though my main focus now is on grandparenting. So, the gathering that led to this book was welcome, after twenty-five years, but not unusual. I still keep in touch with Sanjee and Simon, for example, by phone and email every week and meet up when we can, and keep in touch with many others through Facebook.

This approach to life, of walking with others, began with my first visit to the Lake District when I was eighteen. I was born and bred in Bolton, where my wife, Dot, and I still live. Our children, and now grandchildren, have lived further afield but are now reasonably close again to where they grew up with us. We all go to the Lake District every year for Easter week, with lots of walking, as I did with my parents, siblings, and our children. I had walked the coast to coast before I came to Hope. Therefore, it was natural to mark my fiftieth birthday to try a more adventurous walk, the camino. Dot and our four children have all walked with me, at different times, on the camino in Spain, Portugal, and France. Our eldest granddaughter, Seren, aged eleven, walked six days in Galicia with myself and Dot in 2022.

In appraisal, Simon asked me if I wanted to study for a MBA part-time. I said no but I would like to find a master's that did suit and stretch me and would help my work at Hope. I chose the MSc in managing change at Sheffield Hallam. This was a great experience. The school limits the intake to sixteen people who had to be in managerial work, as a large part of it was sharing our stories and coming up with solutions to real challenges being faced by one another. There was a lot of trust involved, especially as initially the students and tutors were strangers to each other and there was much peer assessment. It was pioneering, a word I had associated with Hope, and very stimulating. It was good to see that another university, not based on church foundations, could be so farsighted and so student-focused at postgraduate level. It opened my eyes to good things about our sector, and I have subsequently worked in two other modern universities often described as former polytechnics, Leeds Metropolitan University (running the graduate trainee programme when Simon Lee went on to be vice-chancellor there) and now Manchester Metropolitan University (where I am teaching business and where Pam Donohoe, who had worked in personnel with us at Hope and then at Leeds Met, is now deputy director of HR).

The influential adviser to the vice-chancellor of Liverpool John Moores, Stuart, was in my set for this MS, so that was interesting in itself.

My enthusiasm for how refreshing it was to study part-time at another institution might have encouraged others to follow suit. Hope was generous in paying fees and allowing some time to other colleagues to pursue their masters. I am sure the people, the institution, and the sector as a whole benefit from this kind of commitment to continuing personal development.

Did this master's help me to manage change? It certainly showed how many people at all kinds of work are reluctant to change. The best way to change the culture in these circumstances is to show people that their employment is at the very edge of a cliff, that the ground beneath them is going to crumble if they don't face up to the erosion of their place in the scheme of things. People have to shore up their positions or make the radical decision to move. I could see that we had been complacent in church colleges, thinking that the world would always need teachers. We hadn't faced up to the threats, for example, how the prestige of university titles had given polytechnics such a boost or how aggressive they would be in competing for our students.

This was where we could have been bolder. We had two really good features of our curriculum, teacher training and a combined honours degree, which could lead, depending on which subjects you took, to a BA or a BS. This was attractive to many of our students, and it also meant that they were well-funded under the old scheme, before fees, because the government gave increased funding to institutions if their subjects had higher costs, reasonably enough, and many of our students did a subject in those higher bands. In Simon's time, we added business studies to that combined honours programme, which gave a huge boost to recruitment. Another suggestion of his was just a step too far for other managers, and we didn't try to introduce nursing. His thinking was that we were one of six big providers of teacher training in the Northwest, the others being Chester, St Martin's (now part of Cumbria), Edge Hill, Manchester Metropolitan, and Liverpool John Moores, but the others all had a similar stream of students, funded by the NHS. Both teaching and nursing had been ways into the professions for women in the nineteenth century, before the successes of those women made the authorities recognise that they were graduate level. Simon's theory was that the Catholic background of two of our three colleges meant those running them were wary of the NHS, principally over the issue of conscientious objection to abortion, and vice versa. For whatever reasons, our benchmarking with those two Anglican colleges, Chester and St Martin's, showed the strengths nursing brought to their portfolios. Anyway, we didn't have a go at nursing.

We did admire what Liverpool John Moores had done in rescuing buildings in the city centre, and we could see that students were increasingly attracted to living in the middle of all that. Even though I had been an undergraduate at the University of Liverpool and like the centre of the city, by now I used to get a lift down the motorways to work and quite liked Hope's location in Childwall, at the end of the M62, on the outskirts of Liverpool. It seemed odd to Simon, however, that we weren't in town. He sensed that students wanted that and it would make us more visible; he could see that some of the areas could do with the boost that out students could bring.

Like people on a cliff where other houses had fallen into the sea, we were in what had been an attractive location but we now needed to be elsewhere. Or to put it another way, we had been too inward looking and slow to adapt, focused on our own internal mergers, rather than noticing that the landscape outside was changing fast. This is why the Sheffield

Hallam master's programme was so brilliant for me. It was based around Harvard Professor John Kotter's eight-step process of change:

1. Create a sense of urgency
2. Build a guiding coalition for change
3. Form a sense of vision and initiatives
4. Enlist a volunteer army
5. Enable action by removing barriers
6. Generate short-term wins
7. Sustain acceleration
8. Institute change[1]

That's exactly what we were doing at Hope, as well as what I was studying, so I would recommend any institution sending managers on a master's like that. It all helped us in listening, thinking laterally, using our imaginations, and creating something distinctive. The other church colleges became intrigued by what they were hearing about Hope, so they wanted to meet in Liverpool, check us out, and poach some of our initiatives. That gave our team a sense of pride, that we were ahead of the competition. When it came towards the end of the long process of gaining degree-awarding powers, we were visited by lots of leading figures in universities, inspecting us, questioning those who worked with me, and again there was great pride as we presented the campuses in the best possible light and answered their questions well. It was a classic illustration of John Kotter's analysis.

After eight years, I think Simon did the right thing in moving on; that's the most effective way to keep up the momentum of rapid change. As Kotter says, you've got to sustain acceleration. Again, we had a year to find the successor. By this time, I was the deputy chief executive. Prof. Pillay had his own strengths, taking forward the campuses and the research reputation of Hope. However, he did not have the same respect for all staff, thinking managers were less important and should be paid less than professors. Many professional managers and administrators decided to leave, including me after three years. I asked for early retirement after being accused of not being fully behind his policies.

---

1. See Kotter, 'Eight Steps.'

When the opportunity presented itself to help Simon Lee in his next role at Leeds Metropolitan University, I was delighted. I enjoyed leading his innovative programme of 'graduate trainees', selecting ten graduating students a year to work for the university for two years while they were studying part-time for a master's, and then coaching them as they rotated through different parts of the administration. When Simon left there, so did I, 'retiring' again but this time teaching business students part-time in Manchester Metropolitan University, which I still do, alongside grand-parenting. We are still in touch with those trainees, who are lovely people, proud of their time in another university.

What about me? That's not the end of my story. I like Bob Dylan's "Not Dark Yet." He wrote it at the time we are reflecting on, in 1997, when he was fifty-six. Dylan captures the shadows that are falling, the sense of time running away, and darkness that is getting there.

Camino

Pilgrimage is the movement of a traveller or group of travellers making a journey for religious purposes, nowadays also called a traditional religious or modern secular journey.[2] Can pilgrimage be seen as touristic? Collins-Kreiner states that religious organisations and pilgrims do not consider pilgrimage as touristic, but from the industry's point of view pilgrims can be treated as tourists. The apostle Saint James lived from about 5 BC to AD 44. He is the patron saint of Spain and the patron saint of pilgrims. He was a fisherman, brother of John, and son of Zebedee and Salome. Dante called him the Apostle of Hope.

The bishop of Santiago in 850 encouraged the idea that St James's (Sant Iago's) relics, his remains, were buried underneath the cathedral. Pilgrimages followed in the spirit of seeking acceptance, forgiveness, and redemption, much as Christians in those times undertook pilgrimages to Rome or Jerusalem. Rather like the pandemic, the plague curtailed inter-national journeys. The Reformation also undermined the idea of relics. Political unrest made travel in the sixteenth century more uncertain. Two developments made a difference after four centuries of few pilgrims. In 1987, the Camino di Santiago was designated the first European Cultural Route.

2. Collins-Kreiner, "Researching Pilgrimage," 441.

Then, Martin Sheen, the actor, starred in a 2010 movie, *The Way*, which brought American pilgrims on the Camino. He was big in the USA as the star of *West Wing*, and the fact that he was born in this region of Spain, Galicia, was a revelation to many.

In a way, Hope needed its own couple of boosts, perhaps the Freedom of the City of Liverpool and our Queen's Anniversary Prize in 1996. Certainly, the growth in the numbers of pilgrims on the Camino since *The Way*, which coincided with a holy year in 2010, has been astonishing. We were amazed at Hope when we more than doubled our student numbers, but look at these figures below!

1985	690
1986	1,801
1991	7, 274
1993 (Holy Year)	99,436
1997	25,719
1999 (Holy Year)	154,613
2000	55,004
2004 (Holy Year)	179,891
2005	93,924
2007	114,466
2010 (Holy Year)	272,417
2013	215,879
2016	277,854
2017	301,036
2019	347,578

A holy year is a year when the Feast of St James, 25 July, falls on a Sunday. It is an extra national holiday in Spain when it falls on a weekday.[3]

There are various reasons why people go on the camino, including the following: religious pilgrimage, travel and sport, challenge, spiritual adventure, and retreat. The increase of foreign pilgrims is huge – in just over ten years, almost 300 percent more pilgrims. In holy years, the number of Spanish pilgrims increases in a very significant way.

There are four or five ways of finding out whether the camino is for you. The first is that you can just go and try it out. The second way is

3. Table information from "Camino de Santiago."

to read about the camino in one of the following books: *The Pilgrimage* (Coelho), *The Camino* (MacLaine), *The Roads to Santiago de Compostela* (Confraternity of Saint James), or *I'm Off Then* (Kerkeling). The third way to learn about the Camino is to watch Martin Sheen's film, *The Way*, and the fourth option is to look at the website of the Confraternity of St James.[4] I said four or five ways, and the fifth includes watching my own videos on Facebook, addressing the myths that put people off trying the Camino.[5] So far, I've made five videos of about twenty minutes each. The first challenges six wrong assumptions about the camino, specifically, that the walks are only for young people; there's only one road to Santiago, the Camino Frances; you must stay in an *albergue*; you have to carry your luggage; you need to be religious; and you need to use a travel company.

Two of those might need a bit of explanation. To illustrate that second point from my first video, the Camino Frances is called that because it is a route from France, from the foot of the Pyrenees. It took me five weeks to walk the five hundred miles along that way to Santiago in 1999, and we had to get there by Eurostar to Paris, and then two more train journeys to the very south of France. Another route is just to fly to Porto, in Portugal, and walk much more easily up the coast, just five miles away from the airport, all the way to Santiago. The word *albergue*, or hostel, means dormitory accommodation where people sleep with a dozen or twenty or more sleeping in a big space. That's not for everyone, but people can do the camino their own ways, perhaps in small hotels. One can find my videos of me simply chatting to the camera with a map or two on my YouTube channel.

If I hadn't said all that in videos, I'd be writing it in the rest of this essay, but one might understand from those six points, and for the purposes of this reunion of people from Hope, there are obvious parallels. In my time at Hope, we also challenged six wrong assumptions about university: university is only for young people; there's only one way to get to university, straight from school; you have to stay in a hall of residence on a campus; you have to deal with your own baggage; you need to be religious to go to a church college; and you need to apply through the Universities and Colleges Admissions Service (UCAS) and get booked up a year in advance.

4. https://www.csj.org.uk.

5. https://www.youtube.com/watch?v=H-IkEOGIK7Q.

To refute a couple of those, I will offer that if you have, say, dyslexia or a bad experience of school for some other reason, a university can help you unload that 'baggage' with practical help like special screens or computer programmes that read out texts and, if you want it, counselling. UCAS has two ways into university – applying a year in advance or at the last minute through clearing. The second of those can be as good as the first, and people can join a university nowadays in other ways as a mature student. For example, we were told by heads of sixth forms further north in the Northwest that their students who went away to university were often homesick for Cumbria. They didn't want to go back after their Christmas vacation at home. So, we recruited from Cumbria, through word of mouth with teachers, for a January start, and adapted our curriculum so students could begin in the second semester. By all means, students should try for a big university somewhere farther away, and good luck, but if a person wants somewhere a bit more like home, we thought we could help out in Hope. This was in Simon's time. Prof. Pillay was keener on good A-level grades, so it might not be the same at Hope now, but there will be other universities offering that second chance.

Another Pathway of Hope

For ten years I was a trustee of the UK Friends of Abraham Path (UK-FAP) with Max Farrar, whom I got to know when working at Leeds Met. In 2014, I got the opportunity to walk for six days on Abraham's Path in Jordan with my wife, Dot; sister, Phil; and her husband, Joe. We stayed in family homes and ate with the families. While in Jordan we visited two Syrian refugee camps and spent a day in one of the camps entertaining children with building blocks and drawing materials that we had brought with us from home. I don't need to say any more about this because the UK and the US friends of this initiative have put it really well. This is how UKFAP describes itself:

> Through education and information, UKFAP aims to support the growing network of Middle Eastern hiking trails which follow the legendary stories of Abraham/Ibrahim. We encourage and help British walkers in their journeys to experience the beautiful landscapes, traditional hospitality and deep friendship of the people who live there; and so to bring home the values and practices of trust, openness, inclusiveness, listening and hospitality.

Our fundraising has three aims: to support local projects and people who work at developing and sustaining the trails; to promote education about walking in the Middle East and about the values of Abraham/Ibrahim. to lead journeys and offer bursaries to help people in the UK experience the Middle East in this way. In 2020/21 we are particularly fundraising for the Zagros Trail in Iraqi Kurdistan; and for Bedouin initiatives in the Sinai.[6]

There are a couple of sentences on the Abraham Path Initiative website, which could be a judgement, in the world of lifelong learning, on our time together at Liverpool Hope University College, where Stephen Heintz says, 'While many in the world are building walls, the Abraham Path Initiative is building paths. They are building pathways of hope.' The way they tell their story, and explain my love of walking, is this:

In 2006, twenty-five people embarked on a trip from Urfa to Hebron, following Abraham's legendary walk from what may have been his place of birth, to the place he is believed to be buried. This journey, from womb to tomb, laid the foundation for a visionary and hopeful project: the development of walking trails approximating the travels of Abraham and his family in Mesopotamia, who shared hospitality with people they met along the way. Stories related to this first family of monotheism abound in the region, from today's Iraq to the Sinai Peninsula. By 2020, nearly 80,000 visitors have walked the network of trails inspired by the Abraham Path project. They've told tens of thousands of stories about the people of the region, their families, traditions, art, architecture, languages, recipes, and agricultural practices. Walkers foster friendships across sometimes challenging divides, boost local economic development, and enrich understanding of this region and its peoples for audiences around the globe.

Walking is a tool for deepening understanding of self and other; it allows an experience of culture that is unattainable from the seat of a bus. The simple act of walking has connected people around the world since time immemorial, with the Eastern Mediterranean an active crossroad between Africa and Asia. The Abraham Path Initiative (API) has seeded walking trails here in order to reintroduce this storied region as one

---

6. Although the above and below texts no longer appears online, readers may visit the current website of the UK Friends of Abraham's Path at https://abrahampath.org.uk/about-us/.

of irrepressibly hospitable people. By shining light on traditions of hospitality, API evokes the beloved regional origin story that shows up in everyday life: residents welcome strangers in honor of Abraham (Ibrahim, in Arabic), a spiritual ancestor of over half of humanity.

The Abraham Path Initiative (API) is a non-profit organization established to develop walking trails or tourists to learn about and enjoy the peoples and cultures of Southwest Asia (the Middle East). Since 2007, API has worked with local partners create over 2000 miles of scenic trails in Turkey, Jordan, Palestine, Sinai, and Iraq, providing economic benefits to local communities and opportunities for walkers to have positive intercultural encounters. Since the Coronavirus crisis of 2020, API has introduced people from around the world to the people, landscapes, and storied cities of Southwest Asia through webinars and live, online tours. Our commitment to catalyzing appreciation for this complex area of our planet is shaped by respect for the widespread traditions of hospitality and kindness to strangers, as exemplified by the legendary Ibrahim/Abraham, a spiritual ancestor of over half of humanity, and the regional residents who honor his memory and traditions.

Conclusion

One day in France, walking with Ruth and Danny, we came across a French man sat down against a tree. He had a bar in a ski resort and worked with VIPs at Glastonbury. He obtained work for Danny, driving VIPs at two Glastonbury events. We often use a phrase he gave us, 'the camino never ends.'

I began with Nelson Mandela's reflection on life and with my enjoyment of walking. So, I leave you for now with the concluding stanza of a poem that was composed not for a twenty-fifth anniversary, but for a fiftieth. Henry Wadsworth Longfellow was writing for the fiftieth reunion of the class of 1825 at Bowdoin. When people ask, 'Why do the camino now in my seventies?', I quote this from 'Morituri Salutamus':

> What then? Shall we sit idly down and say
> The night has come; it is no longer day?
> The night hath not yet come. . . .
> For age is opportunity no less
> Than youth itself, though in another dress,
> And as the evening twilight fades away,

The sky is filled with stars, invisible by day.

The camino never ends.

Bibliography

"Camino de Santiago." Wikipedia, last edited 13 Apr. 2023. https://en.wikipedia.org/wiki/Camino_de_Santiago.

Coelho, Paulo. *The Pilgrimage: A Contemporary Quest for Ancient Wisdom*. Translated by Alan Clarke. San Francisco: HarperSanFrancisco, 1995.

Collins-Kreiner, N. "Researching Pilgrimage: Continuity and Transformations." *Annals of Tourism Research* 37 (2010) 440–56. https://doi.org/10.1016/j.annals.2009.10.016.

Confraternity of St. James. *The Roads to Santiago de Compostela*. N.p.: Confraternity of Saint James, 2007.

Estevez, Emilio. *The Way*. Starring Martin Sheen et al. Barcelona: Filmax, 2010.

Kerkeling, Hape. *I'm Off Then: My Journey along the Camino de Santiago*. Translated by Shelley Frisch. New York: Free, 2009.

Kotter, John P. 'The 8 Steps for Leading Change.' Kotter Inc., n.d. https://www.kotterinc.com/methodology/8-steps/.

Longfellow, Henry Wadsworth. 'Morituri Salutamus: Poem for the Fiftieth Anniversary of the Class of 1825 in Bowdoin College.' Poetry Foundation, 1875. https://www.poetryfoundation.org/poems/44639/morituri-salutamus-poem-for-the-fiftieth-anniversary-of-the-class-of-1825-in-bowdoin-college.

MacLaine, Shirley. *Camino: A Journey of the Spirit*. New York: Pocket, 2000.

10

Collegiality in Higher Education

JOHN ELFORD

THERE ARE TWO ISSUES that need to be as clear as can be about before discussing collegiality. The first is the personally transforming nature of higher education (HE) at a crucial time in the lives of students, regardless of their age. The second is the impact of modern communications technology. Familiar though we all may be with both, we might yet well remain impervious, for our purpose, to their impact.

The personally transforming power of HE is, of course, something it shares with primary and secondary education, but remains distinct from them both. All have the power to enhance pupils' lives, improve social mobility, and accrue financial benefit. This is as true of education in underdeveloped countries as it is of it in developed ones. Both provide the opportunities to improve their students' lot as well as that of the communities in which they live. Little wonder, therefore, that all education raises such politically and economically sensitive issues. In the UK and elsewhere it is generally accepted that the state bears the costs of primary- and secondary-level education. However, the funding of HE, which was once part of this state arrangement, has recently changed, and the cost is now born by its students. One reason for this is because numbers of students in HE have risen dramatically ever since Margaret Thatcher initiated a reorganization of higher education with an emphasis on accessibility. This led to the rapid expansion of HE provision, including the upgrade of universities to all the polytechnics, as well as the foundation of numerous new universities. One consequence of this is the now perceived shortage of a skill-based workforce, which was previously partly provided by the polytechnics. Another raises the questions about whether we now have an HE system that neither the students nor the state can afford and, furthermore, whether it is actually needed. The currently alarming spectacle of a growing number of graduates being forced to take formerly nongraduate jobs is just one concerning evidence of this. This is laudable in that it does not tax those excluded from university education to pay through their taxes for those that can go. However, it does understandably raise the concerns of graduates now in low-paid jobs with extensive financial liabilities. The debate about all this has scarce begun. It needs to continue with more urgency.

Like so much else in our society, this has been further complicated by the coronavirus pandemic. Many universities, which are now effectively run as businesses, find themselves trying to charge students, who are now effectively their customers, for teaching and accommodation which the students have been unable to take part in because of the pandemic restrictions. For these and other reasons, the government has even accepted that, just like other businesses, some universities might even go bankrupt. This was unthinkable under former state-provided arrangements, and it remains to be seen how all this will be resolved.

All this is unsettling for the students, as well as for the government, and should be for all of us. This is because HE is different from primary and secondary education for a number of reasons. It requires, for the most part, students to leave home and, therefore, incur living costs. It also requires them to do this for three years before they graduate as the costs inexorably mount up. HE is also the denouement of its students' education before they enter the job market and prepare to settle in the direction of the rest of their lives, though they may change direction. This is the first of the two reasons we need to keep in mind before we begin to understand collegiality.

The second is modern information technology. Since the invention of the internet in 1983 it has now become, for many, a central way in which knowledge is accessed and shared, in particular by students. One consequence is that usable knowledge, which was formerly only acquired by attending lectures and learning how to use academic libraries, is now readily accessible at the click of a keyboard. For the most part, universities have been struggling to come to terms with this dramatic transformation in knowledge accessibility. Little wonder that many historians liken the invention of the internet to the effect of the invention of the printing press in the sixteenth century.

This ready access to knowledge, and its seemingly exponential use by students, creates problems for universities. One is because of their now widespread use of coursework assessment in their degree studies, as well as in their final examinations, which settle degree grades. This has enabled students to display in their coursework a far greater knowledge than they are able to do in their final and unseen examinations. Furthermore, no plagiarism technology, which is now widely used, can possibly help to redress this. An outcome of this is that students are often awarded degrees that they do not deserve on the basis of their learnt knowledge. It might yet be decided that this is no handicap to them, because they will continue to use the internet in their professions. For our purpose, however, it remains to be asked: if universities are not now in such large part not responsible for the communication of knowledge, what are they for?

Interestingly, the last occasion when the universities had to come to terms with rapidly developing technology led to the founding of the Open University in 1969. It responded by spotting the simple potential of using television for the delivery of lectures. Its subsequent phenomenal success has to be attributed, of course, to its many other radical innovations. These included the following: the abolition of entry qualifications and of any time restrictions on degree completion, with the creation of modular studies supported by study packs, summer schools, and personal tutors. Many traditional universities, often surreptitiously, have also embraced many of these reforms; this alone has raised many questions for the OU about its continued direction. Its once ready embrace of new technology, however, still presents an example which older universities have yet to come to terms with.

These two issues, HE being life transforming and its use of modern technology, will now become, for the reasons already partly explained, the formative influences on our discussion of collegiality.

At a basic level the word 'collegiality' simply designates any collaboration between colleagues in any setting. However, in the context of HE it has, of course, been taken to mean much more than that. From classical times, students have been attracted to live near scholars of their choice, and presumably because of growing demand, this eventually led to the foundation of modern universities in mediaeval Europe. What is meant by collegiality in HE grew out of all this as providing accommodation for expanding student numbers. As a result, colleges did far more than just provide the basic needs of accommodation. They also provided two more important things. The first was to create opportunity for students to live together and interact with each other. This was, and remains, a vital part of college life and the educational process it is designed to facilitate. The second thing colleges facilitated was daily interaction between students and their tutors. All those who have ever had the privilege to experience life in an educational college will know how important both of these things are. The reason for this is because learning in HE is much more than just amassing information. It is also, and importantly, knowing how to exercise critical judgement whilst doing so, as well as to integrate that with one's own values and lifestyle. Doing all this can be personally traumatic. At their best, both colleges and their tutors are alert to all this and able to respond promptly and accordingly. This is why pastoral care became, and remains, such an important part of everyday college life. Over the centuries, none of this has changed. Colleges still exist in HE for exactly the same reasons. Moreover, they invariably attract both staff and students for doing so. It is for this reason that collegiality in HE means more than simply collaboration between colleagues in any setting. In college life, the setting is an integral part of the shared human educational endeavour between staff and students. Both know this equally and respond accordingly as an important part of the reason for their life together. These are just some of the reasons why the word collegiality attains its distinctive meaning in an educational setting. As explained, it stands for the deep and highly personal, even at times raw, experiences for all involved in the final formal part of the educational process.

If universities are no longer largely responsible for the transfer of knowledge, collegiality might now become more, and not less, important in the tertiary educational process. For this reason, it might have to change fundamentally the understanding what it brings to it. The question is, how must it do so?

One answer to this question might well be that it must enable students to *discern* the importance of what information is relevant in their studies from what is not. Of course, this has always been the case, because students have been provided with guided reading to enhance their studies. At its best, this discernment has had the effect of focusing their minds on what exactly it is that is so important for them to understand. Perhaps, even, the sheer energy, discipline, and focus of having to locate and read books was, in itself, an important part of the learning process. However, there is now not a little anecdotal evidence that students on basic degree courses spend less time in academic libraries than they once did. For many of them it is an unattractive and laborious alternative to accessing instant knowledge at the click of a keyboard.

In order for us to understand what such *discernment* entails it is important for us also to understand the *purpose* for which it is required. This might be perfectly clear in preparation for the many specific professions for reasons that are easy to understand. All specialist careers have their specific demands, and many require, for this reason, further years of postgraduate education. Indeed, trying to understand what is specifically important to us from a mass of readily accessible information is part of the everyday experience of most of us. Examples are found in the many ways in which we might well surf the internet for information about our medical, legal, financial, or whatever problems, but still need to turn to professionals in those and many other fields to obtain advice before taking any specifically required action. This is because those professionals have a proven skill in responding to the sort of clarification we might need. Even in this internet age, the continuing need for their services is assured!

Requiring such practical on-the-job experience is now commonplace in training for the professions. Teacher education is just one example of this because of an increasingly large amount of the time they take in training is now spent in the classroom and not at university. Another is the recently reported example of training for entry into general medical practice. Yet another is the example of the many now successful solicitors who have always trained simply by doing their jobs. Clearly, both discernment and purpose can be derived only from experience. This might be well assisted by internet access because relevant information can be summoned remotely of libraries and instantly.

The link between discernment and purpose is clearly able to be understood in the established professions in this way. But there is more to what collegiality in tertiary education entails. This is evidenced by the common fact that many graduates enter professions that are not related to the subject of their degree studies. They might do this immediately after their degree studies or do so subsequently as their careers develop and diversify. Continuing to be a professional in an ever changing and rapidly developing society has already become, for many, a common experience. Collegiality must, therefore, also include preparation of this more ongoing definition of what it means to be a graduate.

For all these reasons, in the history of the expansion of universities, the importance of collegiality has been well recognised. It was done so, for example, in the creation of the so-called red brick universities where halls of residence were created for this very purpose. Many of these universities have also now expanded beyond their ability to provide accommodation for all their students for the duration of their degree studies. However, they have endeavoured to maintain its provision for as many as they can during the first year of them. I am privileged to have once had the experience of responsibility for one of them. Whilst it was a challenge in many ways, it was also very revealing. On reviving the activities of its old members' association, it soon became clear to me that the memory of the accommodation hall in the lives of many of those who are long successful in their careers survived more vividly than their academic studies have done. This had, for them, the clear effect of becoming and remaining the focus of the appreciation and gratitude for their university experience. Indeed, this might well be yet another example of the fact that, as we undergo the graduate experience, we are inevitably more influenced in the long run by the things were least aware of at the time. Understanding the meaning of collegiality must take this into account, however much it might now have to be adapted because of new ways of acquiring knowledge.

Colleges, so understood, provide at their best an often intense and necessarily limited period of interaction between students and staff alike. In Western culture this has historically been why so many of them have had and still have Christian foundations, though these might well now survive only as trusts, which provide real estate. Others will provide more than this by also investing in, and maintaining, distinctly Christian traditions such as worship, the music it requires at its best, prayer, and chaplains. They will also endeavour to appoint academic staff who are either Christians or those not so, but who are in sympathy with the Christian foundation. In a subsequent career experience, I also had responsibility for leading such a college. It was S. Katherines, then the Anglican part of the Liverpool Institute of Higher Education, now of Liverpool Hope University. The other college was the Roman Catholic Christ's and Notre Dame, itself a prior amalgamation. At the same time, I was a part of the management executive as well as being a trustee of the foundation, and for our purpose, three memories of all this remain with me.

The first memory is that it was a period of rapid change in the expansion of higher education, which we have already noted. That raised many questions about the expansion of student numbers, the development of the curriculum, the status of the institute, and the part the college had once played and continued to have in it all. To say that all this was a challenge is an understatement. It was broadly met by accepting that everything was in a necessary transition and that a range of even radical changes had to be made for the college to continue its long-established and widely respected work.

The second was the importance of maintaining the Christian tradition in ways that always kept it open to staff and students alike who were either members of other religions or had no religious affiliation whatsoever. Achieving this was, of course, greatly assisted by the Anglican and ecumenical foundation with the Roman Catholic College. I was inspired through it all, and remain so, by the Elizabethan Settlement, which made Anglicanism into a Church with a specific obligation to serve the nation. The openness that this obligation always requires is of its very essence. It was to prove its value in so many ways during the process of transition. One, which I then was and remain struck by, is the way in which so many of the staff and students alike who did not consider themselves to be Christians not only accepted but also actively took part in the wider doings of the Christian foundation. So many of the avowedly non-Christian staff, for example, shared the concern and care for students that was clearly motivated for others by their Christian faith. All this can only be described as a 'happy contagion' in which we all worked together to a common purpose, which was that of always serving the best interests of the students above all else in everything we did together.

Many of the academic staff who were not Christians were frequently and understandably concerned about whether working in the institution in any way limited their academic freedom. I was personally able to give them the assurance that it would most certainly not. This was because many of my own academic opinions were, in fact, antiestablishment and that I had never encountered any established academic resistance to them that ever discouraged me from holding them. Whilst undergoing all these, for me, invaluable experiences in my everyday job I was also a governor of an Anglican secondary school. This was confirmational because it also endorsed the principles of combining foundational integrity with openness and with equal success. The same must be said of so many other church schools and colleges throughout the country.

The third memory I cherish throughout all this period of rapid institutional change was because I shared, with others, the experience of being a trustee and at the same time a member of the executive management group. In the founding documents of the Liverpool Institute of

Higher Education the trustees reserved the right to veto any actions taken by the executive. Whilst this could be interpreted as a negative influence, and once memorably was in my experience, I never considered it to be so. This was because we were living in a time when so many other church colleges of higher education were distancing themselves from their trust-ees because they considered it in their interests to promote their secular profile. Throughout my time as a trustee and member of the executive, this was never even contemplated, so there was also never any experience of encountering any conflicts of interest. The wisdom of all this has, of course, now been verified by Liverpool Hope University. It has success-fully promoted itself as an ecumenical Christian University and, indeed, even claimed its uniqueness as a strength in doing so.

In the light of all this experience of collegial Christian responsibil-ity amid so much rapid social change, it is clear to me that reconciling openness with commitment to a faith most certainly does not present any insurmountable difficulties. This is not to say, of course, that it can never do so in other contexts. There are far too many instances of allowing dis-cernment to be dominated by the desire to promote religious self-interest to claim that it can never happen. For this reason alone, it always has to be remembered that promoting self-interest in secular society in this way can never be allowed.

I will now conclude with a reconstruction of what collegiality in higher education might now mean in the light of all this. To do that, this discussion will now have to become more personalized.

The founding rector and chief executive of the Liverpool Institute of Higher Education, Dr James Burke, retired in 1995 and was then re-placed by Professor Simon Lee. It now needs to recalled why at this time higher education was going through a rapid period of expansion and change. The Thatcher reforms, which we have already mentioned, were at this time working themselves through a system. Many institutions were responding to them and others not so. The Liverpool Institute of Higher Education, or LIHE as it had in an ungainly way become known, had not responded. For example, its total student number was still only just over three thousand and this often more by accident than design. One reason for this was because, as I recall, there was considerable internal staff and other resistance to any expansion as well as to the curriculum innova-tion and widespread change that it would clearly require. Elsewhere in the city of Liverpool, other HE institutions had already responded with both an increase in their student numbers and the many other changes it required. Most notably, the former Liverpool Polytechnic (now the John Moores University) had risen from some four thousand students to over twenty thousand. LIHE was clearly in danger of being left out of all this and would have to face the serious and probably terminal implications of doing so. All this faced Professor Lee with considerable problems as he took over as rector and chief executive. From the very beginning, he applied his then youthful energy and wide experience particularly of ecumenism in Northern Ireland to every aspect of the organisation. Things were clearly now going to be very different, and the organisation was to make up rapidly for the past resistance to change at every level. As someone who lived and worked through all this in collaboration with him as a pro-rector and head of college, I am convinced on reflection that we had to succeed for the organisation even to survive at all. The stakes could not have been higher. That Professor Lee succeeded to meet this challenge as he did is now history.

As head of S. Katherines, I realised at the time that there was no alternative but to embrace these reforms and to follow Prof. Lee's leadership and, moreover, to do so willingly and helpfully in any way that I could. This very soon became a pleasure as we got to know each other and shared, in particular, many of our common academic interests, invariably with good humour.

In all this, the total student number veritably rocketed to over seven thousand with all the many changes at every level of the organisation that that required. I cannot resist here saying how thankful I then was, because I believed the future was not only secure but that it also became promising in so many ways. Not least in all this I was delighted to learn that Professor Lee also brought with him, from his own experience and life of the Christian faith, a knowledge of the vital role that collegiality played in higher education. As it all turned out, by the time I retired, he often used to remark that I was pleased to leave the future of S. Katherines to him because it was all that I had ever hoped for it. To this I used to reply 'and the more Simon'. These many years later I still think that, with added gratitude to all those who have preserved what S. Katherines and its sister college stand for in the university ever since.

It soon became clear that the organisation was infused with a new energy and purpose that had been previously lacking. Evidence of this appeared throughout. Among them was the priority of seeking a new name, which had long since fallen into the doldrums of disagreement. Professor Lee proposed Liverpool Hope, and this very soon received agreement. Its discussion was no longer to take up and effectively waste inordinate amounts of time. Other evidence included the need to appoint innumerable new members of the academic staff to cope with the increased student numbers. As it gained momentum, the effect of this was to bring what can only be described as a colossal infusion of yet more energy and experience from elsewhere. Notably, this included new professorial appointments. A central example of which was the appointment of Ian Markham as professor of theology under the guidance of Professor Keith Ward, the Regius Professor of Theology at Oxford University who kindly agreed to be a member of the appointing committee. On his arrival, Ian immediately set about engendering and supervising a new focus on theological research in preparation, for the first time ever, for entry for the organisation into the national Research Assessment Exercise, as it was then known. I was personally caught up in all this because Ian came into my room one day and asked, 'What have you got that you have never published?' I gave him a manuscript that I had long since worked on, and he brought it back the next morning and told me that it had to be published. The book, *The Pastoral Nature of Theology*, I understand, is still in print and now in its fourth edition. Ian had the same effect on all the theologians who were capable of published research, with the result that we achieved what we understood was a good grade, four out of a top grade of five in the subsequent national research assessment. This had the effect of encouraging other subjects throughout the organisation to follow suit, which many of them did but without the spectacular result of the theologians. I was personally grateful to Ian because he relaunched my own publishing career, which, now as an octogenarian, I am still enjoying. Many of the new academic appointments were encouraged to leave their careers in universities elsewhere and accept employment at Hope because this assured them of sympathy with their own plans for research and publishing.

This rapid expansion in staff and student numbers soon brought other transforming developments, including one of which I was to personally benefit richly from in an unexpected opportunity. I readily accepted this for both personal and professional reasons. The former was because, after years of literally following me about the country as my own career required, my wife, Anne, had been appointed to the headship of Windsor Community School in Toxteth. She remained there for some fourteen years and came to love and respect children and the local people. Her career there ended with the remarkable success of the school attaining an excellent Ofsted rating. The professional reason for my accepting the new opportunity was that heads of the colleges and pro-rectors were rapidly becoming an anachronism in the now rapidly changing institutional structures. I recall, in fact, that I was the last one standing of this breed, which had been invented, of convenience, when LIHE was created in 1995.

That opportunity was for me to retire and accept the, effectively, consultant post of overall responsibility for a new campus at Everton along with promoting the interests of Liverpool Hope in the city with which I was by then long familiar. Prof. Lee had been managing this development as well as doing everything else required every day by all the innovation and expansion. As well as this benefitting my wife, it also left me with a previously unexpected opportunity to have time to pursue my lifetime interest and career in boating of one sort and another. The four years of having this responsibility were, for me, among my happiest at Hope. I became involved with the local community and the regeneration activity in the wider city at an exciting time of its development. Very soon, all the staff and some of the students at Hope at Everton became friends, and there was a general excitement about the opportunities the new space gave to all the subjects. I always encouraged them to work together in this, and they readily accepted the opportunities of doing so. So many memories of this have for me long (too long) been forgotten, and I am welcoming of this opportunity to recall them. They centre on a vision I had for the project. That was to turn it into a veritable Bauhaus of creativity,[1] which, in as many ways as it could, tapped itself into the remarkable creativity energy of the arts in the of the city of Liverpool. This sounds like, and probably was at the time, a very ambitious aspiration. However, it very soon became a realisable one for a simple reason. That was because all the academic staff in the three subjects of fine art, music, and drama were keen to support it in every way they could. Memories of how they did so abound. We had string quartets playing in the atrium at art exhibitions. The first of these was a memorable exhibition of the Methodist Modern Art Collection, and many such were soon to follow. Other memories include a very fine and entertaining drama production on the history of the building written and produced by Dr John Bennett. As well as all this, working connections with the city and its art activities began to occur regularly. Memorable among them was the use made

---

1. For the Bauhaus movement, see https://mymodernmet.com/what-is-bauhaus -art-movement/.

of the central hall by the Liverpool Philharmonic for rehearsals and the collaboration with it in helping to meet the schools' attendance requirements, which were often attached as a condition of its many grants.

Ever-growing numbers of mature students soon brought even more enrichment to this explosion of creativity. This is well illustrated by my vivid memory of one of them whose name I remember well. He was George Kingdom who came to study for a degree in music and fine art. On his arrival he asked the head of music if he could be absent for a few days because he had a gig. When asked where, he replied 'at Ronnie Scott's'. Clearly, he was already an accomplished jazz musician who came, I recall from conversations with him, to enrich his knowledge of music. Soon he also became an accomplished painter, whose work I also admired. He was a memorable example of a student whose keenness for learning was an inspiration to us all and, in particular, to all the younger students of his subjects. A fine example, that is, of what so many other mature students contributed to everything we were trying to achieve.

As news of what we were all doing at Hope at Everton became known in the city, it came to the attention of the then lord lieutenant. He rapidly understood because of his detailed knowledge of the city and that of his educational history on the site. His staff member came for a visit and brought with him scouts from the office of the Prince of Wales. When I showed them all around and explained the vision of it all, they enquired of the great hall, which was locked and still under construction at the time. They insisted on seeing it and, on doing so, said that the prince must see it and know of all we were already beginning to achieve. That resulted in his memorable subsequent visit at which he clearly paid particular attention to the students in a relaxed, charming, and often humourous way. The students, like all of us, were both hugely impressed and grateful for his visit.

The new campus on Shaw Street became such a necessary innovation because the ever-space-demanding subjects of fine arts, music, and drama had seriously outgrown the provision we were able to make for them on the main campus. This was in spite of them being rehoused together only a few years earlier in what became known as the Benedict Arts Centre. Again, rapid increases in student numbers for all of them were the reason for this. As well as having shared responsibility for these subjects in their new quarters, I was also responsible for raising money for the project and managing the construction developments when we received it. This included formally chairing the monthly meeting of all the participants, including the contractors. In this I was greatly assisted by the presence throughout of Mr Sean Gallagher, the finance director, and by the governor chair of the finance committee, Mr Nigel Bromage. They both enabled me to report developments with confidence to Professor Lee and, through him, to the governing council.

All this expansion and innovation in the life of Liverpool Hope found its expression in many ways. One was the occupation of space in the Albert Dock for Hope on the Waterfront as it became known. This had the effect of noticeably raising our profile in the city that, for many years, had been scarcely even aware of our existence. Membership of the city's Freedom Roll of Associations soon followed, as did the annual use of the site during graduation celebrations, for which it was ideally suited. Moreover, it did this in an area of Liverpool that had for too long been excluded from them. This deserves special mention here as our attempt to understand collegiality, as I hope will become clear below.

When I took up my post as pro-rector and head of S. Katherine's College in 1988, I discovered that it was customary after the graduation ceremonies for us all to visit the University of Liverpool Students' Union for sherry. This immediately struck me as being less than ideal, not least because student union buildings, to say the most in their favour, are not ideal locations for such a celebration. To be frank, my experience of it struck me as being a perfunctory, inappropriate, and somewhat condescending gesture. I decided, therefore, that we should never do it again. In its place we moved the focus of all degree celebrations for our students to S. Katherines College Chapel, its quadrangle, and dining hall. This proved to be an instant success. The main reason for this was because both the academic and service staff alike unstintingly rose to the occasion by willingly, visibly, and invariably joyfully joining in. The LIHE governors were also invited to attend. A chapel service took place for all who wished to attend. This was followed by rejoicing and drinks in the quadrangle, which was bedecked with sparkling white tablecloths and extensive seating for the elderly. I have a treasured and vivid memory of one visitor, after a first glance at it all, saying, 'It's just like Brideshead.' To which I replied, 'It's not on television, and it's for you all.' This was followed by lunch in the refectory before leaving en masse for the graduation ceremonies in the philharmonic hall. This new arrangement proved an instant success and was then repeated annually. Eventually, it was further strengthened by Christ's and Notre Dame College following suit. The result was that the whole campus then became en fête. Again, this was willingly supported by the gardening, cleaning, and catering staff alike who all welcomed the opportunity to make their contributions. Graduation days, in this way, became occasions of celebration for the whole of the then institute community. They soon became widely anticipated and supported. In creating them in this way I was greatly and willingly supported by the hard work of the college senior tutor, Mr Jeffrey Brache, who was able to spend much more time with the student body than I was able to do. It was always a joy to receive expressions of gratitude for these celebrations, from students as well as from visiting parents and others. Jeffrey was also very good at helping to arranging student attendance at early evening sherry receptions in my room, which became another feature of the celebration of college life. These, and other such developments, greatly enhanced the recruitment of students to the college simply because it was encouraged by the students themselves who clearly enjoyed the changes. One of them once remarked to me that 'S. Katherine's is the place to be.'

You can imagine my relief when, on his arrival, Simon Lee not only approved of these graduation day and other developments, he both warmly welcomed and set about developing them in ways I was unable to achieve. Very soon the ceremonies were transferred from the philharmonic hall to the two cathedrals, annually in turn. In this way they became major annual celebrations, visible to all in the city, of all that was excellent in the life of Liverpool Hope.

I am enjoying the memory of all these long-forgotten developments, but it is important for me to return here to our discussion of collegiality and to explain why I think they all played an essential part in its understanding at Liverpool Hope.

First recall, if you kindly will, that I mentioned earlier that I was struck by the fact that former students at Manchester University valued the memory of what St Anselm Hall contributed to the memory of their university experience more than their academic studies have done. The innovations I introduced in 1989 were largely prompted by this, in the desire that we could make it so for all our students. As the celebrations soon developed under Professor Lee, not the least evidence of this was that there was a clear connection between them and the steady response to the recruitment of the many new students required in the expansion of the college. That evidence was in the fact that we sent our students away with a very positive and appreciative attitude to everything we had achieved with them. They, therefore, became our ambassadors at large. Another evidence of this was the revival of attendance at reunion days was clearly given a new impetus. Again, these were encouraged and many of them attended by Jeffrey Brache. Clearly, in all this, students came to value their time with us and to appreciate that it was an important part of their graduation experience. Of course, many other new developments also contributed to this. They were, namely, the provision of enhanced student services, accommodation, and the visible structural improvements made to the campus throughout, including the ones at Hope at Everton. I now rejoice, these years later, that all these campus developments have been not only maintained but also visibly improved upon.

From all this hands-on experience I am, therefore, convinced that collegiality begins with colleges not only being satisfied with what they do, but also embodying it in their activities in every way they can. Only in this way can they communicate it to their students in the hope that it will create the sort of memories that become engrained and hopefully endure for the rest of their lives. This is what happens naturally, of course, in so many of our older universities in which alumni activities flourish as they do, not the least because they are invariably linked to fundraising. For the reasons I am explaining, it is incumbent on newer universities to do the same in every way they can if they are to lay the initial foundations of collegiality. Even this, however, is not sufficient; there is so much more that it is important for them to achieve.

First, this has to do with the nature of higher education learning itself. So often many students are tired of the rigours of learning by the time they enter higher education in spite of everything many of their schools might have done to prevent this. One of the main differences in learning that universities have to instill in everything they do is to make clear that *all* learning, even that acquired previously, now has to embrace two simple things: energy and excitement. The energy is required to help them, to sustain a lifelong and natural curiosity in everything they subsequently do. The excitement with which they do so then becomes the evidence of that curiosity. These seemingly simple elements should be the hallmarks of a person educated to graduate level. When they succeed in this, graduates, of course, want to continue with postgraduate studies, as so many of them often do. This experience alone should help them to enter a lifetime of energetic and excited engagement with anything their careers throw at them. Interestingly, this is why many mature students want to take up higher education often for the first time. Their varied experiences of life have invariably raised for them questions which they enter higher education to seek answers to. This is why it is so often a joy to have them in seminar discussions with younger people for whom all these rich experiences are yet to come.

As so much of this essay is based on my experiences at Hope, I cannot resist here relating an anecdote that, for me, clearly serves as an illustration of this. I vividly remember once walking the corridor outside my room to encounter an eighty-year-old mature student, who was well known to me, completely unselfconsciously conducting a tour on an open day for eager teenagers who, as I observed, were paying rapt attention to him. I have never forgotten, and I hope never will, that he was clearly communicating to them all the excitement and pleasure of being a college member. This incident is so etched on my memory that I dare to hope that you will understand why it so well illustrates the point I am making about collegiality. It is a fundamental and richly lived experience, which is to be embraced and treasured for the jewel that it is.

But there is, of course, more to understanding collegiality than even all this. The quality of its teaching and all its related support for students has to be of the very highest quality. This is now seemingly endlessly inspected and reported upon in published league tables. This is necessary to enable students to choose where to study for their higher education at a time when it involves them in so much expense. In fact, it may not be too far from the truth to suspect that the widely noted degree level inflation to historically excessive first-class categories is crudely encouraged by some universities simply for recruiting purposes. Higher education institutions, which go to the sort of lengths we have discussed to encourage a sense of collegiality, cannot, however, even hope to succeed unless they also provide academic teaching and learning of the very highest standard. This focuses on the staff they appoint for the purpose and, in turn, the provision they make for them to succeed in their careers. I have been moved by the fact that so many of the new appointees at Hope have recently commented that I chaired the appointment committee that gave them their first start at Hope where they still remain. I am moved by that because, in a varied career, I had forgotten that I ever did anything as important as that! All the new appointees, as I recall, also brought new energy and expectation to the college after so many years in which new appointments were a rarity and only ever mainly required because of retirements. Above all, they brought a determination to succeed in their academic research, as well as their teaching careers. Their teaching success is dependent on the former; engendering collegiality by bringing teaching alive is widely proven. Students rightly expect their lecturers to be up to date and informed, preferably by publishing themselves. Unless this happens, all else that we have discussed to encourage a sense of collegiality in institutions will certainly prove to be of no avail. Unless excitement and energy are created in the lecture room, students will not graduate with those qualities they will most certainly need in their careers. They are among the most important hallmarks of graduate-ness, which will serve them lastingly well. Current knowledge will be succeeded by being ever renewed and brought up to date. Graduates who have once learnt, and importantly continue to learn, how to handle it will prove, as the years progress, to be the most successful ones. To be educated to graduate level means nothing less than this. It is in knowing how to welcome and use new knowledge that will make graduates welcome in any situations their careers might throw at them. If their lecturers succeed in teaching that by example, they will have taught something far more important than the material they use when doing so. It will certainly last the longer.

In this discussion, I have tried to show why it is that collegiality is so important to the experience of higher education. I have also dared to suggest that it is more, rather than less so, in this internet age when knowledge can be accessed at the click of a computer. Exactly how this is already working itself out in the management of higher education is something I am not familiar with after these long years of retirement. What I am sure of, however, is that it must do so for the final formal stage in the educational process to retain its centuries-old, and now wordwide, responsibilities of keeping pace with rapid technological process. Even at the time I retired over twenty years ago, progress of this kind was scarcely being made. This was because back then we were clearly underestimating the scale and complexity of the task. What I have dared to suggest in this discussion is that paying attention to collegiality will now play a larger part in that discussion than even back when we imagined. However, I have also been daring to suggest that we, all those years ago, were not oblivious of its importance and did all we could to facilitate it.

I have also stressed that achieving any progress in this task cannot be made without enlisting the support of all the employees in the institution, academic and nonacademic alike, as well as all the executive management, the governing bodies, and their trustees. It really is that demanding on everyone involved. If they all lead together, the evidence of our time at Hope is that, by far, the majority of students will respond enthusiastically and appreciatively. I have also shown why that appreciation grows so much over the years, and even becomes the principal recollection of their time at university.

Because higher education marks the final formal stage in the education process for most people, it is vital that it does so in ways that are life-lasting and enriching. A report published in 1936, and quoted by Simon Lee at the conclusion of his inaugural lecture as vice-chancellor of Leeds Metropolitan University in 2007, stressed this in the following way. I include it here at my conclusion because they express succinctly also all that I have been trying to say.

> An education for life may be achieved in many different ways. Certainly it is not achieved solely in the lecture room, the laboratory or the library. The mere acquirement of knowledge is not enough. Notoriously the most subtle and potent educational influences in the older universities of this country have been those which, being indirect, come not with observation, and were probably originally unforeseen and unintended. The excitement of being plunged into a new environment and more spacious mode of life, with all its possibilities of congenial study and congenial companionship; the sense of privilege in being made heirs to a great tradition . . . these are the influences which stimulate thought and enlarge its boundaries, develop the faculty of judgement and arouse in students that energy of the soul which Aristotle found the essence of true well-being. To evoke in its students such an energy of the soul in pursuit of excellence must be the principal aim of any University.[2]

As I have been trying to say, with far less eloquence, this is exactly what I think collegiality achieves. Without it, universities that attempt to achieve it without also having soul cannot ever hope do so. To the extent to which this is what religions at their best also achieve, then universities, or at least parts of them, without those foundations might even have a head start on those without it.

2. For the inaugural lecture at Leeds Metropolitan University, see the private papers of Professor Simon Lee. For the 1936 report, see 'Universities of Great Britain: Education for a Living and for Life,' *Nature* 137 (1936) 1057–59 (https://doi.org/10.1038/137105 7a0).

PIONEERING LEARNING AT A DISTANCE AND IN PARTNER-SHIPS

11

Mothership

VICKY BAKER

TWENTY-FIVE YEARS ON FROM my experience teaching at Liverpool Hope University, I was pleased to be asked to join a group symposium online, reflecting on our shared time there and addressing ways in which our period at Hope has shaped us. I was looking forward to seeing old faces again but really struggled with the idea that having entered full-time motherhood, it would be difficult to introduce myself with the appropriate title. I settled on 'home engineer' as I thought it sounded more impressive than 'stay-at-home mum.'

When I arrived at Hope, in my twenties, I was at the start of an academic career that I thought I would journey through until I retire. Perhaps I should explain that I had come to Hope primarily because my doctoral supervisor at Exeter, Professor Ian Markham, was the foundation dean, building an exciting team, and also the ecumenical nature of Hope appealed to me. Furthermore, I knew of the chief executive, Professor Simon Lee, as both he and I had written about Muslim communities and Salman Rushdie's *The Satanic Verses*.

Twenty-five years later, taking care of a chronically sick child, it was initially hard to think of any connection between my time at Hope and what I spend most of my days doing now. However, with a little more thought, I realise that are two rather solid connections: The first is around 'disability' and what it means to educate a disadvantaged person, and second are notions around 'flexibility of care' that have shaped who I have become – a full-time career. Both these connections are intrinsically linked.

I was employed by Liverpool Hope as a member of the theology team. Liverpool Hope, by the time of my arrival, had instigated a programme of widening participation and was heavily committed to recruiting and educating people from underrepresented backgrounds – particularly those of an older age group, those who were socially disadvantaged, and those from different cultural traditions for whom higher education was perhaps a more difficult option to pursue. The Network of Hope, at various sixth form colleges located around the Northeast, provided students with higher education during the evenings and attracted learners from all different ages and backgrounds. The programme was successful, providing strong links between the academic institution of Liverpool Hope and its local community. It was a start for me in thinking differently about what it means to be a student – that there was no *one* universal fit.

However, a stronger challenge to any fixed ideas of 'student-hood' came about with my involvement with the Peabody/Hope project in London. Peabody is one of the largest housing associations in London and provides affordable housing in communities in London, supporting people who would otherwise have no adequate home. Dr Carey and Professor Lee had been approached by the Peabody Trust in London because Peabody could see in Hope's community partnership, working in the Northwest, that the institutions were kindred souls. Peabody could have chosen any London university as their educational partner, but they had the vision to see that mission alignment was more important than geographical proximity. According to Dr Carey, both institutions shared the same intrinsic values, and both had already taken a proactive approach to widening participation.

So, in 2001, Peabody fostered a partnership with Liverpool Hope in two main sites in London to make accessible university places to its residents (who consisted of a significant proportion of those from minority ethnic, refugee, and migrant backgrounds). Peabody/Hope offered these students a pre-access and access course in law and social studies; the hub was located in Liverpool with dedicated staff working on the material and delivery. The teaching material focused on issues to do with family life – in the spheres of law, sociology, and psychology. Such a focus meant that the students could all participate and relate to the main areas of study.

The programme benefitted from a central commitment in Hope and in Peabody to the vision of bringing learning to the wider community, as well as a desire to improve integration and community cohesion. At a practical level, it was beset with a few hurdles. It was a hard programme to market to the more deprived communities who found it difficult to contemplate a university place after three years devoted to study. Many of the residents wanted to find employment faster; but for those who did come on board, it certainly gave them some confidence to find employment, albeit in a social sense, even if they did not want to embark on the longer process to a degree qualification.

> All institutions committed to widening participation are confronted by the necessity to encourage those who would not normally consider higher education to begin to do so. Such young people are predominantly from working-class backgrounds and their cultural tradition means that they have to make a conscious decision to go into higher education. Recruiting them represents a daunting challenge to all those involved in working to extend access to under-represented groups.[1]

As a tutor on the programme, I must admit to feeling a little intimidated when confronted with the challenge of teaching such a diverse group of students, but the experience soon became a privilege as the groups made real connections with each other and with myself. Some students slowly began to open up about the difficulties they faced with integration within an unknown host community and the immensely tricky decision, coated with homesickness, on leaving behind the familiarity of their own countries and, in some cases, their family and friends.

I learnt the importance of being tactful and treading carefully when asking about students to talk about themselves and their own experiences. Muteeb Hamdan, a teacher of English at the Asraq Camp in Jordan, recounts his own experiences teaching refugees:

> Before teaching refugees, I wish I had heard learners' individual stories. This is not only to gain learners' trust but also to avoid embarrassing, hurtful and unnecessary questions, especially when planning self-introduction activities. One day, I asked my learners to introduce themselves and then to talk about their families. During the first lesson I asked a teenage learner to introduce himself. During the conservation, I asked about his father's job. He appeared upset by the question. After a moment of silence, he told me that several of his close relatives, including his father, had been killed.[2]

1. Elford, *Widening Participation*, 59.
2. Le Franc et al., 'What I Wish.'

Overall, what did strike me by many of my own learners at Peabody/Hope was their positivity in the face of adversity along with a desire to integrate and improve their position of themselves and their families in society. Ofttimes, they would cite improving the lives of their children as the primary motivating factor for their studies. They wanted to be educated (in England) so that they became enabled in smoothing their children's own educational paths. For many of the migrant and refugee communities, education was key to making a success of their lives in a new country. The programme itself was called REACHOut to Parents and was thus specifically targeted at parents. The positivity and hope of a new kind of life shone through the homesickness and frustration in relation to lives left behind.

Such positivity serves to inspire more during times of adversity in lockdown and associated uncertainties about what the imminent future holds. Filippo Grandi, UN high commissioner for refugees, says,

> As we worry about when we can be reunited with our friends and family and resume our normal lives, it is worth remembering that those displaced by conflict, violence and persecution are faced with these uncertainties, and many more, every day. The grace and fortitude with which they respond can be an inspiration to us all.[3]

Collectively, the learners at Peabody/Hope taught me more life lessons than I could ever impart to them – namely, perseverance in times of struggle, determination, and lots of enthusiasm, despite and in spite of a real worry for relatives left behind in a troubled country, for some of the refugee community, as well as a tangible homesickness for their own country, for many of the migrant community. It must be stated, however, that the fortitude and determination of some of the learners were not solely restricted to migrant communities, as there were many learners from more underprivileged backgrounds who really desired another chance at learning, and who also wanted to help their children navigate their own educational paths.

In terms of reflection, the ridding of the notion that 'one student size' fits has contributed immensely to my confidence and optimism in caring for my chronically sick son. Whilst it is certainly true that his educational journey will not conform to standard expectations and perhaps not be as smooth sailing as that of a healthy child, as a family we remain

---

3. Grandi, 'Why We Must Help.'

sanguine about his educational future and opportunities. In this way, my time at Liverpool Hope opened my mind to an alternative way of education without the constraints that can prove such a hurdle for those disadvantaged students whose cultural, physical, and social barriers can seem to preclude them from higher education.

'Flexibility of learning' is admittedly a rather trite expression, but for want of a better turn of phrase, it captures my experience at Hope and has filtered its way through to my understanding of what it means to be the main educator of a sick child – my sick child. Inclusive pedagogue or a learner-centered pedagogue, which emerged from teaching such a diverse classroom of learners, has impacted how I have chosen to educate my son. Alongside the help from his teachers, his tutor, and his school, a flexible approach to his learning has meant that he has been able to progress well alongside his peers.

Ironically, lockdown, with the increased use of technology in sharing lessons, has probably been beneficial to many homeschooling parents. In fact, when the media highlighted the difficulty that parents were facing during lockdown with homeschooling their children (and this could have been for many factors, including many parents having to manage jobs and their children's education), we found it much easier. Technology, instigated during the lockdown period, enabled us to access the more formal teaching materials and to follow the curriculum that my son's peers were following. It is my hope that the school will continue to use this technology in the classroom, having equipped all the students with laptops and, in this way, providing the stay-at-home students with the same information and learning materials that everyone else has access to by their physical presence in the classroom. If this practice becomes widespread, it would be a real boon for those many parents who have to homeschool their children who have certain disabilities that precludes them from normal attendance.

Inclusive education most certainly involves flexibility. For many of the students at Peabody/Hope, English was a second language. Students struggled with communicating their thoughts in written format, and as a tutor marking their work, a certain amount of flexibility was needed to encourage both their efforts and abilities, looking beyond the communication difficulties (with a steady plan to improve these written skills). Flexibility and maintaining standards were always difficult balls to juggle. However, during my time with Peabody Hope, the former needed to be a conscious effort, and for the most part, the latter took care of itself as the learners progressed in an increasingly assured manner and growing enthusiasm. Educating a child with a chronic medical condition needs this same flexibility of learning. In 2018, Matthew J. Schuelka, at the University of Birmingham, compiled a helpdesk report for UK government departments highlighting what it means to successfully implement an inclusive approach to education and clearly highlighting the link between those learners with disabilities and those from diverse backgrounds. He writes,

> Often, the term 'inclusive education' becomes synonymous with education for children with disabilities. Whilst this may still be the primary motivation for inclusive education, successful inclusive practices will be successful for *all* children with many different attributes such as ethnicity, language, gender, and socio-economic status.[4]

Regardless of academic success, and some children with medical conditions can show great determination to succeed, there must be a real flexibility in approach to learning. Learners who suffer from physical conditions can suffer from lack of confidence in their own communication skills, especially when returning to school after a prolonged absence due to a flare-up of symptoms or the start of a new medication. Overcoming adversity, alongside a determination to succeed, evinced by the Peabody/Hope students contributed to an overriding sense of resilience and hope that I have tried my best to imbue my own child with – both qualities being essential and perhaps difficult to hold onto all of the time.

Intertwined with flexibility of learning is flexibility of care. During my time at Hope, I was lucky enough to receive flexibility of care. As a result of the pandemic, in the UK, there is much talk about businesses and their approach to flexible employment and hybrid working. In relation to women, some women have desired more time working from home as a way to achieve a better work/life balance, and others have stressed the importance of an office, away from home, in order to have the time and peace to work more productively. Individual needs demand individual tailoring – again, there is 'no one size fits all'.

Although I greatly enjoyed teaching at Liverpool Hope, I was suffering from missing my family and friends who resided in a different part of the country. I was desperate to keep teaching so was in a bit of a quandary

---

4. Schuelka, 'Implementing Inclusive Education,' 2.

as to what to do next. The CEO of that time, at Liverpool Hope, was Professor Simon Lee.

In his Hiroshima lecture (unpublished), Professor Lee discusses the importance of inclusivity. The main point I took away from reading his lecture was the importance of the individual and how university practices should incorporate an individual knowledge of the student body. As a fan of Pink Floyd, I cannot help but bring up the image of pupils conforming on an assembly line, in the video of one of their hits – 'Another Brick in the Wall'. The pupils are depicted as one brainwashed unit, processed and spat out as sausage meat. Now, there is a real dichotomy between the image created in this video and the prevalent atmosphere at Liverpool Hope when I taught there. Students had diverse learning needs, and as much as was possible, these needs were embraced and an inclusive community formed. As evinced by the graduations, individual knowledge between student and tutor was central to such inclusivity:

> Where there is such a knowledge of each other, there will also be a strong sense of community.[5]

This was extended to Professor Lee's own knowledge of his staff and their individual needs. This inclusive atmosphere that embraced diverse needs and aspirations of students also meant that such flexibility of care was shown towards staff at the college. After I admitted to my homesickness and my consequent desire to leave Liverpool, Professor Lee (alongside Professor Markham and Dr Carey), presented me with an option – to work for Peabody/Hope in London. In that way, I could continue teaching, whilst being geographically nearer to my own family and friends. Professor Lee even insisted that I continued my own research in theology.

Flexibility of care and inclusive learning involves putting the individual first and offering a pathway that endeavours to suit that individual's primary needs and aspirations. Such flexibility opens one's mind as to what is possible. Rather than thinking in terms of 'disability', Liverpool Hope expanded my ideas of what education is primarily all about. With the appropriate care, the journey may not conform to the norm, but it can be eye-opening as to what diverse learners can bring to the table – what they are capable of achieving and what they teach others by their own unique experiences and struggles.

I was embarrassed joining the symposium, having become a full-time career and mother, despite the fact that these are roles that I enjoy.

5. Lee, 'Hiroshima.'

The symposium and Professor Lee have challenged these insecurities. Hence, I have entitled this chapter 'Mothership'– the classrooms at Peabody Hope were themselves micro-communities where learners could feel bonded and learn in an inclusive environment with inclusive materials that they could relate to, despite their background, race, or social status. For now, I am, hopefully, a mothership to my own son, who can eventually launch himself successfully, in his own direction.

Bibliography

Elford, R. John. 'Widening Participation in Higher Education.' In *The Foundation of Hope: Turning Dreams into Reality*, edited by R. John Elford, 50–63. Liverpool: Liverpool University Press, 2003.

Grandi, Filippo. 'Why We Must Help—and Learn From—Refugees This Ramadan.' *Al-Jazeera*, 18 May 2020. http://www.aljazeera.com/opinions/2020/5/18/why-we-must-help-and-learn-from-refugees-this-ramadan.

Le Franc, Alexis, et al. 'What I Wish I'd Known When I Began Teaching English to Refugees.' British Council, 21 Mar. 2019. https://www.britishcouncil.org/voices-magazine/what-i-wish-id-known-teaching-english-refugees.

Lee, Simon. 'Hiroshima.' Unpublished lecture, 2007.

Schuelka, Matthew J. 'Implementing Inclusive Education.' K4D, 29 Aug. 2018. https://assets.publishing.service.gov.uk/media/5c6eb77340f0b647b214c599/374_Implementing_Inclusive_Education.pdf.

12

Preparing Students for Their Future, Not Our Past

HELEN O'SULLIVAN

Introduction

WHEN I WAS INVITED to write this chapter, I was a few months away from taking up the role of provost and deputy vice-chancellor at the University of Chester. I rightly concluded that it would give me the opportunity to think through my views about the nature of higher education and how we will have to reimagine that vision for a post-COVID new reality. What I hadn't expected was how useful it was to reflect on the most valuable roles and experiences that have shaped that understanding. This chapter is therefore in two parts; the first section discusses four roles and what I have learnt from each of them. Although the roles are very different, they converge to inform shape the new model presented for a post-pandemic university.

Four Roles That Shaped My Understanding of the Real Purpose of Education

1. Network of Hope

The inspiration for the development of the Network of Hope and a detailed description of how it came into operation can be found in the first chapter of this book. My role was to develop a combined subjects programme in Heath that could be delivered on a part-time basis in the network. The plan was to eventually deliver the programme at Hope Park to more traditional full-time students, but it was extremely usual at that time to plan a course specifically aimed at part-time students who were probably returning to learning after a break from formal education. At the same time, my colleague in the music department was asked to develop a parallel programme in identity studies. Incidentally, that colleague, Professor Jonathan Powles, is now vice-principal for learning and students at the University of the West of Scotland while I am deputy vice-chancellor and provost at the University of Chester. It is interesting to speculate on whether that very early opportunity to develop creative and innovative curricula (we were both so young!) was a stepping stone to leadership or whether Simon Lee recognised our potential. Probably a bit of both.

Reflecting back on my involvement in the Network of Hope over the years, it has become clear to me how that experience underpinned so much of what was to follow. I realised that I love curriculum development and thinking about new ways of doing things and that I really love working collaboratively with a range of people who come at a task from a different perspective. It was also the first time that I understood how elements of online learning could have an impact. Hope was a pioneer in the space that would become known as the virtual learning environment – the VLE. This space is now dominated by commercial products such as Canvass and Blackboard as well as the popular open-source platform Moodle. In the mid-90s one of the members of the Hope psychology team, Roger Clark, developed a way for students to link together electronically called the Module Communication Centre or MCC. One of the key features of the MCC was a discussion board. I set up an MCC discussion board for each module on the Heath programme, but it was accessible to all students who were studying that module across the Network. In that way, a student from St John Rigby could share ideas with a student from Holy Cross and so on. At the time, there was only one computer in the department that was permanently connected to 'JANet' (a forerunner of the World Wide Web), and that was in the secretary's office. I used to have a routine of connecting to the MCC via that one computer at 8 a.m. each Tuesday morning where I posted new discussion items, replied to or commented on posts, and generally moderated the discussions. Even using those early systems, I could see the potential for students to connect with each other wherever they were and whatever time of day they wanted to contribute. It was inspiring to see students who had never met physically discussing their work, explaining difficult concepts to colleagues, and supporting each other through assignments. Finally, the Network of Hope was a lesson in how a collective endeavour can be greater than the sum of its parts. The idea of a number of institutions who share a mission coming together was significantly ahead of its time and had a lasting impact on those institutions that were a part of it. As institutions that provide higher education get more diverse, more fragmented, and more global, it is timely to remind our self of this collective power.

2. CETL and Medical Professionalism

In late 2005, I was in the last year of my term as dean of sciences and social sciences at Liverpool Hope. I was starting to wonder what I would do when my term was up when I visited an online academic jobsite to check if one of our vacancies was live. I came across an advert for the director of the CETL at Liverpool University. The opportunity was to lead a centre that would find innovative ways to develop and assess those aspects of a doctor's training that were becoming known as medical professionalism. CETLs – or Centres of Excellence in Teaching and Learning – was an initiative funded by the Higher Education Funding Council for England in order to redress the perceived imbalance towards rewarding and recognising research that was taking hold of universities in the wake of the introduction of the Research Assessment Exercise – the RAE, which is now the Research Excellence Framework, the REF. The CETL initiative had two main aims: to reward excellent teaching practice and to further invest in that practice so that CETLs' funding delivered substantial benefits to students, teachers, and institutions. Funding was provided for seventy-four CETLs, representing an investment of over £315 million over five years from 2005 to 2010. I was already familiar with the concept, having been peripherally involved in the establishment of Hope's two CETLs. Despite having neither a formal qualification in education or being medically qualified (the two essential criteria listed on the job description!), I was appointed to the role and started in March 2006. The role was pivotal to my academic career, enabling me to reinvent myself in the supportive world of medical education and paving the way for my promotion to a personal chair. However, the most significant impact was to shape my ideas about how best to develop and assess what might be called 'soft' or 'transferable' skills. In addition, I learnt the importance of such theoretical constructs as experiential learning, legitimate peripheral participation, and situated learning, as well as the importance of authentic assessment – you can't assess whether a student has developed skills in empathic communion through a multiple-choice test! I became particularly interested in the role that emotional intelligence (EI) plays in developing professionalism and leadership in medical students and junior doctors, and helped to establish EI as a credible theoretical framework with objective measures. We established that EI could be taught, or at least developed, when it was previously believed to be an immutable part of the personality that you are born with, and we showed that EI training could contribute to professional development programmes. Finding ways to develop and measure the so-called 'soft' skills has been a fundamental part of my pedagogic approach ever since.

3. Managing Online Programmes

After five years, the CETL funding came to an end, and I reverted to a portfolio of varied activities supporting the faculty of health and life sciences. One of these was to take the lead for taught postgraduate programmes. There was nervousness in the faculty leadership at the time about two particular master's programmes that had been developed as part of Liverpool's partnership with Laureate Online Education, part of the business that ran a network of private universities across the globe. The partnership was groundbreaking for the sector and enabled Liverpool to be one of the first universities in Britain to move into the online market. By the time of my involvement, the partnership had around ten thousand students studying in around 150 countries. However, because of the way that the partnership had been set up, the operation was seen by most academics as completely separate. Laureate was viewed with suspicion in many parts of the University, and the studenst were referred to as 'Laureate students' when they were University of Liverpool students and 'Laureate programmes' when they were University of Liverpool programmes. By accepting the request from my senior college Eileen Thornton to 'keep an eye' on those two programmes, I stepped on a path that led to me becoming associate pro-vice-chancellor for online education and managing the partnership with Laureate. I learnt a lot about education and leadership during that time, but two particular lessons have shaped my approach to both in the time since.

The first lesson was really to understand what was important to students and what motivated them to undertake demanding further study, often at points in their career and personal lives when space, time, and energy were at an absolute premium. About half of our online students travelled to Liverpool for their graduation ceremony, and we put on a series of receptions, meet and greet events, and celebrations through the week. The highlight of the week was a celebration for all of our online graduates that took place in the crypt of the Metropolitan Cathedral. We encouraged the graduates and graduands to dress up and bring their families, and we gave out the awards and prizes for that cohort. I took the opportunity to talk to as many of our students and their families as possible during that week, and what struck me was the depth of friendships and communities that they had developed with fellow students. They had supported each other and built professional and personal networks that they intended to keep up after graduation. Many of these networks had developed alongside the platform that we used to deliver online education, through common social media apps, but a contributing factor to this was that all of the online programmes were designed with the underpinning pedagogical approach of co-constructivism. This meant that students were taking the knowledge and theoretical constructs delivered in the source materials and adding to it from their own work, experience, and understanding. Because we required students to interact with each other as part of the assessment for each module, students were creating new knowledge and understanding as a group. During this collaborative process, students got to know each other and were engaged and motivated to learn. They could test out their understanding by applying it in the workplace and then come back to the group and discuss how it had gone. All of this took place before the recent improvement in the accessibility and reliability of video-based communication technology and was mostly asynchronous and text based. Some students commented to me that working in an online classroom with students from different countries and different cultural beliefs had helped them professionally, as they had learnt how to collaborate with colleagues who may be in a completely different sector, industry, and time zone. It is perhaps ironic that students who were completely online and, therefore, remote from each other and the geographical embodiment of their university got so much out of the social connection. Through this work I learnt the importance of designing programmes and courses to specifically require this connection and led me to a pedagogical approach that I articulate as social learning.

The second lesson that I learnt was the importance of taking a businesslike approach to running higher education. Our partners, Laureate, were a for-profit company (although at the time did not have shareholders) and had a very specific mission in widening access and were committed to the transformative power of higher education. I felt that because they could be very honest about their need to make a profit, it gave them the freedom to be very clear about their mission and the most effective way of achieving it. There was a significant clash of cultures between a UK Russell Group university and a for-profit organisation that ran a network of private universities, especially when colleagues in each organisation that were more peripherally involved with the partnership got involved. Laureate was frankly baffled and deeply frustrated by some of our processes, and Liverpool colleagues were suspicious of decisions that looked like they were based on containing costs. It is probably true that the vast majority of universities that are in the public sector or equivalent weren't really designed with the changing reality of education in mind, in other words, for an age of rapid technological change, global interconnectedness, and shifting labor market needs. In addition, to do higher education well is expensive, and the cost of delivering high quality education continues to rise across the globe. How do we deal with the scale of change and the investment required? I saw that in the private sector, for Laureate, they were able to respond through market price, competition, and containing costs. In the UK there was a move to place some of this cost onto the student by introducing a tuition fee in 1998. Initially this was set at a relatively modest rate, but in England, the cap was controversially raised to nine thousand pounds in 2012. The consequence of this is that we now have some of the superficial characteristics of a free market – student as consumer, fees for services, etc. – while still being perceived (quite rightly in my opinion) as public sector organisations. I am completely committed to public sector, not-for-profit university education, but I saw that Laureate could be completely transparent about their finances, what programmes were costing, where there was cross-subsidy, and what they were able to devote to philanthropic activity. Although the response to the post-eighteeen review of education and funding (independent panel report, known as the Augar Review[1]) is still to come, there is no sign of

1. https://www.gov.uk/government/publications/post-18-review-of-education -and-funding-independent-panel-report.

a return to free university education in the foreseeable future. Indeed, the most likely result of the upcoming spending review is a reduction in the funding available for some subjects and, therefore, a reduction in the overall income for universities. In my view, there is an ethical imperative to bring that business discipline and transparency to running our universities so that we can continue to offer high-quality, transformative higher education to everyone who can benefit from it.

4. PVC Education during a Global Pandemic

In October 2019, Keele University, where I was then pro-vice-chancellor for education, hosted a meeting in conjunction with Jisc, aimed at exploring effective ways to use Microsoft Teams in teaching and learning. I took the opportunity to launch the start of our digital education strategy. I stated that I thought it would take us three to five years to fully implement the strategy. In reality, events of the following year meant that it took between three to five months to go from emergency remote learning to a fully integrated flexible digital education framework. Every single course, every single member of staff, and all students were forced to engage with digital education and rethink their approach to teaching, learning, and assessment. Of course, it wasn't perfect. Many students struggled with accessing the hardware or Wi-Fi quality that they needed to study wholly online. Others didn't have a private quiet space where they could participate in online classes or have distraction-free study time. Staff had to create new and effective teaching materials whilst striving to keep students engaged, often while having the responsibility of homeschooling small children or worrying about elderly and vulnerable family members. Some staff and students were bereaved, and many fell ill. However, it quickly became clear that something very significant had changed for ever. Whilst a very few members of staff questioned the wisdom of putting in a lot of effort to go online when we would just be going back to normal in a few months, most others realised that we were moving forward into a 'new normal'. Apart from staff exhaustion, the key issue in that early part of the pandemic was how to keep students engaged with their learning as they adapted to being completely online. With lots of support from each other and our central team, colleagues were able to develop and share innovating and creative ways of keeping communities together, promoting social learning, and providing support for individual students.

Because we had been thinking about how best to embrace digital education in the months leading up to the pandemic, we were in a better position than some in that we knew what we were trying to achieve. Keele's Flexible Digital Education framework was quickly finished and used as a basis for structuring the emergency move to remote learning and, importantly, into a future post-COVID world. The purpose of the framework was to support programme and module leads to design educational delivery that is flexible and can be adapted to different contexts, from online-only to different types of blended provision.[2]

The framework emphasises online collaboration, community, and engagement. It provided a foundation for online-only provision when we needed to rely on that mode of education. However, the template also – and emphatically – serves as a more general set of guidelines for educational delivery so that, as we move out of the pandemic, the elements of community collaboration and engagement can be scaffolded into programme and module design.

It suggests elements of digital resource and collaboration that can underscore an authentically blended education – a platform for the social learning that became the heart of my vision for education. The framework can be adapted to faculty or school level to better fit the character of modules delivered in a disciplinary context, but the elements are chosen to be as universal as possible.

The emergency remote learning also spelled the end, at least temporarily, to what might be called 'broadcast lectures' and handwritten, unseen exams. Broadcast lecturers are sessions when the lecturer broadcasts, or talks to, often very large groups of students in a lecture theatre. There is often a series of PowerPoint slides and little or no opportunity for active learning, collaboration, or community building.[3] Finding different ways to deal with content frees up staff and students for more time in active learning and collaborative social learning. This is the basis of the familiar concept of the flipped classroom and has been a key component of many different approaches to education in recent years. A particularly interesting example is the University of Northampton who has been championing this approach as active blended learning for long before the pandemic made it essential for everyone.

2. Keele University, 'Flexible Digital Education.'
3. Schmidt et al., 'On Use and Misuse.'

Handwritten, unseen exams are what many people recognise as a traditional exam. They can be an effective method to test the recall and application of knowledge that has been learnt and recalled under pressure, but I would argue that the number of occasions when this skill is genuinely required in the workplace, or any other form of life outside education, are very limited. The move to emergency remote learning broke our reliance on this mode of assessment, not least with the professional and statutory regulatory bodies, who often mandate this from of assessment in courses before they qualify for recognition. What we found at Keele was that the move to alternative forms of assessment resulted in closing the awarding gaps between different groups of students, and this was mirrored across other intuitions. The large-scale demise of the traditional exams may go on to have a significant impact on our ambitions to improve outcomes for students from widening participations backgrounds.

After spending years championing and advocating for online learning, the pandemic allowed me to feel partly vindicated. However, it is self-evident that most student do not want a fully online experience. They didn't miss the lectures, but they missed the social interaction around lectures. What they do want is the flexibility and convenience that online gives them, and the challenge is to provide that whilst giving as much opportunity as possible for social earning, collaborating, and community building.

No Going Back – Conceptualizing a New Model for Post-Pandemic Higher Education

1. Outcomes, Employment, and Citizenship

In section 2.2 I discussed how important developing the so-called 'soft' skills for medical professions are a critical part of training to be a doctor. It is also widely accepted that these skills are a fundamental part of business success and success as a citizen, and that these 'human' skills are some of the most difficult skills to master. The role of a university is to enable not just the mastery of technical knowledge and skills but also these crucial human skills. The World Economic Forum recently published a report that highlighted the rapidly changing job market globally. They listed the top twenty jobs where there will be the biggest increase in demand and biggest decrease in demand.

Increasing Demand	Decreasing Demand
1 Data Analysts and Scientists	1 Data Entry Clerks
2 AI and Machine Learning Specialists	2 Administrative and Executive Secretaries
3 Big Data Specialists	3 Accounting, Bookkeeping, and Payroll Clerks
4 Digital Marketing and Strategy Specialists	4 Accountants and Auditors
5 Process Automation Specialists	5 Assembly and Factory Workers
6 Business Development Professionals	6 Business Services and Administration Managers
7 Digital Transformation Specialists	7 Client Information and Customer Service Workers
8 Information Security Analysts	8 General and Operations Managers
9 Software and Applications Developers	9 Mechanics and Machinery Repairers
10 Internet of Things Specialists	10 Material-Recording and Stock-Keeping Clerks
11 Project Managers	11 Financial Analysts
12 Business Services and Administration Managers	12 Postal Service Clerks
13 Database and Network Professionals	13 Sales Rep., Wholesale and Manuf., Tech. and Sci. Products
14 Robotics Engineers	14 Relationship Managers
15 Strategic Advisors	15 Bank Tellers and Related Clerks
16 Management and Organization Analysts	16 Door-to-Door Sales, News and Street Vendors
17 FinTech Engineers	17 Electronics and Telecoms Installers and Repairers
18 Mechanics and Machinery Repairers	18 Human Resources Specialists
19 Organizational Development Specialists	19 Training and Development Specialists
20 Risk Management Specialists	20 Construction Laborers

Table 1 Top twenty job roles in increasing and decreasing demand across industries[4]

The report talks about a 'reskilling emergency' driven by the pace of change in the job market. Job and sector destruction driven by technological change will be mostly offset by creation of new jobs and sectors

4. World Economic Forum, *Future of Jobs Report*, 30.

over the next decade. However, economies, industries, and individuals are struggling to keep up with the new skills that will be needed to keep up with these changes. A common refrain from employers is that they can't meet their skills gap. We will need to help our students build these complex human competencies to prepare them for jobs that don't even exist yet. The World Economic Forum report summarised these as ten essential skills for an uncertain future of work:

- Complex problem-solving
- Cognitive flexibility
- Service orientation
- Negotiation
- Emotional intelligence
- Collaboration with others
- People management
- Judgement and decision-making
- Creativity
- Critical thinking
- Collaborative learning design

We need to ensure that all of our curricula specifically develop and assess these skills, and then we need to put them in the student transcript. In doing so, we make a pledge to our graduates' future employers that they have these skills, and it is important that we enable students to recognise that they have developed these skills. There has been a lot of debate in the media recently about the value of an arts and humanities education.[5] The recent government narrative of 'poor quality' or 'low-value' courses is rarely articulated in terms of the actual courses, but there seems to be a prevailing view that some arts and humanities course provide a 'low return on investment', perhaps from the perspective of the government-backed Student Loans Company. An indication of the government's thinking about the relative merits of different types of study can be seen in a speech given by Education Secretary Gavin Williamson to the Social Market Foundation in July 2020, where he said, 'The development of technical and vocational skills, the greater embedding of

---

5. Jeffery, 'In Defense of Arts.'

digital skills – will be vital to charting our course to recovery. There will be a tremendous need for upskilling, reskilling and retraining. Getting people back into work as quickly as possible.' In addition, he commented, 'For too long, we've been training people for jobs that don't exist. We need to train them for the jobs that do exist and will exist in the future. We have to end the focus on qualifications for qualifications' sake. We need fundamental reform: a wholesale rebalancing towards further and technical education. And across our entire post-16 sector, we need a much stronger alignment with the economic and societal needs of the nation.'[6]

In the aftermath of the pandemic and potential economic downturn it is likely that prospective students and their parents will be looking for courses that have a more visible link to the job market. However, if you look at the list of ten essential skills above, it is apparent that many arts and humanities degrees provide graduates with a number of these highly valuable and transferable human skills. By making the development and assessment of these skills transparent in our courses and qualification transcripts, we can demonstrate to future students and their parents that an arts or humanities degree is a secure way to a rewarding career. In addition, as digital transformation of our lives accelerates, creativity and new knowledge will come from the interplay of different disciplinary perspectives. Philosophy and what it means to be human will be a component of artificial intelligence and virtual reality. Until recently, the pattern of life was pretty predictable: play – learn – job – retire. Into the future, the pattern will be more like play – school – post-school education – job, job, job, job, but all underpinned by the ability to learn. We can no longer think in terms of job security but must train our students for career security. The ability to learn will be one of a graduate's most valuable assets.

2. Disruption

Commentators have been discussing disruption in university education for many years. Just as technology has transformed other huge sectors in our economy, the same transformation, it was argued, was coming for higher education. Two thousand twelve was the year of the MOOCs (massive open online courses) with great claims being made for the impact that this form of learning would have. In 2013, the think tank

---

6. Williamson, 'Education Secretary FE Speech.'

the Institute for Public Policy Research published an essay called 'An Avalanche Is Coming: Higher Education and the Revolution Ahead'.[7] The essay described the challenge ahead and the potential threat posed to traditional twentieth-century institutions if university leaders didn't embrace the radical change that was required. In the years following its publication, the essay was treated with scepticism, and then an element of triumphalism crept in – look, it's now 2018, and the avalanche didn't come, and we are all still completely fine, thank you very much! At this point it is wise to recall Amara's Law, which states, 'We tend to over-estimate the effect of a technology in the short run and underestimate the effect in the long run.'[8] Because the essay overemphasised the role of the MOOC in disruption, commentators overlooked many of the other messages that are now starting to look quite prophetic. Although it can't have been in the authors' minds, the avalanche did come in the form of a global pandemic, and we now have a much shorter time frame in which to react.

One of the fundamental principles of this disruption is that knowledge is a currency. Previously, before digital transformation, the currency was the award and the qualification, and universities had a monopoly on those. These are still important as a milestone and a rite of passage and a way to demonstrate that we have achieved certain capstone skills or attributes. The new knowledge currency is where we enable our students (defined broadly as our undergraduate and postgraduate students as well as a range of leaners engaging with us in continued professional development and learning) to curate a digital portfolio of skills and competencies that are verified by the university into what are often called micro-credentials, or digital badges. Demonstrating that they have acquired the skills, attributes, and behaviours should be through competency-based assessment. Once the new currency outweighs the old currency, we may lose the right to run postsecondary school education and be overtaken by Coursera, Google, and Amazon.

So, what might a disrupted university look like? Micro-credentials are defined as a subunit of a credential or credentials (could be micro, meso, mini, etc.) that can be accumulated into larger credentials or qualifications or stay as part of a broader portfolio.[9] On the one hand, uni-

---

7. Barber et al., 'Avalanche Is Coming.'
8. Attributed to Roy Amara.
9. MicroHe, 'Support Future Learning Excellence.'

versities will continue to run higher education or vocational education programmes that result in macro-credits, what we currently call a degree to other qualification, but these might be partly built up through micro- and meso-credits. On the other hand, in order to stay relevant, we will be running pathways for recognition for people who are mainly outside the university in life and work. They will be able to choose from the same portfolio of micro- and meso-credentials and enable to help them build up the micro-credentials that they need to continue learning and continue skills development.

A disrupted university would therefore consist of three core parts:

- The ten essential skills (from section 3.1) built into the curriculum

- A portfolio of micro-credentials aimed at specific skills shortages

- Online programmes aimed at post-formal education learners (working adults) and outside the current usual funding streams. Ability to study completely online or with optional residentials. Will include the micro-credentials choice as well.

The key challenge will be to build a flexible digital education where there are deliberative and purposeful in-person interactions that supplement and add value. Universities are communities, and what we have seen through the emergency response to remote learning is not the same as well-designed, high-quality, pedagogically sound online learning. We now have the opportunity to establish ways of building and supporting those communities in a blended world.

3. Breaking the Mold – Privileging a Boarding-School Model of Universities

In a report by EY titled 'Trends and the Future of Education', it is noted that many students have one or more aspects of being a 'non-traditional student', such as working full- or part-time, having a dependent, having qualifications other than A-levels, being over twenty-one on enrollment, being first in family to participate in higher education, etc. During the recent pandemic, government advice to universities was all predicated on the basis that university is largely for eighteen- to twenty-five-year-olds and that the standard mode of study is to move from home to a residential campus and spend three years studying away from the place that they grew up. This mode of study, characterized as the boarding-school model,[10] is quite unusual internationally and has its roots in history with the dominance of Oxbridge requiring most people to leave home to attend university. University education was once dominated by upper middle class who had been to boarding school and were used to being educated away from home. In Australia, for example, people typically transfer from a local school to a local higher education institution. Of course, the boarding-school model is still very common, especially in the Russell Group and the campus-based pre-'92 institutions and will continue to be important for many. But even at the archetypal campus university, Keele, where there used to be a residential requirement for students and staff, things are changing. Numbers at Keele have increased recently, and much of this expansion has come in what is known as commuter students. Factor in those who are driving students to stay-at-home and commuter students, include the cost of residential accommodation, the need to provide support or care for family members, or the security of part-time employment near to their family home. A survey by the private university accommodation provider Unite, in 2017,[11] showed that students with a disability, those identifying as LGBT, students from black and minority ethnic groups, those from socioeconomic groups D and E, and those who are first in family to attend university are underrepresented in university accommodation. By privileging a boarding-school model, we may be inadvertently exacerbating inequalities. Even before the pandemic, there are lessons that we need to learn about how to ensure that all of our student feel a sense of belonging to their university when they haven't got the safety net of the residential experience.

4. Building Back Better

A. Sustaining Communities in a Digital Age

The narrative has switched from 'emergency remote learning' to 'post-COVID learning'. Everywhere I look across all sectors of society, there are articles and discussions about how we must learn from the positive changes that have occurred during this pandemic. I think there is a small minority of university colleagues who are hoping that things will go back to how they were before the pandemic, but most are planning for a 'new

10. Hillman, 'Can We Learn.'
11. Unite Students, *Everyone In.*

normal' or 'new reality', as I prefer to call it. It seems as though staff and students are conflicted about what comes next. Most people have enjoyed the convenience of working remotely, and for many people, they have spent the time saved on commuting on things that contribute to their health and well-being. On the other hand, one of the single most critical factors in being human, our connection to other humans, has suffered, and we miss the corridor conversation, the pre-meeting discussion, and supportive chat. Students have missed their social life, but also the collaborative, social learning that engages, challenges, and develops critical skills. One thing seems certain – we will be doing more things online, so how do we foster and nurture a sense of community as we accelerate the blurring of our online and in-person lives?

We should have a clear sense of the difference between asynchronous and synchronous online activity and make sure that synchronous activity is prioritized for tasks that build collaboration, creativity, and communication. The same principles apply for student-facing and staff activity – does this really need to be a meeting, or could I post a document that colleagues can work on and comment on asynchronously? Deliberate and purposeful development of in-person activities will complement and add value to the online world.

New ways of building community among staff could be through collaborative course development. Many academics work in teams for research, and team teaching is not new, but the days of a lone academic module leader, creating their own module, is probably over. Relevant and engaging programmes and modules need to be developed and delivered in collaboration with academic teams, learning designers, learning technologies, employers, and students.

We can build genuinely inclusive and supportive communities by having a greater understanding of the challenges that many of our students face as a result of difficult home circumstances and/or unequal access to resources and by recognising the role that institutions and educators have in the care and support of the whole student.

B. Global Partnerships and a Global Network of Hope

As with other sectors, the concept of globalization is widely believed to be creating new markets and forcing an evolution in higher education. One of the stated aims of the partnership between Liverpool University and

Laureate Education referred to in section 2.3 was to improve the global reach of the university. For an institution in the Cathedrals Group, an important aim of working internationally is to build capacity in developing countries and to bring the opportunities to study in a high-quality university to students who wouldn't otherwise have the opportunity.[12] For too many universities, developing international partnerships has been done with the purpose of bringing in higher fee-paying international students. This trend, across all parts of the sector, has contributed to the feeling that universities are too commercial and driven by motives that are more to do with the bottom line than with the transformative academic and personal benefits to individuals.

A potential way to develop a more ethical international policy is to create a network of institutions that share a common mission and goal and for which the total would be greater than the sum of their parts. As a network, they could work collaboratively on research topics of global importance, climate change, sustainability, global health, and social justice and could develop joint degree programmes that enabled students to move physically and virtually between institutions. A strong network could link with other institutions in developing countries to build capacity and broaden opportunities. It would be a global Network of Hope.

5. Foundations of Hope to Serendipity of Hope – Reflecting on Roots and Wings

In 2003, Liverpool University Press published *The Foundation of Hope: Turning Dreams into Reality*. Edited by John Elford, Elford comments in the preface, 'This book is both a celebration and analysis of the creation of Liverpool Hope University College in 1996 and some of its achievements to date.'[13] Chapter 3 is titled 'Maintaining the Integrity of Student Support Services in Mass Higher Education' and was written jointly by Sharron Bassett and Helen O'Sullivan. Although Sharron and I worked in the same institution, we only really got to know each other as we both studied on the same part-time MBA programme. We spent hours and hours discussing how to apply our newly gained insights about leading and managing organisations to ways to improve the services that we

12. For more details on the Cathedrals Group, see https://cathedralsgroup.ac.uk/who-we-are.

13. Elford, *Foundation of Hope*, ix.

provided to students. Looking at it now, it still seems forward thinking with concepts such as one-stop shops and integrated services. Importantly, we thought about the changing needs of students and about new ways that students could access the support they needed; balancing academic support with practical support, such as financial advice; and even thinking about the role that online platforms would play in providing support and guidance. We didn't have the experience of some of the other senior leaders who contributed chapters, but we had ideas, the confidence to express them, and the energy and enthusiasm to implement them.

There are lots of versions of the 'roots and wings' quotations, including one by the Dalai Lama, but my favourite version is attributed to Johann Wolfgang von Goethe: 'There are only two lasting bequests we can hope to give our children. One of these is roots, the other, wings.' The nearly fourteen years that I spent at Liverpool Hope gave me roots and wings. I learnt my craft as a teacher in the structured support of Environmental and Biological Studies (EBS) under the leadership of Bill Chambers and Liz Gayton. EBS was like a family that supported our growth. I got married at Liverpool Hope – literally. I had my wedding reception in Hope Park Refectory, and the evening dancing was 'gate-crashed' by a group of young nuns who were visiting Hope as part of a study tour of the UK. I had both of my children whilst working there. My spiritual and personal development was nurtured by colleagues across the spectrum of 'all faiths and none' from Malcom Rhodes, to Geoff Brach (RIP), to Sr Anne McDowell. The wings were the confidence to innovate and lead, and that confidence came from being given significant responsibility early in my career and being trusted to get on with it. Simon Lee had the ability to spot people with potential and the generosity to give us challenging and meaningful leadership roles.

It is now almost twenty years since I co-wrote that chapter in the *Foundations of Hope*, and I have returned to my roots in the Cathedrals Group. I aspire to be worthy of my predecessors at Hope in reinventing a church-foundation university for contemporary society while remaining true to the values of its founding fathers.

Bibliography

Elford, R. John, ed. *The Foundation of Hope: Turning Dreams into Reality*. Liverpool: Liverpool University Press, 2003.

Hillman, Nick. 'Can We Learn from Boarding Schools to Help Commuter Students Stick?' Higher Education Policy Institute, 20 Nov. 2017. https://www.hepi.ac.uk/2017/11/20/can-learn-boarding-schools-help-commuter-students-stick/.

Barber, Michael, et al. 'An Avalanche Is Coming: Higher Education and the Revolution Ahead.' Institute for Public Policy Research, Mar. 2013. https://www.ippr.org/files/images/media/files/publication/2013/04/avalanche-is-coming_Mar2013_10432.pdf.

Jeffery, Charlie. 'In Defense of Art and Humanities.' WONKHE, 13 Apr. 2021. https://wonkhe.com/blogs/in-defence-of-the-arts-and-humanities/.

Keele University. 'Flexible Digital Education.' Keele University, n.d. https://www.keele.ac.uk/kiite/workingwithstaff/flexibledigitaleducation/.

MicroHe. 'European Micro-Credential Terminology.' MicroHe, n.d. https://microcredentials.eu/terminology/.

———. 'Support Future Learning Excellence through Micro-Credentialing in Higher Education.' European Commission, n.d. https://erasmus-plus.ec.europa.eu/projects/search/details/590161-EPP-1-2017-1-DE-EPPKA3-PI-FORWARD.

Schmidt, Henk G., et al. 'On the Use and Misuse of Lectures in Higher Education.' *Health Professions Education* 1 (Dec. 2015) 12–18.

Unite Students. *Everyone In: Insights from a Diverse Student Population*. Insight Series 2017. https://www.unitegroup.com/wp-content/uploads/2021/10/everyone-in-report.pdf.

Williamson, Gavin. 'Education Secretary FE Speech with Social Market Foundation.' United Kingdom, 9 July 2020. https://www.gov.uk/government/speeches/education-secretary-fe-speech-with-social-market-foundation.

World Economic Forum. *The Future of Jobs Report 2020*. World Economic Forum, Oct. 2020. https://www3.weforum.org/docs/WEF_Future_of_Jobs_2020.pdf.

13

(Pedagogical) Love in a Time of Pandemic

J'ANNINE JOBLING

IT WAS MARCH 2020. Like much of the world at that point, our eyes in the philosophy department of the University of Liverpool were fixed uneasily on the seemingly inexorable advance of the coronavirus thought to have emanated from Wuhan, China. The UK government had yet to announce lockdown measures. The university announced that, nevertheless, in the interests of staff and student well-being, it was going to cancel all face-to-face teaching for nonclinical disciplines with immediate effect for the remainder of the academic year.

That was Saturday. From that Monday, we had to devise and communicate alternative delivery formats for all of our classes. The so-called online pivot had taken place.

In times such as these, concern for student success and well-being becomes especially heightened. It also becomes especially hard to promote and monitor. Students are not always assiduous about keeping up with or responding to electronic communications at the best of times. With all contact digital in nature, in-boxes can become overwhelmed, important information lost, and interpersonal interaction reduced. At the same time, staff faced their own personal challenges as we each coped with our varying experiences of the pandemic and homeworking, whilst retaining our commitment to students. For myself, the priority of this commitment first developed during my formative years of teaching in higher education at Liverpool Hope.

When I arrived at Hope in 1997, it had already embarked upon its journey from a well-established and respected ecumenical church college of higher education to a fully-fledged university with its own teaching and research degree awarding powers. During this journey, its religious roots have remained at the heart, accompanied by the aspiration to be a 'welcoming, hospitable and caring community' whilst building a 'kind, generous and gracious fellowship where all may flourish'.[1] In this environment, commitment to learning and teaching was paramount, including knowing the students one by one, and educating the whole person. It was at Hope, therefore, that I first fully learnt the meaning and significance of what is called by some 'pedagogical love' – on which more later. This student-centered orientation carried over with me to my current employment; by contrast with Hope, Liverpool University has its roots in the overtly secular establishment of 'red brick' civic universities in the nineteenth-century UK, but similarly seeks to incorporate a 'sustained and serious commitment' to student well-being and 'outstanding, research-connected learning and teaching'.[2]

In common with institutions of higher education around the globe, the impact of COVID-19 was heavily felt. The majority of programmes were campus based, and in my department, the typical staff experience of digital learning and teaching interaction was the occasional Skype call with a PhD student. In the flurry of emails between staff following the announcement that face-to-face teaching was to be suspended, 'Zoom' was mentioned and recommended. Many of us had never heard of it. Not all of us had microphones or webcams; technical services rapidly ran out of these items, and shop supplies were soon found to be exhausted. The quality of home internet services was variable. The situation for students was even more patchy and difficult, with some having minimal or no home computing equipment and online access via phone data only.

It was possible, by and large, to address these matters: staff were issued with headsets and granted a modest allowance for purchase of homeworking equipment; COVID-secure offices were provided where homeworking was not possible; and a special fund was established to which students could apply for assistance. Yet many challenges remained.

1. See Liverpool Hope University, 'Our Missions and Values.' The website also details the 'Hope Story', from its founding colleges (St Katharine's 1844, Notre Dame College 1856, and Christ's College 1964) to its establishment as Liverpool Hope University in 2005.

2. The strategy is outlined at University of Liverpool, 'Our Strategy 2026.'

A primary issue for many staff was, of course, a general lack of experience in online teaching platforms, delivery, and pedagogies. However, it was the uniqueness of the situation overall that gave rise to the most trying set of circumstances. The first UK lockdown was announced on 23 March 2020. The strictness of measures varied over the following months through into 2021, but as events transpired, it was not only the remaining weeks of the academic year 2019–2020 that were conducted online, but the entirety of the academic year 2020–2021 also – in total, some eighteen months off campus. National surveys in the autumn of 2020 showed that more than half of students reported a worsening of wellbeing and mental health as a result of the pandemic, 16 percent disagreed or strongly disagreed that they were equipped to handle online learning, 29 percent felt dissatisfied or strongly dissatisfied with their academic experience, and 53 percent felt dissatisfied or strongly dissatisfied with their social experience. Feelings of loneliness had increased significantly.[3]

There follow some autoethnographic reflections on my own experiences of teaching during the pandemic. The discussion is prefaced and framed by an expansion of the concept briefly introduced above: pedagogical love.

Despite a long history associating love with pedagogy, there can be some discomfort in contemplating practice in this sort of way. Cho identifies two forces at work here. The first, and obvious, source of potential unease is a tendency to link love with inappropriate and scandalous relations.[4] The second is the standardization movement, by which teachers 'need only teach to the standards as impartially as possible', and the role of love, if it is even to exist in education, is reductively conceived as 'motivating students to perform to the best of their abilities in the acquisition of knowledge', duly displayed via standardized tests.[5] In relation to the first point, Cho suggests to the contrary that *eros* does have a place in the classroom, referencing bell hooks and her view that 'an eroticized pedagogy does not mean a sexualized pedagogy but one that is passionate and inspiring'. The passion so incited goes beyond desire for knowledge for knowledge's sake and is instead transformative of the way a student looks upon the world. It thus carries the potential to challenge structures

3. Office for National Statistics, 'Coronavirus and the Impact.'

4. Cho, 'Lessons of Love,' in *Psychopedagogy*, 125.

5. Cho, 'Lessons of Love,' in *Psychopedagogy*, 127.

of domination and oppression.[6] This speaks to Cho's rejection of the second contrary force, the standardization movement. For this in itself is seen as a damaging phenomenon, promoting reproduction rather than transformation of knowledge. Teaching, as Paulo Freire insists, cannot simply be 'a process of transference of knowledge from the one teaching to the learner.'[7] Citing Badiou and Lacan, Cho talks of love as 'the name for a radical restructuring of a relation of two people . . . what Badiou means when he calls love a "production of truth".'[8] The love encounter between student and teacher, then, manifests as an enquiry into the world, not each other, an enquiry that takes place in partnership.

Reluctance to embrace the notion of pedagogical love is considered by Smith to emerge from a modernist mindset in which the personal must be sharply distinguished from the professional. Yet this distinction is seen to be false, unsustainable, and a 'modernist conceit'.[9] Expanding on this theme, one might further say that this depersonalization process reinforces relations of hierarchy through neutralization of the teacher as fellow human being and instead posits the teacher as disembodied font of knowledge and authority. This undermines pedagogical trajectories, which are in favour of conceiving the teacher-student relation as one of partnership and reciprocity. Such pedagogical trajectories, in turn, enable the empowerment of student voices and legitimation of their own location as producer and critic of knowledge. As Caraballo and Soleimany argue, this kind of 're-imagination of traditional roles of students and teachers' creates a space 'where the multiple literacies and cultural specificities of marginalized students are acknowledged and valued.'[10]

Pedagogical love thus functions as a spur towards practice which is inclined towards inclusivity, criticality, empowerment, and relationality. Speaking of school contexts, but equally aptly for higher education, Määttä and Uusiautti describe it as creating a setting where learners 'can use and develop their own resources,' individual circumstances are taken into consideration, and 'persistent interest and perseverance' are involved in the support of learners' development.[11] These qualities, I found,

6. Cho, 'Lessons of Love,' in *Psychopedagogy*, 131.

7. Freire, *Teachers as Cultural Workers*, 22.

8. Cho, 'Lessons of Love,' in *Psychopedagogy*, 145.

9. Smith, 'Love and the Child,' 190.

10. Caraballo and Soleimany, 'In the Name,' 85.

11. Määttä and Uusiautti, 'How to Raise Children,' 87.

were of particular importance in navigating the enforced disruption of accustomed teaching patterns over the course of the pandemic.

I shall now relate these reflections on pedagogical love to my own experiences in various teaching-related scenarios. Let us first consider that traditional staple of university educational diets: the lecture.

The model of the typical lecture format has, in any event, come under increasing scrutiny. It is critiqued as promoting a transmission-based model of knowledge exchange, passive learning, and for exceeding optimal length to capture and keep audience attention. Active learning is often preferred, which may involve the so-called flipped classroom, whereby students undertake autonomous knowledge acquisition through engagement with provided materials such as texts and videos, and class time is spent on exploration, discussion, and problem-solving. With the online pivot, policy within my area was to convert lecture materials to asynchronous videos divided into shorter segments ('chunked'), which students could watch at their convenience. The advantages of this are clear. The model is sensitive to difference in student circumstances (itself identified as a dimension of pedagogical love) and does not assume access to an appropriate learning space at a predefined and scheduled timeslot. The shorter durations are in line with research on attention spans. It makes the most of class contact time by reserving that for interaction, albeit virtually, rather than largely one-way information conveyance. It produces a 'reusable learning object', which in the longer term frees up tutor time for more personal support and availability.

I thoroughly disliked it.

In 'normal' practice, our lectures are delivered live and in-person, but are recorded and posted in the dedicated virtual learning environment for a given module, which hosts resources and acts as interface for, e.g., the submission and marking of assignments. The absence of students at point of delivery eroded my communication skills. Lectures, to me, are in some respects a performance. I have colleagues who are better than I am at integrating interaction and active learning into the lecture hall. Nevertheless, it was brought home to me quite strongly that I still fundamentally conceived of lecturing as a two-way, not one-way, process, in which students, even if not contributing, were actively *there*. Addressing my impassioned utterances to a laptop screen felt fake and narcissistic; it also gave rise to excessive self-scrutiny as videos were edited and reedited in pursuit of a satisfactory 'product'.

General student feedback was mixed. The more bite-sized approach in terms of content appeared to meet with approval. However, there was also dissatisfaction with a perceived impersonality. It appeared that the students also valued the intangible benefit of live communication and the sense of being addressed *personally*. This is in keeping with one of the features of pedagogical love identified by Loreman, namely a sense of intimacy and warmth.[12] None of this is to suggest that the asynchronous video cannot function as a highly effective element of good pedagogy; it is a reflection of my own discomfort with the model.

Seminars were conducted live and synchronously, using either Zoom or Teams as a platform. They were not recorded, as even if students formally consented, it might have inhibited them from contribution. Here the quality of the experience varied, and (just as with in-person seminars) the crucial factor was levels of student participation. However, online, it was much easier for students to 'lurk' – even perhaps to be nominally present, as in logged in but actually focused on other activities. Students were encouraged, but not required, to turn on webcams. It was recognised that there may be a diverse range of reasons why students might stay off-camera, relating to factors such as personal comfort zone, stability and strength of their Wi-Fi connection, or reasons of privacy. At its best, these virtual seminars did manage to feel like spaces of intimacy and open discussion, albeit disembodied. Once the initial novelty of the medium had worn off, 'You're on mute!' was a source of gentle group amusement and bonding, not anxiety. Inevitably, technical issues intervened on occasion; the experience of virtual meetings has been likened to a modern séance. 'Sally! Are you there?! Make a sound if you can hear us. We can't see you; can you hear us?'[13] Most daunting of all was the dreaded Screen of Blank Squares, imprinted only with initials. Whilst acknowledging the multiple justifications for students to keep their webcams off, this scenario inhibited interaction between students and between tutor and students. It also made it difficult to 'read the room', which again emerged as a habitual practice previously undertaken without conscious reflection. This close attention to individual body language and expression is also an aspect of pedagogical love and relationality. The antidote to the Screen of Blank Squares was trust and a sense of community. There was a sort of tipping effect; once a couple of students had been persuaded (or implored) to

12. Loreman, *Love as Pedagogy*, 33–48.

13. The provenance of this analogy is unknown. It is widely circulated as an internet meme.

turn on their cameras, others also stepped up. This self-revelation was part of the process of online community-building, which is a further element identified by Loreman as an expression of pedagogical love.

One double-sided feature of the virtual seminars was the sense of being transported into each other's homes and personal spaces. This included the physical surroundings, but also the paraphernalia of domestic life. Cats, dogs, siblings, housemates, parents, children all made cameo appearances from time to time or made their voices heard. On the one hand, this was a valued bridge over the remote context, personalizing and humanizing the experience. On the other, it could be seen as an intrusion, breaching privacy and blurring personal and professional lines for both students and staff. It was important here that people did have a measure of choice; it was possible to deploy a virtual background whilst still keeping the webcam on. Yet, overall, I found the effect to be one that enhanced trust, community, and intimacy. In a way, the nonprofessional contexts fostered personal connections.

Those are some general reflections on my experiences of seeking to teach in a pedagogically loving manner during the pandemic. I turn now to a more specific example, which quite explicitly relates to the model of pedagogical love outlined above with reference to Freire, Cho, and hooks, namely one rooted in a concern for inclusion, social justice, and critical pedagogy. Philosophical Approaches to Conflict is a third-year module that asks students to engage with issues of contemporary sociopolitical contention, particularly where there may be perceived, potential, or actual clashes of rights and freedoms in contexts of diversity. Recent topics include ethics and immigration; free speech, hate speech, and the media; multiculturalism; civil disobedience and protest; and sexual harassment. It also seeks to incorporate socially just and loving pedagogy by empowering students through partnership in learning, teaching, and assessment processes, and by provision of a 'space for active participation, autonomy, and power over what will be learned'.[14] There are no lectures; the classes are student-led weekly discussion workshops, two hours in length. In each session, two students present on issues and examples of their choice within broadly defined curriculum areas based on contemporary public sphere affairs, underpinned by starting point resource packs. The module, therefore, aims to foster inclusive pedagogical practice by offering student-led learning opportunities, both in class and in assessment,

14. Aktaş, 'Enhancing Social Justice.'

in which students can draw on their own interests, experiences, and perspectives.

My involvement in this module proved serendipitous when the online pivot occurred. Its nature helped to overcome potential barriers of alienation and disconnection. The module is dependent on active student engagement with each other and the wider affairs of the world, including peer teaching through the presentations. The tutor's role is that of facilitator and, together with the students, creating a dialogic and respectful learning environment of mutual recognition. Students upload their presentation materials into the class virtual learning environment, and these become a shared class resource, making visible the co-creation of knowledge and diversifying representation of perspective. Student 'ownership' was thus designed into the module, and this bore fruit in the experience of teaching it during the pandemic. There was passionate engagement with the subject matter, and students drew on their own life experiences and perspectives within discussion. This, once more, fostered that intimacy and community recommended by Loreman.[15]

As it (serendipitously) happened, I had changed the final assessment form for this module from an exam to a thousand-word opinion piece aimed at a public audience and for which students choose and research their own examples. This was a tremendous success. Given the likelihood that this was a novel assessment form for most, if not all, a dedicated workshop, samples, and a video tutorial were provided, and the final session offered students the opportunity to peer review each other's work. Once instilled with confidence in how to approach it, students embraced this assessment with enthusiasm. They wrote on a range of pressing concerns: are historic statues 'set in stone'? Should people retain the right to protest during COVID lockdowns? Can, and should, universities do more in relation to sexual harassment? Is 'no-platforming' a valid strategy for student bodies? Student feedback was very positive ('great module'; 'extremely interesting and relevant to current debates'; 'I even enjoyed the assessments!'), and the moderator was moved to read more work than required because it was so interesting. This module, with its inbuilt relatively high level of student involvement, thus proved resilient to the shift online.

Of course, it was not all plain sailing. As with other modules, student participation varied, in particular in correlation with assessment

15. Loreman, *Love as Pedagogy.*

deadlines. There were occasional technological difficulties, and students faced a range of challenges and extenuating circumstances that affected their academic engagement and performance. Communications were not always as clear as they might have been. What all this pointed to was the need for mutual empathy and forgiveness; the latter, indeed, forms part of Loreman's framework in his analysis of love as pedagogy.[16] What it fundamentally boiled down to was the basic precept 'be kind'.

Those, then, are some reflections on the experience of teaching online during the pandemic, related to the principles embedded in the concept of pedagogical love. There were challenges, there were failures, and there were successes. There was learning and new insights, which will impact my practice in the future. Indeed, it is widely thought that there will be a lasting transformation of the sector in consequence. Whilst some thought the 'digital turn to be corrosive to core academic values and the very mission of the university',[17] others saw it as an 'unparalleled opportunity for pedagogical reinvention'.[18] Certainly for me, awareness of the exigencies of the situation from a student point of view has reaffirmed my commitment to learning and teaching, and the aspiration to approach this from a stance of (pedagogical) love.

Bibliography

Aktaş, Carla Briffett. 'Enhancing Social Justice and Socially Just Pedagogy in Higher Education through Participatory Action Research.' *Teaching in Higher Education* (2021). DOI: 10.1080/13562517.2021.1966619.

Caraballo, Limarys, and Sahar Soleimany. 'In the Name of (Pedagogical) Love: A Conceptual Framework for Transformative Teaching Grounded in Critical Youth Research.' *Urban Review* 51 (2019) 81–100.

Cho, K. Daniel. *Psychopedagogy: Freud, Lacan, and the Psychoanalytic Theory of Education.* New York: Palgrave Macmillan, 2009.

Freire, Paulo. *Teachers as Cultural Workers: Letters to Those Who Dare Teach.* Boulder, CO: Westview, 1998.

Liverpool Hope University. 'Our Missions and Values.' Liverpool Hope University, n.d. https://www.hope.ac.uk/aboutus/thehopestory/ourmissionandvalues/.

Loreman, Tim. *Love as Pedagogy.* Rotterdam: Sense, 2011.

Määttä, Kaarina, and Satu Uusiautti. 'How to Raise Children to Be Good People?' *Analytic Teaching and Philosophical Praxis* 33 (2012) 83–91.

16. Loreman, *Pedagogy as Love*, 49–66.

17. Watermeyer et al., 'COVID-19 and Digital Disruption,' 631.

18. Watermeyer et al., 'COVID-19 and Digital Disruption,' 637.

Office for National Statistics. 'Coronavirus and the Impact on Students in Higher Education in England: September to December 2020.' Office for National Statistics, 21 Dec. 2020. https://www.ons.gov.uk/peoplepopulationandcommunity/educationandchildcare/articles/coronavirusandtheimpactonstudentsinhighereducationinengland septembertodecember2020/2020-12-21.

Smith, Mark. 'Love and the Child and Youth Care Relationship.' *Relational Child and Youth Care Practice* 24 (2011) 189–92.

University of Liverpool. 'Our Strategy 2026.' University of Liverpool, n.d. https://www.liverpool.ac.uk/strategy-2026/education/.

Watermeyer, Richard, et al. 'COVID-19 and Digital Disruption in UK Universities: Afflictions and Affordances of Emergency Online Migration.' *Higher Education* 81 (2021) 623–41.

14

The Network of Hope
Reflections Twenty-Three Years On

JOHN CROWLEY

SINCE TAKING PART IN the November 2020 Zoom reunion I have re-flected on how I came to be involved in this exciting and inspirational project. A couple of random incidents in the years up to 1997 acquire a new significance in reflecting on how I was ready to embrace this new project.

In June 1997, during my last term at Holy Cross College, Bury, as deputy principal, I received an invitation to go and see Professor Simon Lee at Liverpool Hope. Twenty-seven years earlier, in 1970, my fiancée, Jacquie's, mother objected very strongly to her marrying a Catholic and said she wouldn't attend any ceremony in a Catholic church in Newcastle. I had grown up in Portsmouth, and we were parishioners of the cathedral there. One Sunday morning at the end of Mass my mother approached Bishop Derek Worlock and explained the situation to him. He said, 'Tell them to come and see me.' Two weeks later we met him. Bishop Derek asked us if we were serious about marriage. He asked, 'Do you under-stand the sacrament? My interpretation is that you marry each other. The priest is there as a witness. And if you are convinced that you want to be together and if it makes things easier to get married in the northeast in an Anglican church, then you can do so with my blessing.' His understand-ing and compassion had a deep impact on us.

So we married at the end of December 1971 and still survive! In the early 1990s we lived next to a vicarage in Penwortham, which is the northernmost outpost of the Archdiocese of Liverpool. I had told our neighbour, the vicar, our story, and one Sunday, across the garden fence, he introduced Archbishop Derek Worlock of Liverpool to us. The archbishop made a point of visiting Anglican churches when he was carrying out his parish visitations in the archdiocese. He remembered us and our conversation in the summer of 1970. We were able to tell him of the impact of his statement on my wife's family. In fact, during her last years, my mother-in-law, who had moved near to us, was visited by our parish priest.

I worked at that time in the local Catholic sixth form college, and my wife taught in the local Catholic high school. The archbishop asked if we had any links with the Anglican schools. He said he wanted church schools to develop closer links across the board with others sharing a Christian mission. Reflecting on those two encounters, I'm convinced that they had an impact on our lives, personally and professionally.

Before going to meet Simon Lee, I learnt about Liverpool Hope and how three higher education institutions had come together with the encouragement of Archbishop Worlock and Bishop David Sheppard.

Archbishop Worlock spoke of mission. When I worked as vice-principal at Holy Cross College, we appointed many staff as we grew from 420 students to over 1400 in my ten years there. Sister Mary Kelly, the principal, made sure that the appointment process for every post was rigourous and thorough. Every time she interviewed for a new teaching member of staff she began by talking about the distinctive mission of the college. Her opening questions probed each candidate's understanding of and commitment to that mission. She used to say, when appointing a teacher, the three questions she asked herself were:

1. Does this person like students, and can they relate to them?

2. Does this person know and love their subject?

3. Can they teach?

The focus of every interview was on teaching and learning related to the mission of the college. Over the years she made many successful appointments. Everybody was asked to speak about a lesson which had gone well. Everyone was asked to think on their feet, to show how they would explain a concept to sixteeen- to eighteen-year-olds.

If staff are being appointed to nonteaching roles in offices, caretaking, for the canteen, they were all asked how they saw their role contributing to students achieving or being fulfilled. The college mission was something that was lived out day to day. And that approach continued when she left and when Mike O'Hare took over as principal.

For six years, from 1987 until 1993, I had responsibility for the students in year thirteen. This involved Universities and Colleges Admissions Service (UCAS) applications and university and higher education links. The college was compact enough for me to read every personal statement, reference, and completed application form before it was sent. In 1992, I was invited to speak to a conference that UCAS had organised for admissions tutors. I gave examples of anonymized personal statements and references we had submitted and spoke of the process we went through to prepare students for higher education. At the end of the question session, one tutor put his hand up to speak. He said that he hadn't wanted his job. He'd been appointed admissions tutor because it was 'Buggins's turn'. His focus was on his research, and he had minimal interest in students and teaching. This provoked a lively discussion, and his view was shared by others.

I remember thinking after that conference about the question of 'mission' in higher education, given the size of institutions and the breadth of staff interests and expertise. Was it even possible to define? So, it was fascinating to go to Hope Park and to hear about the prominence of shared mission and values across staff at what was then University College. Over the next few years, we saw how colleges and schools came together, sharing a common vision, mission, and values and how the Network of Hope came to bloom.

Sixth Form Colleges: The Background

Sixth form colleges grew from small beginnings in the 1970s. In a couple of cases, they were set up as part of strategic local reorganisations of education. In others they were formed as comprehensive education was introduced. Former direct grant grammar schools were converted into post-sixteen institutions or merged with others to form a new sixteen to eighteen college, usually concentrating on Advanced Level work with a programme of re-sit courses (the opportunity for students who had failed their A-levels originally to re-sit the examinations).

A number of Catholic direct grant schools, generally under the trusteeship of religious orders, became the post-sixteeen centre for their area as part of a reorganisation of Catholic education. Some transferred to the trusteeship of the local diocese. For example, in Preston, the former Preston Catholic College, a Jesuit institution, merged with Winckley Square Convent (Sisters of the Holy Child Jesus) and Lark Hill House (Faithful Companions of Jesus) to form Cardinal Newman College. This was under the trusteeship of the Diocese of Lancaster, though the Archdiocese of Liverpool and the Diocese of Salford also had representation supplying foundation governors. In Manchester, though, Loreto College remained under the trusteeship of the Institute of the Blessed Virgin Mary in the Diocese of Salford. They did establish links regionally and nationally through the Association of Catholic Sixth Form Colleges (ACVIC), though this didn't extend to collaboration. In fact, in some areas (Manchester and Salford, Wigan and St Helens), colleges became competitors, and some ruthless recruitment practices were in place in the 1990s.

Incorporation and Designation, 1993–1997

After the incorporation of the former polytechnics and teacher training institutions, Parliament passed the act that approved the incorporation of further education colleges and sixth form colleges in 1993. Colleges left local authority control. The sixth form colleges were included in the provisions, but those drafting the legislation had generally ignored or not been aware of those institutions that had trustees. While this affected a few state colleges (College of Richard Collyer, Horsham, for example), the Catholic sixth form colleges represented an unforeseen problem. Their land was owned by the diocese or the religious order. The solution was to label them as 'designated to receive funding'. This encouraged ACVIC to find a common purpose. As a condition, on their trust deed all these colleges also were bound to deliver religious education to all students. In a tightening financial regime this presented the difficulty of employing staff who were not funded to provide courses for every member of the student body. Sixteen- to eighteen-year-old students were not especially receptive to the fairly prescriptive courses approved by the Catholic Education Service. Colleges worked cooperatively to develop religious education programmes that were appropriate for sixteen- to eighteen-year-old students. In a climate of 'pile them high and teach them cheap', students were applying from outside the Catholic sector. Many of these had had no experience of religious education at all. In addition, the Catholic colleges in places such as Blackburn, Bury, Preston, and Leeds were attracting students from Asian backgrounds. For them and others, the courses were out of date and inappropriate. ACVIC principals were finding that they had common concerns. These provided a professional focus for meetings and encouraged more communication.

St John Rigby College (SJR)

St John Rigby College (SJR) was the first Catholic sixth form college in the country when it opened in 1972. Previously it had been a Catholic boys' grammar school run by the Irish Christian Brothers. It educated students from Wigan and West Lancashire who applied from the designated Catholic partner schools. In 1987, the Archdiocese of Liverpool with St Helens Council opened Carmel College in St Helens. After 1993, Carmel started to pursue an aggressive marketing campaign, targeting, in particular, two high-achieving Catholic high schools: St Peter's in Orrell and St Edmund Arrowsmith in Ashton-in-Makerfield. In Wigan Borough itself, Winstanley College presented itself as a post-sixteen grammar school. The principals of Winstanley and Carmel had both worked previously at SJR and knew the area well. Runshaw Tertiary College in Leyland also pursued potential students aggressively. Runshaw and Winstanley both proclaimed themselves 'the top college in the country' in their marketing materials.

In 1995, St John Rigby suffered a significant fall in numbers. This had a destabilizing effect on the college. There were disputes and differences of opinion at senior level, and governance was not strong. Despite the 1993 changes, there remained a lingering attachment to, and dependence on, the local authority among some governors and senior managers. The college had enjoyed a relatively high level of funding from Wigan Local Authority so that the financial impact didn't hit the college as hard as it might have done. Paradoxically, those colleges that had seen sharp increases in student numbers suffered the most. The 1996 Further Education Funding Council (FEFC) inspection at SJR resulted in an overall 'satisfactory' verdict, though the inspection team was split as to whether a lower grade should have been awarded. The 'satisfactory' judgement was to a large extent political. De La Salle College in Salford had closed and become part of Pendleton College. In Birmingham, the Oratory Fathers closed St Philips, which they didn't consider sufficiently 'Catholic'. So, the funding agency wanted to avoid the possible closure of a third college. The principal and one of the vice-principals both decided to take early retirement. Initially the post of principal was advertised for April 1997 so that the new principal could play a role in admissions and make preparations for the new academic year. However, the outgoing principal decided that he wanted to stay in post until the summer, so the change-over didn't take place until 1 August 1997.

The college's extensive campus is situated outside the borough, in Orrell. Students travel either by bus or train. Neighbouring colleges saw the 1993 act as a green light to market their curriculum offer beyond the traditional 'feeder' schools and across local authority boundaries. Winstanley College, a mile and a half from St John Rigby, promoted itself as a post-sixteen grammar school, stipulating a minimum GCSE grade B for A-level entry. The college's principal had been on the SJR staff in the 1970s, and his wife moved from St John Rigby to Winstanley in 1993. They targeted St Peter's Orrell and St Edmund Arrowsmith, both high-achieving Catholic high schools. Carmel College in St Helens also marketed itself strongly in the Wigan Catholic high schools.

Wigan & Leigh College, strongly supported by local politicians, was always spoken of as 'the college'. It offered A-levels, as well as an extensive range of vocational qualifications, apprenticeships, and its own higher education provision. Principal and governors presented the college as Wigan's post-sixteeen centre. We soon became aware at SJR that year eleven students and their parents were being unofficially advised, 'You don't want to go to St John Rigby. It's going to close.'

I was appointed principal in March 1997 and, as mentioned previously, found out that I couldn't start until 1 August of that year. It was difficult to go into the college. I managed only one visit, and the outgoing principal didn't feel it was advisable for me to talk to any staff apart from him. I visited two of the high schools. I asked the head teacher of St Peter's how the college was seen locally. He told me that the general view was that the college was heading for closure. He summed it up as saying that the College was 'cozy, complacent, run for the staff, not the students. It won't be there long!'

In June 1997, encouraged by Pat Mullin, a college foundation governor who also served on Hope's governing body, I drove to Liverpool to meet Professor Simon Lee for the first time. He showed me the campus and spoke of his plans for Hope, specifically, his ideas for a network of institutions sharing common values and a similar mission. He suggested that we should meet again after I'd started.

During my first week at work at the start of August 1997, I drove in one morning behind a bus that carried the advertisement 'Low GCSE grades? There's a place for you at St John Rigby College.' Over the early part of August I learnt that the financial situation was more difficult than I had thought. The college had no real understanding of the funding mechanism nor of the number of students enrolled. On my second day in post, I was visited by the head of the FEFC regional office who informed me that the college was considered to be at risk. The council would withdraw funding if it saw no signs of progress. I also met with the new college inspector, Christine Crompton, who had been the de facto lead inspector on Holy Cross College's inspection in 1995. In those inspections the FEFC introduced the role of college nominee. As deputy principal I had taken on that role, which involved being a member of the inspection team, part of all discussions but taking no part in grading. I linked with the college staff and governors over the period of the inspection. The college achieved good grades in all areas. However, a grade was awarded for estates, and the FEFC team had concerns about the appropriateness and safety of some of the old convent buildings that were used for teaching and learning. Furthermore, the lead inspector suffered a family bereavement during the week and had to leave. These difficult circumstances built understanding and trust with the lead inspectors, and Christine Crompton proved an invaluable support over the next few years. She skillfully combined rigour and support.

A couple of weeks before the October half term in 1997 I called Professor Lee's office. He returned the call immediately and arranged to visit, arriving on the following day.

He came to St John Rigby, toured the college, and spoke in more detail about his ideas and his vision of the Network of Hope. That was the first of many meetings during a hectic period up to and beyond the launch. I visited the Hope campus regularly and got to know senior staff at Hope who would be involved strategically and on a day-to-day basis. I got to know Hope on the Waterfront and Hope at Everton and saw how the University College, as it was then, was establishing a presence in the city and raising awareness of its mission and its work.

During 1997–1998, Simon Lee would arrive for a cup of coffee and a catch-up on a Friday evening on his way home. This strengthened our personal link and also provided a valuable opportunity to exchange ideas and thoughts. Sean Gallagher, director of resources, also visited regularly and established close personal and institutional links, which led to him joining the SJR governing body. Martin Carey came to explore ways of extending Hope in the Community to Wigan. Bill Chambers and Tony Grayson were also regular visitors. The Wigan politicians and the local FE (further education) college saw SJR as on the edge of closure. Their solution was a merger with Wigan & Leigh College. At an early meeting, three councillors came and introduced themselves to me. Their words of greeting were, 'We aim to shut you down.' The borough's chief education officer was no fan of voluntary aided schools, specifically church-funded institutions. Their vision for St John Rigby was to be a merged campus of Wigan & Leigh College. There was a lack of understanding of the fact that the thirty-five acres of land on which the college stands were owned by the Archdiocese of Liverpool. When I first met the then principal of Wigan & Leigh College, he told me, 'I haven't a bloody clue what your place is for. It serves no useful purpose.' Our embryonic relationship with Hope led immediately to establishing links and connections between the institutions and looking for ways of showing others that SJR was there and planning for a future.

When SJR had found itself in financial difficulties, the then arch-diocesan vicar of finance, Monsignor Michael McKenna, had joined the governing body. He had a clear understanding of the problem and the financial acumen to work to achieve practical solutions. He and Sean Gallagher were used to working together on trusteeship matters. Dr Jim Burke, Simon's predecessor at Christ's and Notre Dame, was also a col-lege governor. He had appointed Sean Gallagher and had a very high regard for him. Tony Grayson, another member of the Hope leadership team, was on the governing body of St Mary's, Astley, at the other side of the borough. The local Anglican high school, the Deanery, was also connected to Hope through its trustees and at governance level. So, over the autumn and winter of 1997–1998, links at local sixth form level were established that were to bear fruit over the following years.

The head of one of the local Catholic high schools, St John Fisher, Dave Burnett was fiercely supportive of the college. His two sons attended as students and achieved good results. His school was also the major pro-vider of the Wigan rugby league team. Several very high-profile interna-tionals had progressed from high school to SJR and then on to professional sport. One of them, Phil Clarke, had captained Great Britain. He had gone on from SJR to university where he achieved a degree in sportssScience.

After the World Cup Final in 1995, he joined Sydney Roosters in Australia. Sadly, in his first season there, he broke his neck and was told by the doctors not to play rugby again. He returned to Wigan and, for a short time, was chief executive of Wigan Warriors Rugby League Club.

With some apprehension, I phoned him and asked if he would consider being a college governor. He immediately agreed and committed himself fully to the role, coming in to college regularly. This had an impact. He met with Simon and Sean and, through his recently established company, built links with Hope, setting up the sports centre at Hope Park.

Our main objective was to establish higher education courses, delivered by Hope lecturers on the college campus from September 1998. The FE model that operated at that time in large colleges such as Wigan & Leigh, Bury, and Blackburn colleges was that those institutions received higher education funding as a separate stream to their FE income. Hope took responsibility for almost all the teaching and quality assurance, and the college provided the accommodation. Simon was on the lookout for options such as Hope on the Waterfront and, for a while, looked at Wigan Pier. Again, local politicians were hostile to interlopers! Between 1997 and 2000, we looked at several options for community involvement, but all were rejected. Hope had a thriving nursery run by Busy Bees and proposed setting up another at our Orrell campus. The planners rejected it immediately. I was approached by the local GP practice about setting up a surgery on the college campus. Again, it was rejected out of hand. In both cases, the trustees were very supportive. As I shall explain more later, a few years afterward a more ambitious project was granted permission.

The establishment of the network had to be formally approved by the SJR governing body in January 1998. We didn't say too much to staff in general until that approval had been granted. We contacted other colleges. Mike O'Hare at Holy Cross College, Bury, and Mike Findlay at St Mary's College, Blackburn, were enthusiastic about the network and began their preparations. Kevin Quigley, principal of Cardinal Newman College in Preston, was wary about trying to compete with Lancashire Polytechnic (later the University of Central Lancashire), which had a wide provision of courses and a high reputation for quality. Similarly, Xaverian College, Manchester, close to Manchester University, was not enthusiastic. Ann Clynch, the principal of Loreto College, was a supporter of links between colleges sharing a common mission and was interested in joining.

On Shrove Tuesday, 24 February 1998, pancakes and champagne were enjoyed by staff and governors to celebrate the partnership of the two establishments. In the remaining months of that academic year the network grew as Holy Cross College in Bury and Saint Mary's College in Blackburn joined the network. Some other colleges were more hesitant about signing up. Carmel College in St Helens had established links with Liverpool University, and the then principal was reluctant to establish links with other Catholic colleges. In Manchester, Loreto and Xaverian College both competed with each other to some extent with recruitment. The principal at Xaverian was very doubtful about the project and favoured maintaining close links with Manchester University. Cardinal Newman College in Preston also joined the Network in 1998.

The SJR governing body agreed to the proposal at its meeting in January 1998. Three weeks later, the college staff in-service training (IN-SET) day was held at Hope Park. Symbolically, this helped to launch the network and also to build ways of all involved in the college starting to look outwards and to set a vision for survival and development. Simon Lee introduced the day, which examined ways forward for the college. Staff from all parts of the college contributed openly and freely, analyzing the college's situation and possible initiatives. At my first staff meeting in September 1997, I had provided all staff with details of the college's financial situation and prospects. Staff were shocked but grateful to be told. I had been advised to embark on a restructuring and redundancy programme immediately when I was new and didn't know individuals. However, I took the view that such a process would have been a distraction. The college's financial situation was such that all jobs, including my own, were at risk if recruitment didn't increase and financial problems weren't controlled. In the event, this provided some staff with the opportunity to reflect on their own professional situation. Several applied for posts in other institutions. I had also made it clear that, in sporting terms, there was no money for new players, so we had to depend on the existing squad. It was against this background that the training day provided the opportunity for imaginative and positive proposals. The restructuring of teaching staff the following summer resulted in fewer drastic outcomes than might have been the case if it had happened earlier.

Two members of the college biology team, Sue Harwood and Trisha Sharples, worked at Hope for part of the spring and summer of 1998, helping to build links with the health care team and to develop courses. Julie Dale, from the English department, also started to become involved and to build links.

I was invited to join the Bishops' Conference on Higher Education, chaired by Bishop Vincent Malone of Liverpool. This gave the network a place at the table, and I was asked to provide updates on the newest developments at each meeting.

Faced with the constant local gossip about the college's impending closure we carried out some small building projects in the summer of 1998. The purpose of these was to give a psychological boost to staff as well as show any visitors to the site that preparations were being carried out for the college's future.

All the colleges took advantage of either existing expertise or re-cruiting staff with an experience of higher education work within a further education setting. Before the launch of the network, with the agreement of Sean Gallagher, director of resources at Hope, Ruth Cu-erden, a member of Hope's finance team, moved to SJR. At Holy Cross the clerk to the governors, John Barton, had extensive experience at Bury College. Pat Temiz who had previously worked at Wigan & Leigh College was appointed to coordinate the Network of Hope work locally. She had extensive knowledge, contacts, and experience of the local area. These individuals built on their established knowledge, previous experience, and local contacts to begin the process of recruitment for the new locally based courses in the autumn of 1998.

Those courses started with good numbers in the autumn of 1998. Student feedback was very positive from the very start. In fact, it was a fea-ture of the development of the network that student views were collected formally and informally, and the organisation was flexible and nimble enough to respond. They didn't have to travel far to an institution. They were known and looked after and built good links among themselves.

Two of the students who began their courses at Orrell in 1998 both had become pregnant at sixteen. This had stopped them continuing their education. The network provided them with the opportunity to put things right. They began their courses in their early thirties. Their studies at SJR, near to home, meant that they could still be full-time mothers, keep their jobs, and study for a degree. Others took courses that hadn't been as widely available when they had been younger, such as IT.

Students welcomed and appreciated the opportunity to be able to study part-time, near to home, in a friendly, compact, and supportive setting. Some had not been able to follow degree courses when younger and enrolled for degrees after their children had grown up.

The Liverpool Hope tutors worked closely with the college-based support teams to ensure that students were kept on track and supported through their studies. In Wigan, Pat Temiz, Ruth Cuerden, and Julia Fleming all lived locally. They knew their communities and developed strong local networks. Juila Fleming completed a degree course herself.

Course numbers remained healthy through from 1998 until 2003. In that year, Louise Tipping took on the role of director of curriculum. She led the Network of Hope organisation in the college and coordinated work with other universities as well as the college's fourteen-to-nineteen provision with local high schools.

Professor Pillay invited me and Kevin McMahon, the principal of St Mary's College, Blackburn, to join the Hope Senate, and this further embedded the network.

Reflections on the Network

For St John Rigby College the network was a key factor, probably the key factor, in ensuring institutional survival and then moving on to success. Hope helped the college and its staff to look outwards, to clarify and live out its mission, and to make a key contribution to the community. These are some of my thoughts on the years I spent there.

Most importantly, the network provided opportunities for many who, for one reason or another, had given up on education, or education had given up on them. Locally based higher education courses, arranged at times to suit work and daily routine, proved the means for them to achieve qualifications, fulfill their potential, build self esteem, and open doors to new career options. Their experience was passed on by word of mouth and contributed to sixteen-year-old contacts and family members enrolling for courses.

The network made us look at the courses we offered for sixteen- to eighteen-year-olds. We introduced vocational courses in business, health care, IT, and other areas that were more suited to the needs of young people.

Members of staff at Hope and in the colleges benefited from fresh career opportunities. Several who may have 'become stuck' or lost motivation grasped the opportunities that the new courses provided and emerged professionally refreshed and reinvigorated.

The reputation proved attractive to staff in other institutions who saw the work being done and chose to apply. When SJR advertised for a head of creative and performing arts in 1998, John Woodley, previously at Liverpool Community College, was appointed. The Hope connection was a key factor in attracting him to the post. John pushed for the purchase of a suite of Apple Mac computers. These helped the college establish new sixteen-to-nineteen courses in art, graphic design, and photography, which attracted many students who might not have considered the college as an option previously. Each summer we ran days for primary school pupils. Many of them displayed precocious design talents.

Links with Deanery High School and St Mary's, Astley, saw staff being shared between departments, GCSE placements providing eleven-to-sixteen and sixteen plus work, and partnership working across the borough.

The Network of Hope was the key factor in the college's transition from the inward-looking, defensive institution of 1997 to the more confident local and regional player of the early to mid-2000s. The network continued to thrive, and SJR dipped its toe in the water with some joint work with Edge Hill as well as an innovative arrangement from 2004 with the University of Liverpool. This concentrated specifically on providing a foundation year for potential medical students from Northern Ireland. The SJR science staff contributed to the teaching of this course.

In the summer of 2003, Dave Whelan, the then owner of Wigan Athletic Football Club and Wigan Warriors Rugby League Club arrived at the college, interested in developing training facilities at SJR. This led to a new state-of-the-art artificial 4G pitch with floodlights, new changing facilities, and a substantial cash donation to the college. The training facilities were opened in March 2004 and hosted a Premier League Football Club as well as a Super League Rugby club. The rugby players, several of them former students, established even closer links to the college. Dean Bell, the inspirational New Zealander who had captained Wigan to many triumphs, was the link. He visited the college at least once a week, spoke to students, ran classes, and proved an exemplary role model. He was helped by Joe Lydon, another former student whose sister was deputy head at St Mary's, Astley. Joe had been a member of Clive Woodward's coaching staff for the England 2003 Rugby World Cup triumph. Dave Whelan sold the rugby club to Ian Leneghan who continued to link up with the college.

These developments led to the college's higher profile in the community. Student enrollments increased rapidly between 2003 and 2008. In 2004, Wigan & Leigh College closed its sixth form centre. Five heads of department moved from the FE college to St John Rigby.

There are educational consultants who earn a living delivering leadership courses. The original 'squad' who worked at SJR when the link was made with Hope took on responsibilities over the period of 1998 to 2003, and several went on to senior posts.

The SJR staff of that period produced:

- Principals of St Mary's College, Blackburn; Holy Cross College, Bury; Winstanley College, Wigan; Priestley College, Warrington
- Head teachers and principals of St Cuthbert's, Rochdale; Ormiston Bolingbroke Academy, Runcorn
- Deputy principals of Cardinal Newman College, Preston; Rainhill High School, St Helens
- Assistant principals of Winstanley College; St John Rigby (internal)

One of the principals wrote to me: 'We learned to manage in adversity as the College moved from survival to success.' The partnership with Liverpool Hope spawned new ideas, a culture of looking for opportunities and grasping those that presented themselves.

When writing about hope, St Thomas Aquinas noted that hope is born from the desire for something good that is difficult but possible to attain. There is no need for hope if we can easily get what we want, but neither is there any reason to hope when what we desire is completely beyond our grasp. But Aquinas also observed that there are far more reasons to be hopeful when we have friends to rely on.[1] If the object of our hopes can extend no further than what we might be able to secure for ourselves, then our hopes will necessarily be rather cautious and limited. But if there are people who not only love us and care for us and want what is best for us but will also help us achieve it, then our hopes can be much more daring and expansive. We do not hope alone, we hope together. Hope requires companions, people who want our good and who help us along our way.

---

1. Aquinas, *Summa theologiae*, II–II, q. 17, a. 8.

15

Building a Community of Hope

Shannon Ledbetter

A YOUNG WOMAN WALKED on her own in downtown Boston, Massachusetts, which was coined the 'city on a hill' by Governor John Winthrop, who was among the first wave of colonists to America in the seventeenth century. This Scripture was cited at the end of Puritan John Winthrop's lecture or treatise 'A Model of Christian Charity', delivered on March 21, 1630, at Holyrood Church in Southampton before his first group of Massachusetts Bay colonists embarked on the ship *Arbella* to settle Boston. The young woman was thinking deeply about her past and future, caught in a seemingly stationary middle despite the lofty aims of the city's name. Her past consisted of extensive travel as an American army brat and of dreams of helping to promote interfaith harmony, peace, justice, and a more compassionate world; and having obtained a theology degree at Virginia Theological Seminary (another place nicknamed 'city on a hill'), she felt restless. For all her grand plans and aspirations, she felt alone and without hope. She was trapped in a cycle of low-paid temporary work, volunteering at her church, and a lack of focus. Then the email came. An invitation to apply for a scholarship to study for a doctorate in theology at a faraway place called Hope.

After much pondering and weighing up my thin options, my decision was made after having applied successfully for the studentship. I would venture forth to pursue my dreams and, after members of my congregation literally took up a collection to pay for my airfare, I found myself on a plane to Liverpool. The initial email had come from an old friend who had just been appointed professor of theology and who would become my PhD supervisor, Ian Markham, who, ironically, subsequently became dean and president of Virginia Theological Seminary. After my having arrived in Liverpool rudderless, the burgeoning community that was Liverpool Hope soon grounded me. There was an air of rebirth and possibility on the campus headed by the vibrant Professor Simon Lee, himself not long in post. The church college, with its noble aims of educating women rooted in Victorian morals, was undergoing a transformation, jubilantly emerging into the twentieth century as a welcoming, diverse, and creative force for change within the higher education sector. The goal was to become a community of hope with the premise that education must be laced with opportunity. Ideas need to be nurtured and rewarded with practical outlets, especially those that are geared to the common good. This outlook was fostered not for the short term, but for a lifetime of service. This is what was exemplified at Liverpool Hope. It was the foundation stone of building community.

As I settled into the rhythm of studying and the lifestyle of a post-graduate student, I also embraced the institution's culture of possibility. It spoke to my creative tendencies and, perhaps more importantly, fostered a sense of community and belonging. I embarked on a dizzying array of roles and jobs – PhD student, lecturer, researcher, and resident advisor, to name just a few. The work we were doing and the camaraderie we were attempting to foster developed a heightened sense of community. There was a sense that we were developing something new and important. Perhaps the former Chief Rabbi Jonathan Sack's definition of community would be helpful here.

> In classical Hebrew there are three different words for community: *edah*, *tzibbur* and *kehillah*; and they signify different kinds of association.
>
> *Edah* comes from the word *ed*, meaning 'witness.' The modern Hebrew noun *te'udah* means 'certificate, document, attestation, aim, object, purpose or mission.' The people who constitute an *edah* have a strong sense of collective identity. They have witnessed the same things. They are bent on the same purpose. The Jewish people become an *edah* – a community of shared faith. . . . The word emphasizes strong identity. It is a group whose members have much in common.
>
> By contrast, the word *tsibbur* [describes a group of people coming together for a particular purpose. They may not know each

other.] . . . They may never meet again. A *tsibbur* is a community in the minimalist sense, a mere aggregate, formed by numbers rather than any sense of identity. . . .

A *kehillah* is different from the other two kinds of community. Its members are different from one another. In that sense, it is like a *tsibbur*. But they are orchestrated together for a collective undertaking – one that involves itself in making a distinctive contribution. . . .

The beauty of a *kehillah* . . . is that when it is driven by constructive purpose, it gathers together the distinct and separate contributions of many individuals, so that each can say, 'I helped to make this.' . . .

Moses was able to turn the *kehillah*, with its diversity, into an *edah*, with its singleness of purpose, while preserving the diversity of the gifts they brought to God.[1]

While the interactions at Liverpool Hope involved all of these forms of community, the institution strove to foster a community that honored the unique contributions of each person. Simon Lee emphasised, 'Any of these communities though has duties to the wider society, to the common good.'

For there to be a community of hope, there needs to be action and a celebration of the uniqueness of each individual. However, it is not simply an attitude of tolerance, but an acknowledgement that without the individual gifts people bring to the collective, life is diminished for everyone. This is what South Africans call *Ubuntu*: 'I am because you are.' As I developed my thesis on a theology of work and vocation and started to lecture in the Theology and Religious Studies Department, I was asked to develop an outreach component of University College, as the institution was named at that time. I was tasked with articulating an ethos for an academic establishment with a Christian foundation, specifically made up of two Roman Catholic colleges and one Church of England college originally set up for teacher training. Initially, I felt little qualified for this challenge. Yet, I soon determined that I was indeed perfect for putting forward a rationale for the aims and ideals for this unique institution called Hope. I had been offered the opportunity to spread my intellectual wings, as well as to pursue my dreams of making a practical difference; I heartily grabbed the opportunity with all of the energy and enthusiasm

1. Sacks, 'Three Types of Community.'

I could muster. The institution's resources had been offered to me with as much support and encouragement as I could have needed. The result was Church and Community Connections, which was set up to promote Liverpool Hope's resources out into the community. The church college's aims of educating the person in mind, body, and soul and turning dreams into reality were to have far-reaching effects.

I could pontificate on the academic machinations of the theological, philosophical, and moral basis for Hope's ethos in mission and how Hope set about educating its students, but I believe part of the beauty of Hope was that it was accessible to all, thereby opening its doors to everyone, even those who never thought themselves capable of entering the academy – the vulnerable, the deprived, and those who needed a helping hand. The blessing of Hope and Church and Community Connections was that opportunity met the prospective student or organisation on their own turf. We did not set out to build an ivory tower where only the few could ascend or to extend the hand of friendship only if the cause was lucrative or came with accolades. Ours was a desire to unlock human potential and to create an extended community of hope.

As I look back on those relatively few years, I can feel much more than nostalgia. I feel a sense of accomplishment and pride. I also feel that it was the making of that young woman. As my research carried me further into an understanding of the subject of my thesis – vocation and how each person's gifts and talents formed the basis of their sense of purpose – Liverpool Hope branched out further into the community. There were international initiatives like Hope One World, in which I participated, which sent students and teachers to schools in India and the Tibetan settlements in India. There were community research projects that aided in understanding vulnerable communities and their needs. There were unique academic projects, including the Doing Theology module that I created to give theology students placements in such diverse workplaces as the School of Tropical Medicine, the Ronald McDonald House, a women's hostel, and an acting company. There were many students who said, in their final presentations, that they had never thought ethics and morals played such a big part in the workplace. This type of thinking went beyond simply the academics but challenged students to reflect on how their career choices would either impinge on or enhance the common good.

This coincided with the breakthrough in my own research when I determined that a traditional view of providence was a false crutch and that each human being had radical free will to determine his or her own destiny. The caveat is that in order to remain faithful and a wholly moral and ethical person, actions and purpose need to make a positive impact on individuals and society at large. This topping off (to borrow a building term) signified my highest point to date. I now knew without a doubt that all of my dreams to build a better world weren't prescribed and that I didn't have to sit back and wait for God to provide. It was as William Ernest Henley proclaimed, 'I am the master of my fate: I am the captain of my soul.'[2] Yet, as much as we are personally motivated, our progress is only successful when, at best, we are surrounded by an entire community or at least by a few like-minded individuals working towards common goals and unity. There are two examples of biblical grammar that help to reinforce these ideas. Again, I turn to Jonathan Sacks. 'Passivity allows bad things to happen – "Wherever it says 'and it came to pass' it is a sign of impending tragedy." . . . Proactivity is the defeat of tragedy: "Wherever it says, 'And there will be' is a sign of impending joy."'[3] And, uniquely, Jesus is referred to as *el verbo* in Spanish. For example, the first verse of John's Gospel has been translated as 'In the beginning was the verb, and the verb was with God, and the verb was God.' This dynamic translation of Jesus coincides with the ultimate conclusion in my thesis. God can change, and not only do we have free will to determine our choices in life, but also those choices can change. We are not stuck on a railway track, nor are we cookie cutter images. In other words, it is okay to fail, it is okay not to reach perfection, and it is okay to try to transform the world one student, one outreach project, at a time. I had become a process theologian. The task of the process theologian had a synergy with the ethos of Liverpool Hope. Both ideologies had an appreciation of the nuances of an iteration between unique people coming together and the creative process of the academy whereby students and staff work together to sharpen their understanding of diverse ideas, give birth to big ideas, and in the case of Liverpool Hope, be offered the platform to take practical action. All of this energy and enthusiasm resulted in victories both small and large as well as false starts and letdowns. However, the acceptance of an unknown outcome with continuous encouragement allayed fears and strengthened community. We were in this together, no matter the outcome.

2. Henley, 'Invictus.'

3. Sacks, 'Three Types of Community.'

This research informed my work with Church and Community Connections, and there are two projects in particular that came under the auspices of that department that I would like to expand upon. The first is a partnership between Liverpool Hope and Liverpool Football Club (LFC). In reaching out to the wider community, I learnt of the deep deprivation of North Liverpool. Both premier league teams in the city were located at either end of a dilapidated Victorian park. The housing was poor, drugs and criminal gangs were rife, school buildings weren't fit for purpose, and health facilities were sparse. People in this area died younger on average than anywhere in Western Europe. On top of it all, it was known as being one of the worst areas for litter and dog fouling. It was just the place for Hope!

As mentioned above, Church and Community Connections's brief was to develop projects outside the university utilising its resources. Talks had been underway between the club and the city and the local residents for some time, but around the year 2000, discussions began in earnest about regeneration of the area and a new stadium for LFC. A steering group had been set up that was made up of representatives from many different sectors from the civic, community, and public realms, including Professor Simon Lee and myself. I had met with various members of the committee to discuss possible ways Liverpool Hope, with its ethos of providing education of the mind, soul, and body to all, could be an asset to the community. This resulted in an invitation to become a conversation partner at the table. There was a real appetite for including not only the commercial aspects of a premier league team, but also a desire to make a difference to the members of the community by improving their quality of life. As talks ensued it was decided that Liverpool Hope would have a mini-campus within the stadium. It was exciting and, we believed, groundbreaking. The prestige of LFC would be a tremendous draw for potential students in that renowned area of deprivation who were searching for meaning and purpose in their lives, not unlike that young woman who had been wandering a few years earlier in Boston. While the new stadium never materialized, Liverpool Hope had been showcased as an educational institution that cared about even those most marginalized and vulnerable and worked hard to give each person an equal opportunity to become the best he or she could be.

The second case study involves the setting up of a housing charity that has become an extension of my heart. It has encompassed my mind, body, and soul, and its legacy can rightly be traced back to Liverpool

Hope and Church and Community Connections. I do believe that in those early days of Professor Lee, Professor Markham, and all the staff and students there was a pioneer spirit that engaged the intellect and passions in a new way. Education had to make way for compassion and pastoral care. What I mean is this: we did not have the luxury to dedicate ourselves purely to intellectual pursuits. We lived in a city in the late twentieth century that was sadly in decline; jobs were in decline, and much of the housing stock was in woeful disrepair. We could not ignore the basic needs of our city or, more importantly, its population. To this end, Church and Community Connections also engaged with what many would say were noneducational schemes or projects. One such initiative was Liverpool Habitat for Humanity.

While Habitat for Humanity was a household name in much of the world, it was virtually unknown in Britain. Coinciding with the completion of my thesis based on a theology of work, I discovered a distinctive outlet for my principle vocation, that of a priest, in the pattern of *el verbo*. While Liverpool Hope had offered me the opportunity to expand my knowledge and solidify my desires to 'be the positive change I wished to see in the world', the institution could not grant me ordination, which I had been pursuing since I left Virginia Theological Seminary. I had to turn to the Church of England for that. However, parish ministry was not as strong a pull as providing ministerial support to those who did not want to be part of a traditional Christian community, while at the same time wanting to advocate for social justice and attempting to improve conditions within health, education, and, most specifically, housing. This combination of wanting to have one foot in church and one in community had perfectly aligned in my journey thus far. The perfection of Liverpool Hope was that it wasn't just the staff that made it special, but that the buzz was created by all the different souls that combined to be a community of Hope. The beauty of Habitat for Humanity was that it only succeeds if all contributions from each person are celebrated and valued to literally build a new community. I was encouraged and supported in the formation of the charity, as it was believed to be an extension of the ethos of the college.

Liverpool Habitat for Humanity, now Housing People, Building Communities (HPBC), as a charity, has been recognised nationally as a builder of communities and with its unique 'sweat equity' model has enabled those who would otherwise never be able to afford their own homes to get on the property ladder. Liverpool Habitat for Humanity was formed a number of years ago when I, as founder, wanted to bring people together to form friendships and provide much-needed affordable, good housing. The model of building your own home and those of your neighbours was a relatively new idea here in England. When I approached the archdiocese about a brownfield site in Toxteth, Liverpool, and which had previously been the site of a RC primary school, they generously agreed to transfer the land to the charity for the benefit of the community. The charity then built thirty-two homes on the site, which were all built utilizing the sweat equity model of home partners; their friends and family put five hundred hours into building the homes (alongside qualified construction professionals), and that counted as a ten-thousand pound deposit for the family. Saint Bernard's Church, which had been closed and was adjacent to the original site, was much loved by the ex-parishioners and the wider community. When we had completed the thirty-two new-build homes, the archdiocese asked if we could transform the church into affordable homes for the local community. We lovingly preserved the church building, providing eleven three-story townhouses within the building itself. There were also four new-build flats and a detached house built on the site using the same model. Housing People, Building Communities is dedicated to creating homes that people will take pride in and to helping build loving communities. The model enables neighbours to support and care for each other, having gotten to know each other while working alongside each other building their homes and creating community.

In completing the forty-eight homes on the site in Granby/Toxteth, many dreams of mine were fulfilled. The development itself had become a 'city on a hill'. Since having been the location of riots in the early 1980s, the area is considered one of the most diverse neighbourhoods in the country and amongst its most deprived. The charity withstood the initial challenge of enlisting support for a new and controversial concept of building homes, criminal gangs burning down the first three homes, and overcoming generations of mistrust and anger towards organisations by the local residents to create a beautiful and loving kaleidoscope of families and home partners living side by side, having built each other's homes together. The charity continues to move forward and is developing new projects in the region – all dedicated to building communities of love, peace, and hope.

I had understood for much of my life that poverty and deprivation creates division and animosity. However, it was not until I was given the freedom and resources to reach out to try to make a difference by developing practical activities out in the community that I felt I had finally found my purpose and some satisfaction with my choices. My doctoral thesis concluded with the thought that our radical free will meant that all jobs, careers, and vocations have worth. However, all activity must further the ends of love and contribute to the common good. Goodness knows that this thesis has been validated in the past year during the COVID crisis with a renewed appreciation for key workers and jobs traditionally perceived as lower paid and unskilled.

In 2001, I was the first student to receive a PhD from the University of Liverpool through Liverpool Hope. It was one of those days when all of the stars aligned and truly was one of the best days of my life. It was an achievement born of encouragement, support, and opportunity. Like the majority of Hope students, I had overcome obstacles to reach that point and could rightly be proud of my accomplishments. The day itself was tremendous with my parents making one of their rare trips from America for the graduation, other friends making the journey from the States, a celebration lunch, the ceremony in the Anglican cathedral, strawberries and cream at the Roman Catholic cathedral, and the party hosted by friends in the evening all combined to create a spectacular and memorable day. I had become part of a community that Hope built.

Post-Hope

In the years after the completion of my doctorate and Simon Lee's and Ian Markham's departures, Liverpool Hope naturally evolved. The newly appointed Professor Pillay wanted to emphasise the academic foundation of the institution, and Liverpool Hope became Liverpool Hope University with its own degree-awarding powers. I continued to lecture in a number of subjects in the Theology and Religious Studies Department and further developed ties with the organisations that were regenerating North Liverpool. The housing charity was continuing to build houses and a significant community. I was ordained in 2002 and served my diaconate in the most delightful parish, St Mary's, Knowsley Village, known as 'Dibley'. When I was made redundant in the reorganisation after Professor Pillay arrived, I went to work for Liverpool City Council as project manager, New Anfield, while also serving as a priest in Knowsley, then St Mary's, West Derby. It was a natural progression to involve myself more deeply in helping to improve the built environment and looking to increase opportunities and support for people living in more deprived neighbourhoods. In improving conditions and opportunities, I believed I was helping people to spread their own wings, providing support as they followed their dreams. The stronger the communities were, the easier it would be for people to discover their true joy and purpose. During this time, I also set up a consultancy called Ubuntu Unlimited and worked with organisations to develop similar projects, as well as researching ways for them to improve their services out in the communities (e.g., the Primary Care Trust).

In 2011, I accepted a job as the first community canon within the Anglican Communion at Blackburn Cathedral where I worked to develop community cohesion and social justice projects. Blackburn, and much of East Lancashire, has been considered one of the most segregated towns in Britain, according to a report by a Home Office review team in 2001.[4] If there was anywhere in the country where my views were needed on how to build a community of Hope, it was in Lancashire. One of the highlights of this time was opening a community café (BB1 for Life) in the town centre, which aimed to be a welcoming place for people from different backgrounds and diverse groups to do things together 'for life', in order to break down barriers and build relationships . . . as well having the best cappuccino in town. Four years later I left the cathedral and was diagnosed with breast cancer. I spent three years going through treatments and surgeries. Despite the challenges, hope was never far away, and my yearning to make a difference was only heightened by my ordeal.

When I was once again physically able to hit the ground running, I was offered yet another unique opportunity to build community with the Lancashire Collaborative Ministry as the social justice minister developing projects for the common good. I found myself in a rather odd position. I was an Anglican priest working with the Unitarians based on the free Christian tradition. However, serendipity yet again played a part in this role. The Unitarians have a long and noble history of faithfully actively engaging with their communities to promote social justice issues and increase tolerance of all God's children in all of their diversity. It is a role I both relish and cherish. Jesus for Unitarians is most definitely *el verbo*! Amongst the many activities being developed, including interfaith and social cohesion projects, there is one I am especially proud of: the

---

4. Independent Review Team, *Community Cohesion*.

offering of free legal advice sessions in partnership with the Open University and the University of Lancaster. The aim is to alleviate the strain caused by unresolved legal issues, thereby lessening stress and improving health and well-being for those who don't have the same access to legal services that others with more resources might have. In yet another wonderful moment of serendipity, I find myself working with Professor Lee again who is a trustee of the Open University. It does make me smile. The community we all built and the dreams we all hold remain strong.

Doing things together breaks down barriers and builds bridges in a way dialogue never can. While we can all say hello and try to spark a conversation while out shopping or walking, creating opportunities to engage with each other in a more substantial way requires organisation and resources. It is a reality that the bulk of the burden for bringing people together rests with those with resources and organisational skills, whether it be a litter-picking group, sports team, growing on an allotment, luncheon club, or any other group activity. Any attempt to break down barriers, like sharing food, is positive, but opportunity that improves the quality of life and lessens poverty needs to be fostered by communities of hope. Otherwise, relief is short lived and in the long run often results in the opposite of what was intended. Real efforts need to be made to create inroads into communities of deprivation and loneliness. The task can be overwhelming, but I am convinced that with the sharing of opportunity, resources, and compassion we can build that community of hope.

Reminiscing is always bittersweet. This exercise of pondering the past has cemented my long-held convictions of justice, equity, and harmony. Writing this has also renewed my thankfulness for such a supportive and caring environment at Liverpool Hope, without which, much would not have been accomplished. This contrasts with periods of my life where that support and encouragement was not there. When I was a little girl, I used to love Cat Stevens, especially his song "Oh Very Young." I used to listen to the words of that song on long trips in the car and vowed to respond to those lyrics that captured our short dance on earth.

From those early formative years to walking in Boston and the many journeys in between, I always felt a responsibility to make a positive difference to the world. My dreams were lofty and my faith was sure, but I discovered that to achieve those goals in isolation was impossible. What Liverpool Hope afforded me was the freedom to spread my wings and the support while in flight, whether I soared or fell. This lesson in building true community, or *Ubuntu*, was the secret to making dreams become reality and one which I pledge to carry on.

Ultimately, though, my entire philosophy of life can be summed up in one line from a song by that great sage, Elvis: 'A little less conversation, a little more action . . .'[5]

Bibliography

Henley, William Ernest. 'Invictus.' Poetry Foundation, n.d. https://www.poetry foundation.org/poems/51642/invictus.

Davis, Mac, and Billy Strange. 'A Little Less Conversation.' Elvis Presley. Recorded 7 Mar. 1968. RCA Victor, 1968, LP. B-side of *Almost in Love*.

Independent Review Team. *Community Cohesion: A Report of the Independent Review Team*. Ted Cantle, Dec. 2001. https://tedcantle.co.uk/pdf/communitycohesion%20 cantlereport.pdf.

Sacks, Jonathan. 'Three Types of Community.' AISH, n.d. https://aish.com/195235991/.

Stevens, Cat. 'Oh Very Young.' Recorded Feb. 1974. Island, 1974, LP. A-side of *Buddha and the Chocolate Box*.

5. Davis and Strange, 'Little Less Conversation.'

SERVING ALONGSIDE THE MARGINALIZED

Walking On, with Hope in Our Hearts

16

Prison-Visiting

MAUREEN MCKNIGHT, SND

WHEN I ARRIVED IN Childwall in 1990, I was following a long line of Sisters of Notre Dame who had been involved in education in Liverpool for well over a hundred years. Throughout this time, I lived on the campus. In those interesting years, change was all around. When I began, we were the Liverpool Institute of Education (LIHE), which became Liverpool Hope University College, and when I left in 2000, were moving to university status. By then I had completed almost thirty years in education. Time for another change!

After a sabbatical period exploring what to do next, I have been involved in a variety of ministries, including hospital chaplaincy (2001–2004), parish team ministry (2004–2011), service of pastoral leadership in the Notre Dame Childwall community (2005–2011), and member of the Congregational Chapter Planning Committee for the General Chapter in Washington, DC (2012–2014).

At the end of 2014, I had major cancer surgery, but happily I got the 'all clear' in 2019. I continued in service of pastoral leadership in the Notre Dame Birkdale community from 2019 to present. However, my primary ministry has been in the prison service, 2001 to present. This was, for me, a response to one of the articles (no. 17) in the Constitutions of the Sisters of Notre Dame, which states, 'In fidelity to Julie's preference for the poor in the most abandoned places, we choose to stand with poor people as they struggle for adequate means for human life and dignity.'

In this ministry, I began as a volunteer prison visitor and in 2014 was asked to become a part-time Catholic chaplain alongside the visiting.

When I reflected on Simon's letter of invitation to us, the phrase in the opening paragraph that caught my attention was 'a commitment to widening participation and access for non-traditional students'.

My experience during my time at Hope was that in encouraging such students, we were giving them 'a future full of hope' (Jer 29.12), and their presence on campus enriched us.

In the various ministries I have undertaken since leaving Hope, the thread that has run through all that I have been involved in has been this: somehow to share with others a growing awareness of their innate dignity and to journey with them as they discover that in their lives, no matter the circumstances, there *is* a future full of hope. It has been for me both challenging and enriching. It is also an immense privilege.

17

The Mirror and the Kindness of Strangers

The Building of the Cornerstone at Liverpool Hope University

DAVID TOREVELL

Jesus said to them, 'Have you never read in the Scriptures: The stone that the builders rejected has become the cornerstone. This is what the Lord has done and it is wonderful in our eyes?'

—MATT 21.42 CSB

Continue to love each other like brothers, and remember always to welcome strangers, for by doing this, some people have entertained angels without knowing it.

—HEB 13.1 NJB

'Woe to him that is alone, for when he falls, he has none to lift him up'. He is entirely alone who is without a friend.

—AELRED OF RIEVAULX

Introduction

THE CHRISTIAN IMPERATIVE TO love oneself, one's neighbour, and one's enemy sets a task for church universities, stretching their mission to breaking point. This chapter explores the dynamics of this teaching with reference to those who exist on the margins of society and those who feel isolated and alone in a world sometimes cruel and uncaring to those it misunderstands. On my first visit to the newly built Cornerstone campus in Everton, devoted to the creative and performing arts, I had to park my car a little distance away. Suddenly, I was approached by a sex worker. Apparently, the area had temporarily become a red-light district after the building works had started, but the street workers vowed to move on once the campus was up and running. My encounter with the woman proved to be providential, however, as it got me thinking about all those in our society who have been forgotten and perhaps unfairly judged.[1] How would Liverpool Hope respond to such people? I reflected on how the arts, in particular, might address this challenge. There had already been significant research conducted by three Liverpool Hope staff on inner-city prostitution, and I began to muse on how Cornerstone could extend their work and put into practice Jesus's teaching about the nature of love. I draw from Tennessee Williams's play *A Streetcar Named Desire* and Georges Rouault's painting *Prostitute at Her Mirror* to illuminate how two extraordinary examples of the arts might encourage this New Testament command, and contend that such provision at both undergraduate and postgraduate levels is of supreme significance for Christian universities, since without the inclusion of the arts, it is less likely that staff and students will come to appreciate the importance of the kindness of strangers. I also situate in my account the writings of St Aelred of Rievaulx on charity to support my claim.

A Streetcar Named Desire

Liverpool Hope has significantly developed its portfolio of courses in the creative and performing arts over the last twenty-one years since its first tentative steps. It now offers undergraduate and postgraduate degrees in the following concentrations: music (it is one of only six all-Steinway schools in English higher education), music production, dance, film, fine art, and graphic design. Drama and theatre studies (BA Hons single and combined) and musical theatre (BA Hons combined) plus a postgraduate

---

1. See Elliott's study of providence and its relationship to hope: 'The Christian faith *trusts* in the living God, with a very sober form of ecstasy that is located in the ground for hope, in that God is more forgiving and more in control of events than we will ever be' (Elliott, *Providence*, ch. 6).

MA in performance continue to play a large part in the curriculum based at the Cornerstone campus. The space boasts two beautiful Grade II listed buildings, a magnificent great hall, and two theatres. The 2022 prospectus states that students will 'be challenged to reflect on how theatre and performance relate to contemporary social and ethical contexts,' helping them 'to understand the critical place of performance in 21st-century society.' I now examine how Williams's play does just this.

At the end of Tennessee Williams's highly acclaimed tragedy *A Streetcar Named Desire* (1943), Blanche DuBois, the drama's central figure, says to the doctor who escorts her to a mental asylum and whose arm she tightly holds, 'Whoever you are—I have always depended on the kindness of strangers.'[2] In an earlier scene, she confesses to her new boyfriend, Mitch, that before meeting him, 'Yes, I had many intimacies with strangers', by which she means casual sex with men, even a seventeen-year-old boy. Her reason for this was out of 'panic' of being alone; they were desperate attempts to fill 'her empty heart', 'hunting for some protection—here and there, in the most—unlikely places.'[3] The affairs took place after the suicide of her first lover, Allan, whom she discovered, after their marriage, to be homosexual. In this short sequence, we encounter central themes that pervade the whole play and indeed Williams's entire oeuvre, as well as his own personal life.[4] As Eyre and Wright comment, Williams has tended to become the 'mouthpiece for the dispossessed—women, gays, blacks, the mad, the wayward, the lonely.'[5]

The drama unfolds the stages of guilt-ridden Blanche's life (due to the death of Allan and her own promiscuity) and plots her tortured mind, which relishes the shadows and the dark – a life characterized by

2. T. Williams, *Plays*, 563.

3. T. Williams, *Plays*, 546.

4. Tennessee Williams (1911–1983) was the son of a travelling shoe salesman, who was an alcoholic, and of a minister's daughter, who became a patient in a psychiatric hospital. He drew the religious allusions in his plays from the time he spent in his grandfather's rectories while his father was away on the road. He was devoted to his sister Rose, who was diagnosed in her teens with schizophrenia and who was given a prefrontal lobotomy, which Tennessee knew nothing about until it had been performed. Tennessee knew from personal experience what it felt like to be marginalized, unfairly judged, and lonely, because he was a gay man growing up in the American South of the Depression years, 'where to be gay and white was barely better than being black, and he observed the sober, heterosexual, clubbable, gullible subscribers to the American Dream with the eye of the outcast' (Eyre and Wright, *Changing Stages*, 180). T. Williams, *Plays*, 180.

5. Eyre and Wright, *Changing Stages*, 180.

the refusal to face the truth about herself. 'I like the dark,' she comments. Like strangers, 'the dark is comforting to me.'[6] The paper lantern covering the lightbulb becomes the visible symbol on stage for Blanche's desire to live an illusion. She fantasizes about her life and tells lies about her companions to cover up the truth. Mitch comments, 'You never want to go out till after six and then it's always some place that's not lighted.'[7] Like a prostitute's place of work, bathed in artificial light, the lighting through-out the play gives a strong sense of unreality and subterfuge. Blanche acclaims, 'I'll tell you what I want. Magic!'[8] and explains to the audience how she tries to 'give that to people', a clear reference to her many sexual clients and, more generally, to her myriad of relationships. Her brother-in-law, Stanley, confronts her ruthlessly with her dissembling. Although shamed, she adds, 'If that be sinful, then let me be damned for it!',[9] which gives a strong indication she does not feel it is wrong at all. This is partly because Blanche has come to believe that the only way to live in a cruel world is to pretend to be who you are not. As Raymond Williams writes about such stances taken up by many of Williams's characters, 'It is in their consciousness, their ideals, their dreams, their illusions that they lose themselves and become pathetic sleepwalkers.'[10] Make-believe leads to downfall. When asked about the meaning of his work, the playwright replied, 'The ravishment of the tender, the sensitive, the delicate, by the savage and brutal forces of modern society.'[11] Smith-Howard and Heintzelman argue that 'all the characters in *Streetcar* have been ravished by life to some degree.'[12] As I will later allude to, when referring to Rouault's painting *Prostitute at Her Mirror*, there is a sad vulnerability and, at the same time, brave attempt at resilience in Blanche's profile. She relies on others to bring her hope, kindness, and comfort, rather than abuse.

The symbol of the mirror features significantly in the play. In scene 10, Williams's stage directions add that Blanche is placing '*the rhinestone tiara on her head before the mirror of the dressing table and murmuring*

---

6. T. Williams, *Plays*, 544.

7. T. Williams, *Plays*, 544.

8. T. Williams, *Plays*, 545.

9. T. Williams, *Plays*, 545.

10. R. Williams, *Modern Tragedy*, 119.

11. Quoted in Smith-Howard and Heintzelman, *Tennessee Williams*, 273.

12. Smith-Howard and Heintzelman, *Tennessee Williams*, 273.

excitedly as if to a group of spectral admirers.[13] She fantasizes about being desired by others, who are in reality mere figments of her own imagination. Later in the scene, Stanley ruthlessly mocks her regal pretentions and her refusal to look at herself honestly, 'And look at yourself! Take a look at yourself in that worn-out Mardi Gras outfit. . . . You come in here . . . and cover the lightbulb with a paper lantern and lo and behold the place has turned into Egypt and you are the Queen of the Nile!'[14] What she dresses up to see in the mirror is an illusion. Near the close of the play, Blanche comments 'How strange!' that she has not had a call from her invented boyfriend, Shep Huntleigh. The stage directions add, *'Blanche stands quite still for some moments—the silverbacked mirror in her hand and a look of sorrowful perplexity as though all human experience shows on her face.'*[15] Williams presents his audience with a character who has to endure the cruelty of others as they force her to confront herself. Cabral writes, 'The illusory reflection of a non-existent desired life that keeps Blanche Dubois weakly tied to reality is cut loose when Stanley Kowalski breaks the mirror of romantic fantasies she has tried to build.'[16] It is equivalent to Merton's examination of the construction of the 'false self'.[17]

Blanche's own downfall is largely due to her inability to forgive herself for her sexual lapses and to face the reality of the shame she feels. The Greek word *aidoia* means 'genitals' and is a derivative of the word *aidos*, which translates as 'shame'; similar terms are found in other languages. Blanche's reaction is to hide from shame, like Adam and Eve in the garden. As Bernard Williams argues, the common response to shame is 'to cover oneself or to hide, and people naturally took steps to avoid situations which called for it.'[18] However, just as influential on Blanche's downfall is the cruel treatment of others, which she abhors. She says, 'Deliberate cruelty is not forgivable. It is the one unforgivable thing in my opinion and it is the one thing of which I have never, never been guilty.'[19] Nevertheless, in spite of all this, Blanche believes that the best way of dealing with desire is to live a refined life. This is the main reason why she

13. T. Williams, *Plays*, 548.

14. T. Williams, *Plays*, 552.

15. T. Williams, *Plays*, page number unavailable.

16. Cabral, 'Blanche through the Looking-Glass,' page number unavailable.

17. Torevell, 'Distractions, Illusion and Need.'

18. B. Williams, *Shame and Necessity*, 78.

19. T. Williams, *Plays*, 552.

fell in love with 'the boy who wrote poetry' and 'worshipped the ground he walked on!'[20] and why she is grateful 'such things as art—as poetry and music—such kinds of new light have come into the world,'[21] an allusion to the light of Christ in St John's prologue.

Stanley represents someone who seems to withstand far better than Blanche the 'arrows of outrageous fortune', but he does not completely avoid their sting.[22] He is scarred, like Mitch, by his experience of World War II and succumbs like Blanche, to addiction – in her case, alcohol, and in his, alcohol and gambling. His character, if played by a seductively handsome actor like Marlon Brando (who took on the role in the Broadway production in 1947 and in the 1951 film version), can become attractive and 'an object of straight male envy and a universal object of gay and [heterosexual] female lust'.[23] But he, too, longs for the comfort of someone else's arms and after hitting his wife in a drunken rage cries out in desperation 'Stella! My baby doll's left me!' The stage directions are *'he throws back his head like a baying hound and bellows his wife's name*:

20. T. Williams, *Plays*, 533.

21. T. Williams, *Plays*, 511.

22. Thompson's insightful study of Williams's plays in terms of memory, myth, and symbol argues that the dramatic *agon* between Stanley and Blanche 'represents an externalization of their own inner conflict: the struggle between the brutal desires of the flesh and the transcendent aspirations of the spirit or soul. . . . Stanley embodies the Dionysian antithesis to Blanche's romantic dreams and moral pretensions, the personified projection of her own libidinous impulses. Thus Blanche's animosity towards Stanley's "animal force" and "bestial sexuality" is also self-disgust at her own irrepressible carnality for in Jungian terms "that which one passionately hates is sure to represent an aspect of his own fate"' (Thompson *Tennessee Williams' Plays*, 37–38). Williams studied Greek at the University of Washington and knew its mythical stories well. The myth of Dionysius is one of the archetypal foundations of Williams's work. Roche-Lajtha writes that 'Dionysius was a god of paradoxes, who could be the most gentle and yet the most terrible of divinities. . . . The god brought ecstatic bliss to his worshippers but hunted his enemies down with the utmost ferocity. This duality is dramatized in Euripides's *Bacchae*, which . . . is a structural analogue to Streetcar' (Roche-Lajtha, 'Dionysius, Orpheus and Androgyn,' 62). The dramatic use of myth and ritual should not be underestimated in Williams's work. In an age bereft of a commonly shared mythos, Thompson persuasively argues that Williams attempts to restore symbolic meaning to the modern existential condition and encourages a granting of religious significance and value to human relationships, however limited and compensatory they may be. He offers no solution for loneliness other than the rare and transient embrace with one's fellow human being, but in this embrace resides a degree of redemption. Williams's dramas thus endow acts of human kindness with religious and metaphysical value.

23. Eyre and Wright, *Changing Stages*, 180.

"Stella! Stella, sweetheart! Stella!"[24] A little later the text adds, 'Stanley *(with heaven-splitting violence)*: "STELL-LAHHHHH." There might be a raw animal urgency about this outburst, but like Blanche, he craves affection and the comfort and kindness of another human being in a world he finds difficult to negotiate. Williams's attitude to Stanley is double edged and ambiguous.

Vivien Leigh as Blanche and Marlon Brando as Stanley in the 1951 film version.[25]

Bigsby is right to suggest that 'he dominates existence and in such a way commands Williams's respect, even if he represents a brutalism which frightens a writer who is drawn instinctively to the fate of those less equipped to confront the modern world.'[26] Thus, in one sense, Williams admires his ability to survive, but he also knows this is combined with a potentially violent sexuality and susceptibility to anger; indeed, he hits his wife and rapes her sister, Blanche, who becomes the enemy in the house, potentially destroying his marriage. In the final moments of the play, the audience experience this tension, a toxic cocktail of deep affection and raw lust: 'Now, honey. Now, love. Now, now, love. *(He kneels besides her and his fingers find the opening of her blouse)* Now, now, love, Now, love . . .'[27] The final, telling line of the drama is spoken by Steve, one of the poker players, who says, 'This game is seven-card stud'; and Stanley knows how to win at it.

24. Williams, *Plays*, 502.
25. Kazan, *Streetcar Named Desire*.
26. Bigsby, *Critical Introduction*, 2:60.
27. Williams, *Plays*, 564.

I partly agree with Bigsby's claim that Stanley is a Lawrentian figure: 'Animal joy in his being is implicit in all his movement and attitudes. Since earliest manhood the center of his life has been pleasure with women, the giving and taking of it, not with weak indulgency, dependently, but with the power and pride of a richly feathered male bird among hens.'[28] It also needs saying that Stanley is as vulnerable as Blanche when comfort is taken away from him. What characterizes both characters is their ruthless and relentless internal battle between the body and the spirt, a combat every human being knows. Raymond Williams argues that Williams offers a tragic vision of life precisely due to this tension:

> Tennessee's characters are isolated beings who desire and eat and fight alone, who struggle feverishly with the primary and related energies of love and death. At their most satisfying they are animals; the rest is a covering of humanity and is destructive. . . . The human condition is tragic because of the entry of the mind on the fierce, and in itself tragic, animal struggle of sex and death. The purpose of the drama is to cut through these mental illusions to the actual primary rhythms. But the one redemptive thing in all this bleakness, is the power of art to assuage this desperate battle with sympathy for others who feel like you.[29]

For Tennessee Williams, the theatre can become an arena where 'our hearts are wrung by recognition and pity so that the dusky shell of the auditorium where we gathered anonymously together is flooded with an almost liquid warmth of unchecked human sympathy.'[30] As such, the audience are the strangers who give comfort to the *dramatis personae* and to each other by their sympathy for, and empathy with, the characters on stage; the actors exhibit feelings similar to their own, if somewhat more vehemently.

Prostitute at Her Mirror

The study of fine art and design is central to Liverpool Hope's mission. It offers a BA Hons (single) degree in fine art, a BA Hons (single) degree in graphic design, a BA Hons (combined) in art and design history, and an

28. Bigsby, *Critical Introduction*, 2:60.
29. R. Williams, *Modern Tragedy*, 119.
30. Quoted in R. Williams, *Modern Tragedy*, 120.

MA in art history and curating at the Cornerstone campus. The prospectus states, 'The newest addiction to the campus, the Arts Centre features a large, refurbished warehouse space as well as smaller studios for Fine and Applied Art students to hone their practice.' The campus houses the Cornerstore Gallery, 'which supplements the student experience via a series of contemporary art exhibitions, student-led seminars and some of the best examples of current professional practice.' It also has an international artist-in-residence programme. Its presence deeply influenced my own appreciation of art.

One painter studied within the programme is Georges Rouault (1871–1958), a French artist steeped in the mediaevalist tradition. He began his career apprenticed to a stained glass worker admiring the windows of Gothic cathedrals with their splashes of bold colour and their thick, binding black lines. He converted to Catholicism in 1895 and was influenced by the Christian socialism of Léon Bloy and the ardent Catholics, Charles Péguy and Joris-Karl Huysmans, also converts. Rouault's artistic mentors were Moreau, Forain, Rodin, Carrière, and above all, Paul Cézanne. Rouault's depictions of prostitutes plainly owe something to Cézanne's paintings of bathers. His representations of prostitutes and clowns echo the unique significance of stained glass windows – they only work if redemptive light shines through their darkened frames. In his *Prostitute at Her Mirror* (1904), dark and light interact creatively – the sad, somber eyes, the deep red lips, the jet-black hair coexist with the woman's creamy white body, which is reflected back to her in the mirror, offering some possibility of redemptive change. Hergott and Whitfield comments that Rouault is adept at displaying the complexity and vulnerability of human beings behind the external mask for he 'shows us the dark aspect of each individual lying behind the superficial mask of the brothel. . . . What the prostitutes share with the clowns and the judges is the great disparity that exists between the professional garb and the individual who wears it. Rouault treats the prostitute's physical nudity as a disguise, which he removes as he paints.'[31] He also does another remarkable thing – he button-holes the onlooker and takes her inside the frame, from which she has difficulty extricating herself.[32] She then sees signs of herself in the figure and, by moving very close to her, sees her plight with the opportunity given to her to offer compassion and kindness. Rouault

---

31. Hergott and Whitfield, *Georges Rouault*, 24.
32. Hergott and Whitfield, *Georges Rouault*, 25.

often painted pictures of himself as a clown, and, no doubt, if he had painted gigolos, he would have done the same thing. He offers in his portraits aspects of himself while suggesting they are also true of everyone else too. Like *Streetcar*, the painting offers a visual representation of what Blanche has always sought and never experienced for very long, only in brief, sexual encounters – the kindness of strangers. Those who look at the prostitute look at themselves. What do they see, and what questions do they ask themselves? Am I, too, a fallen person? Do I give comfort to strangers? Do I feel ashamed and guilty about my propensity to sin? Am I capable of redemption? Is there hope for tomorrow?

Georges Rouault, *Prostitute at Her Mirror* (1904)

Rouault and Williams, like the author of Song of Songs, know that human sexual desire is a strong and vital drive, epitomized by longing and absence.[33] In her elucidatory commentary on this scriptural text, Exum argues that although this erotic love poem has been allegorized

---

33. Palmer and Torevell, 'Sweet Pain of Life.'

over time, the text is *not* an allegory. It celebrates the God-given, joyous desire of all lovers; the beauty of human love is the central dynamic in Song. The voices of the poem are our voices, their amorous flesh, our flesh, their longings for intimacy, our longings, their kisses, our kisses. The text affirms the biblical notion of the consoling pleasures of the flesh, the strength of love, and the beauty of the created world.[34] And, just as in *Streetcar*, desire is always on the brink of fulfilment. The author offers a vision of romantic love where both desire and sexual pleasure are dignified and views positively the human search for happiness through the trajectory of sexual longing. Its creative and original use of metaphor and rhythm prevent any descent into an over-eroticization or pornographic voyeurism.

Blanche knows the meaning of Song of Songs 8.6 all too well, 'Love is strong as death.' Williams, who had a deep sense of the passage of time and death, believed that the invention of art and literature was a defense against such transience. In scene 9, a mood of mortality pervades, as a vendor selling 'gaudy tin flowers that lower class Mexicans display at funerals'[35] enters the stage. Blanche tells her that death had often been 'as close as you are' to her, but 'the opposite is desire.' Desire, as strong as death, counters it with its own, momentous force. It should not be surprising to the audience that they are told, 'before we had lost Belle Reve, was a camp where they trained young soldiers. On Saturday night they would go into town to get drunk . . . and on the way back they would stagger onto my lawn and call – Blanche, Blanche! . . . sometimes I slipped outside to answer their calls.'[36] At times desire causes death. Blanche speaks of the soldiers in these terms, 'Later the paddy-wagon would gather them up like daisies . . . the long way home.'[37] A little later she adds, 'You know what I shall die of? *(She plucks a grape)* I shall die of eating an unwashed grape one day out on the ocean.' But she shall not be damned for this aberration, for 'that unwashed grape has transported her soul to heaven.'[38] Williams offers here the central conundrum of the play, a dilemma that he never solved in his own life nor in his philosophy. Blanche says, 'I will die—with my hand in the hand of some nice-looking

34. Exum, *Song of Songs.*
35. T. Williams, *Plays*, 546.
36. T. Williams, *Plays*, 547.
37. T. Williams, *Plays*, 547.
38. T. Williams, *Plays*, 559.

ship's doctor, a very young one with a small blond moustache.'[39] 'The power of sex to redeem or destroy is at the heart of *A Streetcar Named Desire*, write Eyre and Wright.[40] Spoto contends it is about 'the clash between desire and death.'[41] The world might name Allan a 'degenerate' and Blanche a 'destitute woman' and 'morally unfit for her position' as an English teacher, but the marginalized and abused know this is not the whole story of their lives, even if they are wracked with guilt and shame they cannot easily assuage.

For Williams, Rouault, and Aelred, it is important to offer kindness to strangers and neighbours, for they have the same nature and suscep-tibilities as ourselves. At times they depend on such kindness for their very survival. Compassionate others are able become a place of refuge for those in need. Williams alludes to the Song of Songs 2.14 in Blanche's reply to Mitch, 'I thanked God for you . . . gentle . . . a cleft in the rock of the world that I could hide in . . . a little Peace.'[42] She sees her lovers as places of safety in which she can find peace and rest. Griffiths indicates that the word *cleft*, as he translates it from the Vulgate *chink (foramen)*, means 'a narrow opening'. The lover in Song beckons his beloved to come from the rock where she is hidden so he might see her face and hear her voice. The text also signals 'a place of safety; the Lord says he will put Moses in a chink in the rock while he passes by.'[43] Psalm 30 speaks of God as a place of refuge for those who, like Blanche, have 'become the object of scorn' (v. 12) and who need to hide from the cruelties of the world. God will 'hide them in the shelter' of God's 'presence/from the plotting of men' (Ps 30.22). Mitch offers no such comfort, for he abandons Blanche after he is told she has had sexual relations with many men. She is unfit to marry him. Mitch declares, 'You're not clean enough to bring in the house with my mother.'[44] Because of such attitudes, Blanche speaks of herself as someone fighting against being 'a single girl, a girl alone in the world has got to keep a firm hold on her emotions, or she'll be lost.'[45]

39. T. Williams, *Plays*, 559.

40. Eyre and Wright, *Changing Stages*, 180.

41. Spoto, *Kindness of Strangers*, 129.

42. T. Williams, *Plays*, 546.

43. Griffiths, *Song of Songs*, 69.

44. T. Williams, *Plays*, 547.

45. T. Williams, *Plays*, 522.

Saint Augustine responds to this dilemma by teaching that if one feels lost or seems destined to be lost because this, that, or another person has let you down, this is not the whole picture, for it is possible to redirect your hope away from human beings toward God, because 'all who fix their hopes on mortals are under a curse.'[46] The Christian gospel encourages its followers to offer the kindness of strangers *and* to rely on God. Chapter 1 of Pope Francis's encyclical *Fratelli Tutti*, 'Stranger on the Road', is a direct reference to the parable of the Good Samaritan. 'The parable shows us how a community can be rebuilt by men and women who identify with the vulnerability of others, who reject the creation of a society of exclusion, and act instead as neighbors lifting up and rehabilitating the fallen for the sake of the common good.'[47] We have all been strangers, as Exod 22.21 reminds us, 'Know the heart of the stranger, for you were strangers in the land of Egypt.'[48] Jesus refers to himself as such: 'I was a stranger and you welcomed me.'[49] In offering the kindness of strangers to the abandoned, we meet Christ himself.

Ignatieff's examination of the plight and needs of strangers refers to Bosch's painting *The Garden of Earthly Delights*, but he could easily have chosen Rouault's paintings of prostitutes or Williams's play instead. He asks, 'Bosch's reflection centered on a problem intrinsic to all Christian metaphysics: whether spiritual need forms part of the natural yearnings of unredeemed human nature?'[50] Both artworks seem to suggest this *is* the case, for they exhibit what Charles Taylor refers to as the desire for a transcendental horizon that beckons them to a life more fulfilling than the one they presently endure.[51] Beckett suggests, 'The picture does not depress but holds out hope of redemption.'[52] Although, like Blanche, the unnamed prostitute is representative of abuse and an 'indictment of human cruelty', a sentiment Williams would have endorsed, Beckett actually compares her to Rouault's pictures of Christ: 'She is a travesty of femininity. . . . She is a sad version of his tortured Christs, a figure mocked and scorned,

46. Augustine, *Essential Exposition of Psalms*, 308.

47. Francis, 'Fratelli Tutti', 35–36.

48. Francis, 'Fratelli Tutti', 33.

49. Francis, 'Fratelli Tutti', 39.

50. Ignatieff, *Needs of Strangers*, 72.

51. Taylor, *Secular Age*.

52. Beckett, *Sister Wendy's*, 180.

held in disrepute.'[53] Rouault, like Williams, 'does not judge . . . the terrible compassion with which he shows his wretched figures makes a powerful impression.'[54] They become for both artists 'angels without knowing it' (Heb 13.1) in their hope of finding something better in their lives.

Saint Aelred of Rievaulx

Liverpool Hope places the study of theology, biblical studies, religion, ethics, and philosophy at the heart of its curriculum. The examination of the vital intersection between religion, theology, and the arts has played a significant role in its provision, and I initiated a specific module on this topic, Religious and Philosophical Aesthetics, to encourage students to explore further this cross-disciplinary dynamic.

I will now discuss Aelred of Rievaulx's *The Mirror of Charity* in order to cast light on what I perceive to be one crucial aspect of the mission integrity of Liverpool Hope University, to which I have already referred – love of oneself, love of one's neighbour, and love of one's enemy. It will complement my foregoing analysis of *Streetcar* and *Prostitute at Her Mirror*. The twelfth-century Cistercian monk makes a distinction between a human being made in the *image* of God and in the *likeness* of God, using the metaphor of the mirror to elucidate his teaching. Unlike Blanche, Aelred's formation as a monk encouraged him to look honestly at himself; he was horrified by what he saw. 'I was terrified by the loathsome image of my unhappy soul,'[55] a line that echoes St Augustine's view of his own self-hatred in *Confessions*. However, he noticed this displeasure only when God started to become pleasing to him and was near suicide until he discovered 'how much joy there is in your love, how much tranquility in that joy and how much security with that tranquility.'[56] He begins to see that his own broken image can be repaired and that the shattered glass can be mended by the charity of Christ's coming and his own remembering of this 'by the text of sacred Scripture.'[57] Aelred writes, 'The likeness of God may be tarnished in human beings, but the image of God remains as defining our true nature. . . . capacity to love . . . in loving

---

53. Beckett, *Sister Wendy's*, 180.
54. Beckett, *Sister Wendy's*, 180.
55. Aelred, *Mirror of Charity*, 134.
56. Aelred, *Mirror of Charity*, 135.
57. Aelred, *Mirror of Charity*, 55.

the likeness of God is restored.'[58] The 'image' is static and unchangeable, but the 'likeness' is constantly shifting due to acts of selflessness or self-ishness. To live the Christian life is to find a 'sabbath rest' in oneself by offering kindness and love to oneself, to one's 'non-enemy', and to God.[59] There are two reasons why this virtue should be forthcoming. The first is because, by 'reason of nature,' our neighbours are human beings and are like us.[60] The second is because God has given us a precept to love our neighbour as ourselves. The extent to which we improve ourselves by acts of love determines how godlike we become. The love of our neighbour should always be absolute because her nature reflects God's, even when it becomes dulled by sin and its likeness is blemished. Blanche touches on this teaching when she comments, 'Maybe we are a long way from being made in God's image, but Stella—my sister—there has been some progress since then!'[61]

Aelred describes a person's spiritual goal in terms of 'rest' or 'sab-bath', saying, 'Let love of self, then, be man's first sabbath, love of neighbor the second, and love of God the sabbath of sabbaths . . . . the spiritual sabbath is rest for the spirit, peace of heart, and tranquility of mind.'[62] It is incumbent upon each person to master these three loves as skillfully as possible, for an interrelation and marvelous bond exists between them; each is found in all and all in each. When one wavers, they all diminish,

58. Aelred, *Mirror of Charity*, 376.

59. The teaching of loving-kindness towards oneself, to others, and to one's ene-mies is prevalent in other religious traditions. For example, in Judaism, the word *hesed* is central to its value system. The three most important aspects of Jewish character are modesty, compassion, and kindness. Just as God's *hesed* humanizes the world, so we are called to act kindly to one another, irrespective of who they are. Sara, writing about this quality, adds that the world does not operate solely on impersonal principles, but 'on the deeply personal basis of vulnerability, attachment, care and concern, recogniz-ing us as individuals with unique needs and potentialities' (H. Sara, 'The Kindness of Strangers,' in Sacks, *Essays on Ethics*, 31). Buddhism also has a strong emphasis on *metta*, which translates as 'loving-kindness'. A popular meditation is devoted to increasing this moral quality. The practice begins from developing loving-kindness towards oneself, then to one's neighbour, and finally to all those to whom one feels hostile. Harvey writes, 'Thus his mind becomes accustomed to spreading its circle of loving-kindness into increasingly difficult territory. . . . The aim is to break down barriers which make the mind friendly towards only a limited selection of beings: to cultivate an all-pervading kindness' (Harvey, *Introduction to Buddhism*, 248.)

60. Aelred, *Mirror of Charity*, 249.

61. T. Williams, *Plays*, 510–11.

62. Aelred, *Mirror of Charity*, 223.

since these three loves 'are engendered by one another, nourished by one another, and fanned into flame by one another.'[63] All three might be understood in relation to 'kindness to strangers'. The three sabbaths have wholesome consequences. The first brings security, joy, and jubilation. The second, through brotherly affection shown to each other in the monastic community, increases one's capacity to love. The third promotes love of God, as they all do. Once we become engaged in these loves, we are able to rest in the shalom of God. Unsurprisingly, this triangular loving journey to the everlasting kingdom requires the affection of friends. God's loving plan is that we should need one another.[64] In *Spiritual Friendship* Aelred writes, 'Here we are, you and I, and I hope Christ is the third in our midst!'[65] Friendship might slip into selfishness at times, but Aelred is most forgiving of this tendency because he knows from experience the traps of desire, but also the need to receive from and give kindness to others. Not all slippages are as drastic as Stanley's rape. His monastic friend, Walter Daniel, in chapter 31 of *Vita* writes about those Abbots who, 'if a monk takes a brother's hand in his own . . . demand his cowl, strip and expel him. *Non sic Aelredus, non sic.* Not so, Aelred, not so.'[66]

The tragedy for Blanche rests upon her inability to look at herself in the mirror in full daylight, to love herself unreservedly. Her crippling sensitivity to the damaging of her likeness to God prevents her from believing she is created in the image of God. Her family and friends fail to love her too. Mitch and Stanley (and Sheila, but to a far lesser degree) turn their backs on her. They stop loving their neighbour, even when she is their potential lover, their sister, and their sister-in-law. The school authorities give up on her too. We might see now why Williams describes his play as 'the ravishment of the tender' by a cruel world. The metaphor of the sabbath as personal rest, God's shalom, so prevalent in *The Mirror of Charity*, is something Blanche sought throughout her life. It is a rest she never finds.

---

63. Aelred, *Mirror of Charity*, 224.

64. See Dunbar, *Friends*, on the vital importance of friends.

65. Aelred, *Spiritual Friendship*, 30.

66. Quoted in Callaghan, 'Aelred of Rievaulx.'

Conclusion: Hope as a Mirror

Having discussed *Streetcar*, *Prostitute at Her Mirror*, and the spiritual teachings of St Aelred, I end by drawing out their implications for the on-going work and mission of Liverpool Hope University and how it might reflect, as in a mirror for all to see, their central educational concerns. I have emphasised throughout the imperative to love ourselves, our neighbour, and our God. There is no exception to this law of love. Those who manifest failings in their lives and suffer as a result, open up possible encounters with Christ himself to those who wish to offer 'the kindness of strangers'. The prostitute on Shaw St next to the Cornerstone campus, just as much as the tabernacle in the ecumenical chapel, is the place par excellence for a meeting with the divine. Those who enter the theatre to watch Blanche's struggles near to where they sit and those who move into Rouault's canvas to sit beside the prostitute at her mirror are already taking a significant step towards this meeting. By empathising with them, in the sure knowledge that they themselves are her because they share her nature and undergo her same battles, they extend their love to God himself.

Like the doctor at the end of *Streetcar*, all are invited to take the hand of those who suffer and lead them to a better place. Art allows this effective and spiritual identification to take place. At its best, it invites responses to the question Jesus was asked at the beginning of the parable of the Good Samaritan, 'And who is my neighbour?' (Luke 10.29), as it encourages deep connections between aesthetic and spiritual experience. If this is the case, church universities ought to maintain and expand their arts provision at both undergraduate and postgraduate levels. Boyle endorses this position when he points out that a Catholic approach to art is nonutilitarian and is centered solely on the investigation of truth and the nature of Being – in other words, it is revelatory like sacred Scripture itself, if not in precisely the same degree.[67]

A final note about hope. Christianity makes sense only with reference to death and rebirth. Eagleton avers that Christianity is at one with Marxism in its belief that authentic existence and hope can spring only from a loss of being; to be enduring and well founded, hope needs to be bought at a cost. When there is nothing but hope, when things have been hacked down to almost nothing, 'it is thus that nothing veers on

---

67. Boyle, *Sacred and Secular Scriptures*.

its axis to become something.'[68] The kind of despair Christianity ranks as sinful is the matter of rejecting the long-term possibility of redemption, of concluding that this or that particular effort is doomed. 'Those who lack hope betray the efforts of others and belittle their courage and resilience.'[69] Alluding to St Paul, Eagleton writes, 'The whole of creation is groaning and travailing' towards something better, and 'it is part of God's design that men and women, being the recipients of his grace, will freely co-operate with this project.'[70] The Dominican priest Herbert McCabe puts it like this: 'We are not optimists; we do not present a lovely vision of the world which everyone is expected to fall in love with. We simply have, wherever we are, some small local task to do, on the side of justice, for the poor.'[71] If Liverpool Hope, and the Cornerstone campus in particular, can attempt this, then, in my opinion, they are moving in the right direction towards fulfilling their distinctive mission, and their work will be pleasing to God.

Bibliography

Aelred of Rievaulx. *The Mirror of Charity*. Collegeville, MN: Cistercian, 1990.

———. *Aelred of Rievaulx: Spiritual Friendship*. Edited by Marsha L. Dutton. Translated by and Lawrence C. Braceland. Collegeville, MN: Liturgical, 2010.

Augustine. *Essential Exposition of the Psalms*. Edited by Michael Cameron. Translated by Maria Boulding. New York: New City, 2015.

Beckett, Wendy. *Sister Wendy's 100 Best-Loved Paintings*. London: SPCK, 2019.

Bigsby, C. W. E. *A Critical Introduction to Twentieth-Century American Drama*. 3 vols. Cambridge: Cambridge University Press, 1989.

Boyle, Nicholas. *Sacred and Secular Scriptures: A Catholic Approach to Literature*. London: Darton, Longman & Todd, 2005.

Cabral, Amalia Malanca. 'Blanche through the Looking-Glass.' UNCA, 17 Dec. 2010. https://www.academia.edu/4300674/A_Streetcar_Named_Desire_Blanche_Through_the_Looking_Glass.

Callaghan, Brendan. 'Aelred of Rievaulx.' *The Way* 38 (1998) 375–87. https://www.theway.org.uk/back/38Callaghan1.pdf.

Dunbar, Robin. *Friends: Understanding the Power of our Most Important Relationships*. London: Little Brown, 2021.

Eagleton, Terry. *Hope without Optimism*. Carlottesville: University of Virginia Press, 2015.

68. Eagleton, *Hope without Optimism*, 71.

69. Eagleton, *Hope without Optimism*, 82.

70. Eagleton, *Hope without Optimism*, 99–100.

71. Eagleton, *Hope without Optimism*, quoted before 'Contents.'

Elliott, Mark. *Providence: A Biblical, Historical and Theological Account.* Grand Rapids: Baker Academic, 2020. Ebook.

Exum, J Cheryl. *Song of Songs: A Commentary.* Louisville: Westminster John Knox, 2005.

Eyre, Richard, and Thomas Wright. *Changing Stages: A View of British Theatre in the Twentieth Century.* London: Bloomsbury, 2000.

Francis, Pope. '*Fratelli Tutti:* On Fraternity and Social Friendship.' Vatican, Oct. 3, 2020. https://www.vatican.va/content/francesco/en/encyclicals/documents/papa-francesco_20201003_enciclica-fratelli-tutti.html.

Griffiths, Paul J. *Song of Songs.* Grand Rapids: Brazos, 2011.

Harvey, Peter. *An Introduction to Buddhism: Teachings, History and Practices.* Cambridge: Cambridge University Press, 2003.

Hergott, Fabrice, and Sarah Whitfield. *Georges Rouault: The Early Years 1903–1920.* London: Lund Humphries, 1993.

Ignatieff, Michael. *The Needs of Strangers.* New York: Picador, 2001.

Kazan, Elia, dir. *A Streetcar Named Desire.* By Tennessee Williams. Burbank, CA: Warner Bros, 1951.

Palmer, Clive, and David Torevell. "The Sweet Pain of Life'—Dancing Metaphysical Longing: A Theological Critique of Matthew Bourne's *Swan Lake.' International Journal of Science Studies* 8 (2020) 63–71.

Roche-Lajtha, Agnès. 'Dionysius, Orpheus and the Androgyn: Myth in A Streetcar Named Desire,' *Etudes Anglaises* 64 (2011) 58–73. https://www.cairn-int.info/article.php?ID_ARTICLE=E_ETAN_641_0058.

Sacks, Jonathan. *Essays on Ethics: A Weekly Reading of the Jewish Bible.* Jerusalem: Maggid, 2016.

Smith-Howard, Alysia, and Greta Heintzelman. *Tennessee Williams: A Literary Reference to his Life and Work.* New York: Facts on File, 2005.

Spoto, Donald. *The Kindness of Strangers: The Life of Tennessee Williams.* New York: Da Capo, 1997.

Taylor, Charles. *A Secular Age.* Cambridge, MA: Belknap, 2007.

Thompson, Judith J. *Tennessee Williams' Plays: Memory, Myth and Symbol.* New York: Lang, 2015.

Torevell, David. 'Distractions, Illusion and the Need for a Contemplative Spirituality: A Critique of Thomas Merton's Advice.' *Journal for the Study of Spirituality* 9 (2019) 152–62.

Williams, Bernard. *Shame and Necessity.* Berkeley: University of California Press, 1994.

Williams, Raymond. *Modern Tragedy.* London: Chatto and Windus,1966.

Williams, Tennessee. *Plays 1937–1955.* New York: Library of America, 2000.

18

The Steps We Take Together,
the Strides We Light

John A. Patterson

ALONG THE JOURNEY OF life and the paths we take, I hold to a belief there are *always* plans to prosper and not to harm, 'plans to give you hope and a future' (Jer 29.11). Although we may not always recognise or respond to those plans so readily, observing our journey through a 'dim image in a mirror lens' (1 Cor 13), if we are open to that Spirit of hope, our purpose emerges and is known.

Being prepared to accept a little 'miraculous serendipity', we may see more clearly their full purpose and wider impact not just on our own but on the journey of others. With the aid of hindsight at a pathway chosen, we may see those plans as 'golden threads' weaving through and informing our journey. Whilst momentarily rooted at this 'life crossroad', we also may better comprehend how it provides a guiding light to a potential future.

As a student teacher at LIHE under Professor Lee, and later a senior lecturer at Liverpool Hope University under Professor Pillay, my journey is interwoven with, and blessed by, the learning, experiences, and people I met alongside the constantly evolving 'life journey' of this university itself. Higher education is that space to find, develop, and hone strengths whilst simultaneously building knowledge, skills, and *understanding*. For me, the deepest relevance is how we experience and understand our 'strength accompaniment' value and impact towards others and, indeed, theirs towards us. The journeys we take, or are blessed in being bestowed with, along with the trials and challenges faced, are where we learn of ourselves and what it actually *is* we have to give. Furthermore, they may show us how ready we are to give, how willing we are, and ultimately, how much. A great writer, Guimaraes Rosa, once said, 'The master is not the one who teaches; it's the one who suddenly learns.'[1] In this context, I share here an 'on-the-road' interconnected reflection on my journey, picking out the 'golden threads' I observed through education pathways, which have led me to my current position as principal at St Vincent's School for Sensory Impairment and Other Needs, Liverpool, a non-maintained specialist school for children with visual and hearing impairments (VI/HI).

Here at St Vincent's, my journey comes to sharp focus and action in challenge to internationally high unemployment rates and lower than acceptable access to opportunity and inclusion within society. This fiercely challenging situation for my pupils I consider unjust for them but also a gift for me to overcome, because, as with Rome, this is where all roads travelled were meant to bring me. This has involved to date (and forgive the liberal use of military metaphors) many side roads and blockades, 'dead ends' diverged along, yet trudged back from. That image crafted by Wilfred Owen in 'Dulce et Decorum est' of 'bent double' troops cursing 'through sludge' holds a certain resonance here. Sometimes a journey requires the most extreme of experience to be endured, as Job would certainly attest to. Nonetheless, as with the trenches, it is upon these roads we meet some of the most wonderful people as we accompany each other back to the 'main road', solid ground, and clearer pathways. Trusting outside of our understanding in 'plans to prosper' whilst on rough, winding roads in turbulent conditions may not always be easy, but with help we may perceive those clearer pathways (Prov 3.5–6). I have long marvelled at Dutch writer Corrie ten Boom who thanked God for the smallest of travelling companions. Imprisoned at Ravensbruck concentration camp in 1944 for helping Jews to escape the Nazis, her thanks was for the fleas in keeping guards away. Although we may wait for God in the fire and the storm, it was in that 'still small voice' God spoke to Elijah (1 Kgs 18.20). Like Ten Boom's interloping fleas, I have found that if we are expectant, it's often the little things that speak to us as we grow in understanding our pathways. Their relevance becomes clearer once the 'big things' have happened. Returning again to conflict and extreme of experience, David Jones's epic Great War poem 'In Parenthesis' illustrates for me the power

1. Rosa, *Grande Sertão*, 91.

of that 'still small voice' to impact reflection. His intent in sharing his experiences was to encourage the reader to ask questions about war and life in general. He challenges us to seek meaning in the most painful of experiences, suggesting meaning may lie in the virtue, patience, courage, and kindness of people. Using the infantry soldier as the example, it is noteworthy that Jones's coming to faith was after observing a small Mass and the breaking of bread in some tiny corner of an immense struggle. We can only ponder on what it was revealed to him, what he *saw* at that moment he had not before. Whatever it was, it was that individual, personalized meeting with God where sooner or later, and ultimately, all crossroads and journeys lead and end.

As a snapshot across which my life crossroads are embedded, I entered LIHE teacher education as a former engineer for a sports and English main focus. What I took from LIHE into Liverpool schools eventually saw me seconded onto a European-funded (Objective One) initiative as an education and community consultant to work across the city region in 'raising educational standards through the innovative use of ICT'. With *innovative* being the key in this role, I wrote curricula and piloted a range of ideas and initiatives culminating in the design of the Schools Intergenerational Nurturing and Learning Project (SIGNAL), an interfaith cross-curricular project focused on volunteerism and entrepreneurial learning. The SIGNAL project was simultaneously developed at a time of great activity in some of the most deprived areas of the UK, famed by the Excellence in Cities intervention. As Liverpool had, at the time, five wards in the poorest top ten in the UK, SIGNAL had an auspicious chance to connect in and with them all. The outcomes of this project I took into Liverpool Hope University College (2000) on accepting the position as head of physical education (PE) on teacher education programmes, sharing the community ideas for development with project-based activity and *volunteer* students from my own PE pathways. It was encouraging to share this work at Foundation Hour (an hour at lunchtime when faculty, staff, and students were encouraged to attend and learn about certain mission-related activities) where its inclusion in the book *Foundation of Hope: Turning Dreams into Reality*, was one of those aforementioned 'crossroads' that would shape my destiny in education.[2]

An inclusion in Foundation Hour marked my journey into research and publication and an awareness of its value and importance I had not

2. See Ian Sharp, in Elford, *Foundation of Hope*, 94.

seen before on my journey to date. I connected a deeper understanding of my own faith and service with education and the body of knowledge in synergy with the SIGNAL project 'in the round'. During this time my evolving journey was marked by three publications.[3] The relevance in understanding better the interconnected threads of volunteerism, citizenship education, social capital, and 'third sector' engagement and employment opportunity would later feed directly into the role I now hold at St Vincent's. It is here I brought my MS and PhD research outcomes in the above areas from Liverpool Hope in generating a creative curriculum for VI-centered in the international Sightbox (a toolkit for access to sports and education) as an outcome of the curriculum itself. At the time of writing with Sightbox in some twenty countries, I sense a new journey about to start. Being given the opportunity to write here has created a crossroads moment in itself, for which I am grateful. An awareness of social capital emerges at the front of my thinking as a key journey outcome to date. We are influenced by where we are and the actors we meet, both positive and negative. Social capital may well be measured in terms of lower crime, better health, and increased employment, but social capital is about people. Social capital is about people this university has connected through its history and will continue to do so into its future together, and in turn, our communities are served within the 'common good'.

Before sharing two (golden-thread) illustrative stories, it strikes me that my journey with Liverpool Hope possesses two interrelated parts: that of student and lecturer. Throughout my experience there I, the constant learner, was blessed to encounter those I met 'by chance'. So many times, and far from being 'rejected stones', those I met turned out to be the cornerstone needed (Ps 118.22) at the most incredible life crossroad moments for myself and, as I have observed, for others. People *themselves* can be the golden threads I have referenced. Although we may indeed unknowingly meet angels (Heb 13.2) on our journeys, Scripture teaches we will one day be 'like angels' (Mark 12.25). I certainly feel I've met some who have reflected such a likeness and, more often than not, along the most precarious and isolated of roads, guided me *towards* a fated destination of which 'chance' played no part.

Surrounding this two-part journey reflection, there are similarities with the stories 'The Road to Damascus' and 'The Road to Emmaus'.

3. Patterson and Hamill, 'Citizenship and Values Education'; Patterson, 'Developing Role of "Values"'; Patterson and Loomis, 'Combining Service-Learning.'

Both stories convey a journey *toward* a destination with some sense of the unknown ahead. Both Emmaus and Damascus journeys make reference to 'sight' and 'seeing', holding thus a personal significance across my service with and for VI. However, the Damascus road is associated with the impact of a dramatic and exciting burst of light. The Emmaus road is more a gradual, step-by-step illumination of the 'truth' and its impact built from when and how it touches the heart. The disciples illustrate this as in looking backwards, they realise Christ had been walking with them unrecognised; did not their hearts 'burn within' as he opened the Scriptures to them (Luke 24.32)? Having walked both roads myself, in a sense, my journey destination was always St Vincent's, that golden thread of hope connected to an inner thirst, an urge to seek, to have revealed – that of discernment and seeing what is in front of us when the time is right and we are open. Any 'plan to prosper' and journey may take inspiration from Deut 31.8 in that 'the Lord himself goes before you and will be with you; he will never leave you nor forsake you. Do not be afraid; do not be discouraged.' The 'white cane' we associate with VI mobility and independence reminds me that at times we all walk blindly in some way. Be encouraged, we have the living 'rod' and 'staff' to guide and protect in these moments as promised to us (Ps 23).

Strangely, yet paradoxically, my learning journey is such that everything I have learnt I have gifted back to those who will receive it: the staff and VI pupils at St Vincent's. There is an importance for those in education and their educators to be afforded time in order to reflect and share their journeys. Sharing from the 'chalk face' may not be set within extreme and catastrophic events such as suffered by Corrie ten Boon, Davis, or Owen; yet the 'still small voice', hope within it, and the 'common good' may be recognised throughout as a constant travelling companion. What an honour and privilege it is as students and educators to share in each other's journey stories, lighting better pathways for those following similar pathways.

As a student, the Damascus road for me has synergy with that sudden turning point in life. I was blind to the big picture of education, and entering LIHE caused the 'scales to fall'. I saw a future for myself in education.

My time as a lecturer was my road-to-Emmaus moment. It is here I saw and understood the connections between education, faith, and service. As the well-known Emmaus walks reveal, there has to be in each of us a means to strengthen individual belief in education and to help others undertake the same journey; the 'breaking of bread' and the 'opening of eyes' was, for me, through my academic study, research, and publications and, indeed, my MS and PhD completion. All of this has led me to work within the field of VI where I have seen firsthand the need for change and the need for action. If we continue to hide the smallest of lights, we may dim a pathway to illumination for others. This contributes to a selfish and loveless world; a world without vision is truly blind, in which the 'people perish' (Prov 29.18). I refer to a world still lacking in inclusion and opportunity for VI pupils. Visually impaired young people need encouragement and support to inform how *their* lights and creative strengths, although unseen to themselves, are shining brightly. It is a privilege as an educator to spark their creativity by delivering innovative and diverse learning opportunities. Furthermore, support is needed in making these lights the brightest for *others* to see and to recognise these strengths in creating new and equal opportunities.

My contribution to the world of VI can be found both in the recommendations of my PhD and with the development of the international Sightbox. The Sightbox is delivered through a curriculum focused on generating opportunities for and with VI young people globally. They are shared in a St Vincent's 'crossroad marking' through the article 'Lighting Pathways: Investing in Visually Impaired Creativity' and the book *Visual Impairment: Caring for Yourself and Others*. I will explain this curriculum and the Sightbox outcome in more detail; however, it is best described as a resource kit empowering young people with VI to access sports, education, mobility, and independence so as to ultimately enable wider, further, and longer journey opportunities. This means in the physical and in the remote (i.e., with and through technology) as both a learning space facilitator and as tools towards inclusion, equality, and employability. The option to go alone in order to go fast or to go together to go far is not as accessible, as it first may sound, for VI young people. They may require their needs to be met in different ways, and with varying levels of assistance. The journey towards equality, of better ways of doing and being, is one the VI community does need to be supported on together, but in the right way. The exponential developments in technology are yet to be fully harnessed along individual and collective VI journeys. As we read in the meeting of Bartimaeus, the Lord led us by example. All three Gospels reveal Christ asked Bartimaeus what *he* wanted, allowing time and space for his voice to be heard and for him to request the return of his sight. Christ did not presume. As with all journeys, asking others and listening at their point of need make for the very best of travelling companions; the Sightbox presents a package of reasons and ways to start a journey and to connect with the travelling companions chosen.

The SIGNAL project noted earlier is the cornerstone to the curriculum investigated through my MS and PhD, and now delivers the Sightbox at St Vincent's. First delivered in 1999 when I was an Objective One consultant (i.e., a consultant on spending of an allocation of European Union funds that went to Objective One areas), I later shared this at Foundation Hour in 2003 and further developed it with volunteer students at Liverpool Hope University.

The Liverpool region had one of the lowest access to internet rates in the UK due in part to areas of high unemployment and social deprivation but, as such, qualified for quite a range of funding initiatives to 'close the digital divide'. Following computers into some of the poorest wards in the UK, SIGNAL generated a range of activities connecting with school pupil interests and higher education volunteerism (under service-learning). A celebration of the connected interventions was focused into a musical performance of participating schools culminating at the Olympia Theatre, streamed live onto the internet. This event in real time was connected by an interfaith collaboration, which, as the performance continued, was simultaneously streamed onto the internet. Through this virtual connection, terrestrial, real communities brought a range of items to St George's Hall, depositing them on the steps. Canned food was collected for distribution to those in need identified by the interfaith groups, old tools were collected and sent to several African countries, and old spectacles were distributed to a number of international destinations. SIGNAL was an exemplar of how communities could work together in service to each other locally, nationally, and internationally through education for citizenship.

Sadly, one mishap emerged from SIGNAL, which I now share as my first golden-thread illustrative story. A church elder left his state-of-the-art laptop unattended, which, in watching the film footage made to record the event, could be seen disappearing into a van with a combination of secondhand tools. I am conscious in writing this piece of my old friend Mark Sutcliffe who was on another course at LIHE and whom I met in my first year. He was 'called home' on that final journey recently; however, years ago he qualified as an occupational therapist but became a missionary instead. It is uncanny how he would appear from quite anywhere in the world at so many of the 'crossroad' events in our journeys;

the first SIGNAL project was one of them. It was several years after the event and the laptop mishap, a letter arrived from Ghana thanking us kindly for the computer, which was now supporting a small school and had been used to connect a range of further support. Uncanny yet, Mark would find himself at that very school a few years later quite by chance to build on the work that one laptop had connected. Across that one laptop's journey, some had sown and some watered, yet it was the higher power making things grow and flourish (1 Cor 3.5–11). As co-workers in the vineyard, there was something more in seeing the laptop impact connect across the years. That 'something' is underlined for me in two ways – the connecting power of the technology online and how it drew people together for what happened physically around the computer, i.e., the 'virtual and terrestrial' linking. It was part of a modern-day, new type of journey – journeys made in an instant, anywhere in the world, and inclusive of disabilities. There is a new space with the darkest of roads, calling for new and more intrepid travellers with the clearest of vision to illuminate uncharted pathways. There is a space, perhaps, where our VI young people can lead the sighted. Certainly, as Rev. Dr. Martin Luther King Jr. called for that world where his children would be judged on the content of their character, not the colour of their skin, how VI children interact with those they cannot see has much to teach us all.

That 'something more' is explored further in this second illustrative story. Having been at St Vincent's for some years, I had a phone call requesting a Perkins Brailler to take to a girl in Tanzania. Believing we had some to spare, I, of course, promised one, and as is customary with me on occasions, promptly forgot. Many months later, the last remaining Daughter of Charity teaching Braille in St Vincent's asked to see me. After some forty years at St Vincent's, Sr Francis said she was called to service elsewhere. As she was a prayerful woman, I knew she would be resolute in her decision. As she walked out of the office, she turned and said she had left a present for me outside the door. It was just at that very moment, the office manager came into view saying there was a man with a taxi running, rushing to catch a plane to Tanzania, and here to collect a Brailler. My issue was I had discovered that all spare Braillers were in real need of repair, and I was going to have to renege on my promise. As I walked out the door to make my apologies, a glance saw the present left for me by Sr Francis. Strangely unsurprisingly, it was a Perkins Brailler. A very specific piece of equipment, at the precise moment, for a named girl across the world. Not just any Brailler, the one this sister had used for forty years to bring communication and hope to countless children. Again, what a blessing to feel and understand we were all part in some way of interconnected plans to prosper and give a future; the golden threads shone brightly for us all to see. The Sightbox itself, and its feeding curriculum, is already generating a wealth of such 'something more' stories as now expanded upon.

At St Vincent's, all pupils experience an enriched curriculum. Here, pupils opt into constantly developing, refreshing, innovative, project-based learning surrounding the creative subjects in which they perceive themselves to have strengths, i.e., music, art, dance, drama, sport, information and communication technology, and horticulture. This forms part of the school's educational formula, where the outcomes are clearly focused on inclusion, opportunity, friendship generation, and employment:

Social/Human Capital + Reverse Inclusion + Service-Learning + Creativity = *Outcomes*

Once pupils are confident within a project and their creative strengths, sighted children are invited into school to work on a collaborative project. Here, St Vincent's pupils flip the narrative and lead their sighted peers (re-verse-inclusion), building their confidence and self-belief. At this crossroads, VI pupils are encouraged to conceptualize and design resources that could enable and empower them to better access the world. Sports equipment has been a wonderful starting place, where alongside existing equipment (such as a ball with a bell in it) pupils have presented and designed quite a range of ideas. The best example is the current I-Rugby Ball, currently under second-stage development. To widen a VI awareness and in the barriers faced, preservice student teachers and design engineers (under service-learning) are invited to support the VI design ideas in a reciprocal and valuable way. A range of design ideas generated in this way has been placed in a physical box, i.e., Sightbox; funded by third sector intermediary agencies (Rotary and Lions); and has been supplied to VI schools in over twenty countries, including Pakistan, India, Rwanda, Gambia, Sierra Leone, Nepal, Kenya, Nigeria, Peru, the Virgin Islands, Nepal, Indonesia, Ethiopia, and Malawi. Pupils at St Vincent's are now teaching other VI and HI children how to use the content of Sightbox remotely on Zoom. As with the disappearing and reappearing

Ghana laptop years before, I can only wonder what will come from the Sightbox taken into the Peruvian wilderness by a group of sisters and not heard from since. One day perhaps we will learn of its journey and those impacted by it?

As with all journeys, there are blind spots where we cannot see or respond to what we do not know is there. It is here we need to listen most closely for that still small voice. In this vein whilst driving, that look in a rearview mirror is best observed with a secondary glance in wing mirrors, lest a blind spot catch us out. Perhaps a reflection on this will provide some understanding towards how life must be navigated for a VI young person in a sighted world. On all levels, and at all times, there is always a need for safety checks, whilst the rules require the use of tools, often with little practical help if you cannot see. Adaptations are needed and at times support offered. We must be there encouraging, enabling VI young people to drive their own journeys with access to innovation and creativity being the engine beneath. Reflecting on the coming of wisdom with time, W. B Yeats's shortest of poems reminds us that though the 'leaves are many', yet the 'root is one', and the swaying of his leaves and flowers in the sun is Yeats's life experience, that in old age finally permits him to 'wither into the truth.'[4] I've always found it quite sad that whatever Yeats's personal truth discovered was, it maybe shrank or diminished him, leaving him ultimately an individual alone. What he may have missed, I suggest, is the joy that comes through the accompaniment of others on such a journey, which may have allowed him a 'relaxing into the truth' at the end; a more triumphant blossoming framed by hope and that which encompasses faith.

My thanks to friends and colleagues, fellow travellers met on the journey connected through and by this university. A special thanks for my 'eye opening' alongside the most creative of VI young people. Children who just happen to be blind, but who see things differently, have so much light to share as their strengths and abilities are recognised and invested into.

Bibliography

Elford, R. John, ed. *The Foundation of Hope: Turning Dreams into Reality*. Liverpool: Liverpool University Press, 2003.

4. Yeats, 'Coming of Wisdom.'

Jones, David. *In Parenthesis: Seinnyessit e Gledyf ym Penn Mameu.* London: Faber & Faber, 1937.

Owen, Wilfred. "Dulce et Decorum est." Poetry Foundation, 1921. https://www.poetryfoundation.org/poems/46560/dulce-et-decorum-est.

Patterson, John A. 'Developing the Role of "Values" within Information and Communication Technology: An Introduction to the Schools Intergenerational Nurturing and Learning Project (SIGNAL).' In *Higher Education, Emerging Technologies, and Community Partnerships: Concepts, Models and Practices*, edited by Melody Bowdon and Russell G. Carpenter, 329–339. Hershey, PA: Information Science Reference, 2011.

———. 'Lighting Pathways: Investing in Visually Impaired Creativity.' Impact, 17 Nov. 2020. https://my.chartered.college/impact_article/lighting-pathways-investing-in-visually-impaired-creativity/.

———. *Visual Impairment: Caring for Yourself and Others.* Pastoral Outreach 15. Chawton, UK: Redemptorist, 2019.

Patterson, John A., and Mark Hamill. 'Citizenship and Values Education . . . the Still Small Voice.' In *Re-Imagining Christian Education for the 21ˢᵗ Century*, edited by Andrew B. Morris, page range unavailable. Stockport, UK: James, 2013.

Patterson, John A., and Colleen Loomis. 'Combining Service-Learning and Social Enterprise in Higher Education to Achieve Academic Learning, Business Skills Development, Citizenship Education and Volunteerism.' In *Learning, Teaching and Assessing in Higher Education: Developing Reflective Practice*, edited by Anne Campbell and Lin Norton, Teaching in Higher Education, 120–29. Exeter, UK: Learning Matters, 2007.

Rosa, João Guimarães. *Grande Sertão: Veredas.* São Paulo: Letras, 2019.

Yeats, W. B. "The Coming of Wisdom with Time." Bartleby, 2000. From *Responsibilities and Other Poems* (New York: Macmillan, 1916). https://www.bartleby.com/147/43.html.

19

Slavery Reparations

IAN MARKHAM AND JOE THOMPSON

Hope and Reparations

By Ian Markham

THE LIVERPOOL HOPE YEARS were special. Lesley (my wife) and I arrived with a newborn baby; our son was just three weeks old. We lived at the Bishop's Lodge in Woolton, Liverpool, above Bishop David Shepperd and his wife Grace. We had the upstairs apartment – a bedroom, a small kitchen, and living room. It was the perfect place to learn the craft of parenting. Liverpool Hope was just a five-minute drive away. The Department of Theology and Religious Studies was right on the edge of the campus, overlooking the nursery where Luke spent his first five years.

When Simon Lee persuaded the Governors to rename the college 'Hope', a vision for the institution started to unfold. Hope Street connected the two cathedrals – the Roman Catholic and the Anglican. Hope was the theme of Jürgen Moltmann's work; hope, argued Moltmann, is a Christian conviction that the age to come is one where justice and love triumph, and this vision of society puts a pressure on our current age to provide an aspiration that becomes our goal. Our duty as Christians is to slowly start turning this world into the one that God promises to create:

'thy kingdom come, thy will be done, on earth as it is in heaven' is our prayer.

Turning this world into the world that God always intended became a theme of Hope. Let us provide education to those who have been excluded. Let us bring education closer to those living in the inner city. Let us model ecumenical conversation, especially between Roman Catholics and Anglicans (the two traditions that make up the merged Liverpool Hope). And let us work harder to welcome and include all those who wanted to work, learn, and grow at Hope.

This season at Liverpool Hope was formative for me. One theme became central: if you want to make a difference, then you have to 'do' something. 'Be ye doers of the word, and not hearers only,' the writer of James reminds us: this was the Hope ethos.

Reparations and Virginia Theological Seminary

By Ian Markham and Joseph Thompson

Virginia Theological Seminary was founded in 1823. Virginia Theological Seminary was founded in 1823, less than fifty years after the Revolutionary War had created an independent nation. The Anglican clergy in the United States had overwhelmingly supported the British. As a result, in the decades after the Revolutionary War, congregations in the Anglican tradition struggled. There was precipitous decline; there was a shortage of clergy; there was a real risk that the Anglican tradition might disappear from North America.

So in 1823, the bishop of Virginia – Bishop William Meade – gathered with other Anglican worthies, including William Holland Wilmer and Francis Scott Key, and decided to create a seminary. From this seed came the Virginia Theological Seminary – the strongest seminary (or theological college) in the Anglican Communion.

The above narrative is all true. But it tells only part of the story. Most Americans date the founding of their nation from 1776; however, the roots of chattel slavery in what would become the state of Virginia go back at least to 1619;[1] this was the date when two ships owned by the

---

1. There were enslaved people already in what would become the United States of America prior to this date. However, 1619 remains a helpful date because of the increased numbers of enslaved persons who arrive. From 1618 to 1620, some fifty thousand Africans were forcibly brought to these shores.

English nobleman the Earl of Warwick, Robert Rich, called the White Lion and the Treasurer, delivered Africans to Virginia to be a cruelly exploited form of labor.

The founders of Virginia Theological Seminary all owned enslaved persons. For decades, enslaved people built the buildings, cooked the meals, cleaned the homes, cared for the livestock (for the seminary had a farm), tended to the campus, washed the clothes, cared for the children, and were humiliated, beaten, and killed by their white overseer. All the value of the labor was stolen by the owner of the enslaved person. The sin of slavery made the institution of Virginia Theological Seminary possible.

The temptation (and it is a temptation, in the technical theological sense) for white institutions is to tell the story of their founding as if slavery was an incidental detail. Too often the narrative sounds like this: our brave founders had vision, skill, and determination to create this remarkable institution, but like everyone living in the nineteenth century they could not escape the ubiquitous institution of slavery that sadly was part of their context. This is a narrative that reinforces racism: it is narrative written from the white perspective. It is a narrative that ignores the truth that the founders were parasites on exploited African labor. It is a narrative that ignores the reality that without this labor Virginia Theological Seminary would not have existed and would not have survived over the decades of its founding.

Sadly, there is no evidence in our history of our founders having a sense of disquiet over the institution of slavery. Faculty owned enslaved persons; the institution owned enslaved persons. It constantly advertised for enslaved labor and rented that labor from others. The historical record seems to show an institution that believed that this was the 'natural order of things'.

As change came, the seminary adapted. But a consistent theme was that the exploitation of African Americans was entirely appropriate. The Civil War comes, and ostensibly freedom comes to the African American community. Reconstruction provides glimmers of hope. However, racism has an extraordinary capacity to adapt. White supremacy and terrorism and segregation come to the fore. Whites would not allow African Americans to fully participate in society as human beings. Instead, segregation becomes the norm in Virginia. And Virginia Theological Seminary participates fully in the system of Jim Crow. Humiliation is built in; exploitation is the norm; and access to education and health care is difficult.

'Cancel culture' has become a key phrase in our time, used to dismiss historical accounts that explore the role of racism and white supremacy more fully. The accusation is made that the seminary is seeking to cancel the achievements of Bishop Meade, our founder. There is a deep irony in this allegation. The white history of the seminary has been extremely effective at the work of 'cancel culture'. The entire participation of African Americans was cancelled. Their names forgotten. Their identities cancelled. Their labor exploited. Their descendants denied the appropriate legacy that their ancestors would have created for them if the fruits of their labor had been passed down the generations.

Indeed, it could be said that VTS is attempting to counteract 'cancel culture' by presenting a more thorough narrative of its history. This effort includes not only naming the sins of white supremacy but also learning more about and celebrating the perseverance, resilience, and achievement manifested in African American lives and communities, in spite of oppression. Many African American families that currently reside near VTS have longstanding connections to the institution. In many cases, multiple generations of a family worked at the seminary. They built strong families and institutions of their own, even as they were forced to endure separate and unequal treatment. These include St Cyprian's Chapel (initially begun as the segregated chapel for Blacks in the neighbourhood of VTS), Oakland Baptist Church, and Meade Memorial Episcopal Church.

In 1923, the seminary marked its centenary. The Seminary commissioned a history. Written by W. A. R. Goodwin, the history is straightforward hagiography of the founders.[2] The African American presence in the history is totally ignored. The narrative was triumphalist and celebratory. However, as we approached 2023, we knew that the time had come to tell the entire story of our past. We had to allow the vision of the reign of God – the hope of a state where justice and love coincide – to impact this anniversary. The time had come to not simply tell the complete story of our past, but also to do something about the deep injustice embedded in that story.

---

2. To be completely accurate, W. A. R. (William Archer Rutherford) Goodwin wrote the centennial history in 1923 and does mention several Black laborers. However, these are literally just passing references; the book remains a celebration of the founders, and the history of slavery and Jim Crow are not confronted.

The Reparations Program

By Ian Markham and Joseph Thompson

This part of the story begins in the 1950s. The first African American student at Virginia Theological Seminary was John Walker, who later became the bishop of Washington. The seminary had decided that African Americans were allowed to be educated alongside white students. Each year a small number of African Americans were admitted. However, in a remarkable study by Joseph Constant, the stories of these students make painful reading. All the way through the 1970s, 1980s, and 1990s, African Americans found Virginia Theological Seminary difficult. From stereotypes to humiliation, African American students found themselves in a small minority and having to navigate an environment that did not fully respect them. In 2009, the institution issued an apology to all African American alumni who had to cope with the prejudice and racism on the campus. But this was not adequate. This is a seminary. The seminary is church. We read from a Bible that teaches us that all people are made in the image of God. We know that there is 'no Jew nor Greek, neither bond nor free, we are all one in Christ Jesus.' We know from the Gospel of Luke that our Lord abhors oppression and exploitation. Yet here was a seminary going into the twenty-first century without any real engagement with its history of racism.

Reparations is a simple idea. To simply apologize is insufficient. Words in the end can be cheap. Oftentimes, they literally cost nothing. VTS needed to do something to 'repair' the damage. Most institutions decided that one should tell the story about the past first and then decide what to do. VTS decided to reverse that process. This institution was going to create a fund for reparations and then find the names of those who were exploited.

The other decision made right at the outset was that this was going to be a fund that would make payments to the descendants of those exploited by the seminary. The logic here was simple. When VTS exploited the labor of an African American in the past, then the estate bequeathed to their descendants was also disadvantaged. Therefore, the seminary had a moral obligation to start to put that right. The amount would be modest, but at least a small down payment would be made on the labor exploited by the seminary and the estates thereby deprived.

There was another essential consideration in the decision to make direct payments available to descendants. The modus operandi of slavery and Jim Crow (and indeed of white supremacy to this very day) was to seek total control of African American lives and communities. Thus, VTS felt that the attempt to make amends to descendants should involve the relinquishment of control on the part of the institution, in some way. It sends one signal, for example, to make a descendant apply for a housing grant from a reparations endowment or to apply for some kind of needs-based assistance. It sends another signal to provide them with a share of the endowment fund that they may use however they wish. Very few, if any, controls have ever been placed on the wealth amassed by Americans of European descent in an economic system that has consistently advantaged whiteness. Should reparative acts of the sort undertaken by VTS not provide maximal control to those families who were exploited under that system?

With these themes in mind, in September 2019, Virginia Theological Seminary announced the creation of a reparations endowment fund and the intent to research, uncover, and recognise African Americans who toiled under the oppression of VTS during slavery and throughout the Jim Crow era. The endowment is fully funded by VTS as part of the commitment to recognising the racism in the seminary's past and working toward healing in the future. Additional funds have since been allocated to support the work of African American congregations that have historical ties to the seminary, to create programs that promote justice and inclusion, and to elevate the work and voices of African American alumni and clergy within the Episcopal Church, especially in historically Black congregations. These initiatives also fall under the institution's mission to begin the process of repairing the material consequences of its past sins.

Led by the Office of Multicultural Ministries, the Reparations Program is a twofold initiative that includes a research team, comprised of historical and genealogical experts, and an implementation effort, comprised of the Office of Multicultural Ministries and the reparations subcommittee of the Dean's Task Force on Diversity, Inclusion, and Equity. The research team is tasked with gathering historical documentation of Black persons who labored at VTS during slavery and/or Jim Crow and with conducting genealogical research to find living descendants. The implementation effort is tasked with the administration of the program, which includes fostering relationships with the descendant families to assess their desires as beneficiaries, managing the seminary's commitment to the other aspects of the reparations program, and determining the program's policies.

Unlike most reparation programs, the seminary is virtually alone in creating a reparations program that seeks to recognise that the estates of the ancestors exploited by the seminary were deprived of income. Therefore, we are seeking to make payments to the descendants. We have created the system: on July 1 of each year, there will be an assessment of the funds available for distribution to eligible descendants in the program. In each family, a share of those funds will be provided annually to the members of the generation that is closest to the enslaved person or Jim Crow-era employee. At least one person in that generation must be living for its members to be considered shareholders. If a person in an eligible generation is deceased, then the value of their share will be divided equally among their children.

With regard to the significant historical research necessary to undertake this project, we have started to work with three professional genealogists and historians who have extensive knowledge of the city and region. These three experts are Char McCargo Bah, Maddy McCoy, and Elizabeth Drembus. In addition to conducting archival research with the aim of documenting descendants' connections to VTS, Bah reaches out to known descendants of Jim Crow-era employees (many of whom still reside in the neighbourhood near the seminary), in order to research their families' records and oral traditions regarding their ancestors' experiences at the seminary. McCoy and Drembus focus on using historical records to find the names of enslaved persons who worked on the campus, and then they work forward in time to locate living descendants.

Members of the seminary staff are also crucial to the research effort. Ebonee Davis, the associate for Historical Research for Reparations, coordinates the team's investigative strategy and guides the seminary administration in interpreting and acting upon the findings. Seminary archivist Chris Pote helps the researchers to understand the history of the seminary and the Episcopal Church and expertly facilitates their usage of the seminary's records.

In spite of being at a relatively early stage and being conducted during the global coronavirus pandemic, the research so far has proven quite fruitful. Char Bah has identified at least twelve families whose relatives worked at VTS during the period of de jure segregation. Members of these families worked in various roles at VTS, including cook, laundress, waiter, janitor, and farm laborer. In partnership with the families, Bah has also been able to trace some of them back to free persons of colour who hired their services out to the seminary before the Civil War as wheelwright, carpenter, blacksmith, and bricklayer.

In the antebellum period, McCoy and Drembus have uncovered dozens of names of enslaved persons who worked at the seminary in a variety of roles, including farmhand, laundress, and domestic servant. As of yet, the team has not made contact with any living descendants of enslaved persons. However, they are encouraged by the fact that they have found not only first names but also surnames for many individuals. This information significantly increases the chances that the genealogical research will identify living descendants.

As VTS continues with this important project, one thing is very clear: this effort must be approached with an open-ended mindset. At this stage in the research, it is quite difficult to estimate how long it will take to reasonably exhaust the records and find the bulk of the living descendants. Even beyond the research, the seminary has determined that it will be invested in this project well into the future. The agreements currently being established with descendant shareholders today are designed to go on in perpetuity with their own descendants and designees for many more tomorrows. The reparations program is a trust, both in the ongoing nature of the financial resources and in VTS's commitments to form relationships with descendant families and to tell the truth of the seminary's history. When the Office of Multicultural Ministries contacts descendants, we know that we are attempting to build trust with people who have no particular reason to trust the institution because of its past. But the attempt is a crucial aspect of the project.

Many questions remain: What are the particular ways that families would like to have their ancestors commemorated on campus? How can the growth of the fund be promoted in such a way as to ensure that the allocations to descendants will be even more impactful in the future, even though admittedly small at present? What mechanisms can we use to ensure that the voices of the families are increasingly included in the governance of the program? We have tried to initiate a project that is both clear and decisive today, while at the same time being adaptable in the months and years ahead. We pray that the Holy Spirit will guide this endeavour now and always.

CPSIA information can be obtained
at www.ICGtesting.com
Printed in the USA
JSHW010307230723
45114JS00002B/108

9 781666 737066